# THIS BUSINESS OF WORDS

UNIVERSITY PRESS OF FLORIDA

Florida A&M University, Tallahassee
Florida Atlantic University, Boca Raton
Florida Gulf Coast University, Ft. Myers
Florida International University, Miami
Florida State University, Tallahassee
New College of Florida, Sarasota
University of Central Florida, Orlando
University of Florida, Gainesville
University of North Florida, Jacksonville
University of South Florida, Tampa
University of West Florida, Pensacola

• • •

# This
# Business
# of
# Words

## Reassessing Anne Sexton

• • •

Edited by Amanda Golden

University Press of Florida
Gainesville · Tallahassee · Tampa · Boca Raton
Pensacola · Orlando · Miami · Jacksonville · Ft. Myers · Sarasota

This book may be available in an electronic edition.

First cloth printing, 2016
First paperback printing, 2018

23 22 21 20 19 18   6 5 4 3 2 1

Library of Congress Cataloging-in-Publication Data
Names: Golden, Amanda, 1979– editor.
Title: This business of words : reassessing Anne Sexton / edited by Amanda Golden.
Description: Gainesville : University Press of Florida, 2016. | Includes bibliographical
references and index.
Identifiers: LCCN 2016035946 | ISBN 9780813062204 (cloth)
ISBN 9780813064031 (pbk.)
Subjects: LCSH: Sexton, Anne, 1928–1974—Criticism and interpretation. |
Poets, American—20th century—Criticism and interpretation.
Classification: LCC PS3537.E915 Z94 2016 | DDC 811/.54—dc23
LC record available at https://lccn.loc.gov/2016035946

The University Press of Florida is the scholarly publishing agency for the State University
System of Florida, comprising Florida A&M University, Florida Atlantic University, Florida
Gulf Coast University, Florida International University, Florida State University, New College
of Florida, University of Central Florida, University of Florida, University of North Florida,
University of South Florida, and University of West Florida.

University Press of Florida
15 Northwest 15th Street
Gainesville, FL 32611-2079
http://upress.ufl.edu

# Contents

# Figures

# Acknowledgments

*This Business of Words* began in conversation with David Trinidad, and it contains the work of extraordinary critics and poets. It has been a pleasure to collaborate with such perceptive and generous writers. I am grateful to Linda Gray Sexton for her support of this project. *This Business of Words* would not have been possible without the expertise of Shannon McCarthy at the University Press of Florida. I began the research that led to this volume as a Dissertation Fellow at the Harry Ransom Center for Humanities Research at the University of Texas at Austin and developed the project further as a N. E. H. Post-Doctoral Fellow in Poetics at Emory University's Fox Center for Humanistic Inquiry. As a Marion L. Brittain Postdoctoral Fellow at the Georgia Institute of Technology, the School of Literature, Media, and Communication supported my research, helping to fund the permissions for the photograph on the cover of the hardback edition of this book. I have learned from phenomenal colleagues at the University of Washington, Emory, Agnes Scott College, Georgia Tech, and the New York Institute of Technology. For their thoughtful feedback, I would like to thank Marsha Bryant, Jonathan Goldman, Emily James, Margaret Konkol, Randi Saloman, Dawn Skorczewski, Peter K. Steinberg, Sarah Terry, and Linda Wagner-Martin. Many colleagues and friends have supported my research, including Jane L. Anderson, Keith Anthony, Colette Barlow, the late Bruce Berlind, Elaine Brown, Martine Brownley, Rebecca Burnett, Hal Burton, Sarah-Jane Burton, Laura Butler, Susan Cerasano, Wayne Chapman, Bryan Chitwood, John Coldewey, Stephen Coppolo, Dianna

Coppolo, Michael Coyle, Christine Cozzens, Anthony DiMatteo, Elizabeth Donaldson, Amy Elkins, Amy Erbil, Holly Fils-Aime, Gillian Groszewski, Mark Hussey, Sydney Kaplan, Barbara Ladd, Kevin LaGrandeur, Loraine Lazarus, Megan Miller, John Morgenstern, Christopher Moylan, Richard Oram, Jane Pinchin, Maryse Prezeau, Daniel Quigley, Ronald Schuchard, Rahmat Shoureshi, James Simon, Richard Utz, Sarah Wider, Roger Yu, and Linda Zygutis. My research draws inspiration from the mentorship of Peter Balakian, Anita Helle, Terry Kidner, Karen V. Kukil, and Brian M. Reed. *This Business of Words* could not have become a reality without my family: Shirley Goldfine and Vickie, Andrew, Louise, Ben, Molly, Jack, and Kate Golden.

## Permissions Credits

Anne Sexton's unpublished materials are included with permission of Linda Gray Sexton. Reprinted with permission of SLL/Sterling Lord, Literistic. Copyright by Anne Sexton.

Image of letter by Saul Bellow. Copyright © n.d., 2010 by Saul Bellow, © 2014 by Saul Bellow Estate, used by permission of The Wylie Agency LLC.

Kathleen Ossip's essay was published as "Are We Fake? Images of Anne Sexton, 20th-Century Woman/Poet," *American Poetry Review* 42.3 (May/June 2013): 11-16.

David Trinidad's essay was published as "Two Sweet Ladies: Anne Sexton and Sylvia Plath's Friendship and Mutual Influence," *American Poetry Review* 35.6 (Nov./Dec. 2006): 21–29.

# Abbreviations

| | |
|---|---|
| *AS* | Diane Wood Middlebrook. *Anne Sexton: A Biography.* 1991. New York: Random House, 1992. Print. |
| *APAS* | Audiotapes and papers of Anne Sexton, 1956–88. Schlesinger Library at Radcliffe Institute, Harvard University. |
| *CP* | Anne Sexton. *The Complete Poems.* 1981. New York: Houghton Mifflin, 1999. Print. |
| *NES* | Anne Sexton. *No Evil Star: Selected Essays, Interviews, and Prose.* Ed. Steven E. Colburn. Ann Arbor: U of Michigan P, 1985. Print. |
| Sexton Papers | Anne Sexton Papers. Harry Ransom Center for Humanities Research, University of Texas at Austin. |
| *SPL* | *Anne Sexton: A Self-Portrait in Letters.* 1977. Ed. Linda Gray Sexton and Lois Ames. New York: Houghton Mifflin, 1991. Print. |
| *UJ* | *The Unabridged Journals of Sylvia Plath 1950–1962: Transcribed from the Original Manuscripts at Smith College.* Ed. Karen V. Kukil. New York: Random House, 2000. Print. |

# Introduction

## Reassessing Anne Sexton

AMANDA GOLDEN

In her first volume of poetry, *To Bedlam and Part Way Back* (1960), Anne Sexton's speaker in "Said the Poet to the Analyst" famously proposes, "My business is words" (*CP* 12). Words become material entities: "Words are like labels, / or coins, or better, like swarming bees." She considers their ability to organize, arrange, and archive. But words also have weight and value, and, ultimately, the power to sting. The speaker then turns to the analyst in the second stanza, "Your business is watching my words." For over fifty years, critics and poets have also scrutinized Sexton's words like the persona of "The Ambition Bird" in *The Book of Folly* (1972), for whom "The business of words keeps me awake" (299). The speaker is preserving her words: "all night I am laying / poems away in a long box. // It is my immortality box, / my lay-away plan, / my coffin."[1] As the contributors to this volume demonstrate, Sexton's words exist in material contexts, including manuscripts, archives, and workspaces. Becoming a successful poet meant skillfully approaching various forms of media and developing strategies for teaching, critiquing poems, delivering poetry readings, and giving interviews. *This Business of Words: Reassessing Anne Sexton* examines her industry and her industriousness. Sexton's dedication to *The Book of Folly*, "For Joy, when she comes to this business of words," suggests the value of language in the economy of living (297). The chapters that follow return to the materials of

Sexton's oeuvre to consider the development of her aesthetic, her reception, and the continuing allure of her poetry in the twenty-first century.

Sexton continues to fascinate readers. Her career is in need of a reassessment that considers the wide range of materials in her archive, her influence on contemporary poetry, and directions for future scholarship. While there have been recent collections analyzing the poetry of Sexton's midcentury contemporaries, such as Anita Helle's *The Unraveling Archive: Essays on Sylvia Plath* (2007), there have not been comparable considerations of Sexton's poetry. Several volumes of essays were published from the late seventies to the early nineties, including J. D. McClatchy's *Anne Sexton: The Artist and Her Critics* (1978), Diana Hume George's *Sexton: Selected Criticism* (1988), Stephen E. Colburn's *Anne Sexton: Telling the Tale* (1988), Linda Wagner-Martin's *Critical Essays on Anne Sexton* (1989), and Dave Oliphant's *Rossetti to Sexton: Six Women Poets at Texas* (1992), but there has not been a book that fully engages the scope of Sexton's creative and critical legacy.

Twenty-first century Sexton criticism has considered her poetry from historical, formal, cultural, and psychological approaches. Philip McGowan returns to the construction of Sexton's poetry in his formalist study, *Anne Sexton and Middle Generation Poetry: The Geography of Grief* (2004). Jo Gill's poststructuralist reconsideration of Sexton's poetic strategies in *Anne Sexton's Confessional Poetics* (2007) and Paula M. Salvio's interpretation of Sexton's pedagogical techniques in *Anne Sexton: Teacher of Weird Abundance* (2007) analyze Sexton's teaching materials, poetry manuscripts, and other materials in the University of Texas at Austin's Harry Ransom Center for Humanities Research. More recently, in *An Accident of Hope: The Therapy Tapes of Anne Sexton* (2012), Dawn M. Skorczewski returns to the recordings of Sexton's therapy sessions with Dr. Martin Orne held in the Schlesinger Library at Harvard University's Radcliffe Institute and at the Ransom Center, which Diane Middlebrook had controversially examined in *Anne Sexton: A Biography* (1991). Skorczewski argues that Sexton's therapy tapes "provide a vivid portrait of a woman's transformation from a high school–educated, depressed housewife into a nationally recognized public intellectual" (xviii). While she focuses on the later recordings in which Sexton prepared to cease her treatment with Dr. Orne because he would be relocating to Philadelphia (xix), Skorczewski adds, "the tapes have the potential to transform our understanding of Anne Sexton as a woman poet struggling to establish her identity" (xviii). Skorczewski's findings lay the groundwork for future considerations of the social, cultural, and political factors that shaped Sexton's poetic development.[2]

*This Business of Words* draws new attention to the material dimensions of Sexton's life and work, ranging from the drafts of poems she composed to the income that she earned.[3] Taking her therapy tapes as an example, Sexton's voice alone reflects her time and place, beginning with her accent in pronouncing "Dr. Orne" as "Dr. Arne."[4] Sexton's voice reflects her time; so, too, do the references she makes to her daily life and economic concerns. During Sexton's session on 7 February 1961, on a radio station from Emerson College, an announcer from WERS News Radio states that President Kennedy had requested that Congress increase the minimum wage from one dollar in 1961 to one dollar and twenty-five cents.[5] When accounting for inflation, one dollar in 1961 is equivalent to $7.96 in 2016 and $1.25 is equivalent to $9.95 in 2016, almost two dollars over the actual minimum wage in Massachusetts in 2016, $10.00.[6] In a session the following week, we hear Sexton discussing her concerns regarding an upcoming reading of her work at Amherst College and her pleasant surprise at receiving "$200 plus expenses."[7] When adjusted for inflation, this fee may far exceed poets' compensation in 2016 ($200 in 1961 is the equivalent of $1592.86 in 2016), but it is perhaps more interesting that Sexton was receiving the equivalent of compensation for two hundred hours of work at minimum wage in 1961. Working with archives means that digital tools (such as inflation calculators) are accessible alongside material resources, which enable our interpretations of Sexton's fiscal world in relation to our own, and illustrate one way that, as Helle argues, "archives are, in part, social constructions. They swell, even as we write about them" (11).[8]

The contributors to this volume analyze the contents of Sexton's archives and add to them. In her introduction to *The Boundaries of the Literary Archive: Reclamation and Representation*, Lisa Stead cites Paul Voss and Marta Werner's understanding of "the archive" as "both a physical site—an institutional space enclosed by protective walls—and an imaginative site—a conceptual space whose boundaries are forever changing" (Introduction 2). In *Women's Poetry and Popular Culture* (2011), Marsha Bryant demonstrates the productive relationship between domestic and popular contexts, including advertising. She notes that Sexton not only includes "Bab-o" in "Briar Rose (Sleeping Beauty)" but also that in her poetry "Sexton . . . drew on the dream kitchen and housewifery" (Bryant 130, 146; *CP* 292). As Bryant illustrates, commercial and popular media fueled these kitchen fantasies following the Second World War. Building on Bryant's research, *This Business of Words* considers new facets of Sexton's relationship to popular culture by examining materials ranging from publicity photographs to poems by her fans.[9]

Approaching Sexton's life and work from different perspectives, the critics and poets in this volume shed new light on her efforts in building a career.[10] When an interviewer asked Middlebrook how Sexton was able to become such an accomplished poet without a university education, Middlebrook responded, "that question was the one that attracted me to this project [*Anne Sexton: A Biography*]" (interview). *This Business of Words* returns to this issue and asks new questions about Sexton's role in professionalizing herself. Peter Davison began his well-known recollection of Sexton in *The Fading Smile: Poets in Boston, 1955–1960, from Robert Frost to Robert Lowell to Sylvia Plath* (1994) with the observation, "I don't recall ever having been with Anne Sexton when she did not require someone to take care of her" (131). Davison's sketch of a needy Sexton does not give her enough credit for collecting and curating her own fame and opportunities. But it also draws attention to the ways that she was strategic in meeting people who would help her. She was assembling a network.[11]

*This Business of Words* expands Middlebrook's sense of Sexton's progress from "housewife into poet" in order to consider the ways that she redefines the poetic landscape from outside of academia (67). In her final paragraph of *Anne Sexton's Confessional Poetics*, Gill leaves readers with the significance of Sexton's agency: "Most important of all to the reassessment of Sexton's work I have proposed is the profound self-consciousness with which Sexton approaches the [poetry] field" (192). While Sexton lacked her peers' academic training, Kathleen Ossip notes in her contribution to *This Business of Words* that Sexton's family background shaped the practical business-sense that she brought to the profession, and she "almost innately knew how to milk and grow her initial success" because she was raised in a "family of prosperous businessmen and socialites" (189, this collection). Sexton's poetic development, Gill adds in her chapter of this book, occurred in response to the surroundings of the suburbs and the physicality of her home.

In May 1961, Sexton received a grant from the Radcliffe Institute for Advanced Study that allowed her to build a workroom.[12] As Sexton stressed in a therapy session, she wanted to impress upon her husband the significance of this accomplishment and the space that it provided: "when I got the Radcliffe grant with *my money* this is what I want to shout at him, with the thing that I've done, we built a room, the room is built with the thing I've done" (Skorczewski 92). Sexton's study not only became a location for her writing but also informed her engagement with language and literary texts.

Arriving at her therapy session on 17 October 1961, Sexton handed Dr. Orne a copy of *Newsweek* and asked him to turn to the Education section.[13] When he asked what was in it, she said, "Me!" She was astonished that the photographer had captured her looking "so happy."[14] *Newsweek*'s "Women of Talent" article introducing the Radcliffe Fellows opened with Sexton in her office:

> In her book-lined study in Newton Lower Falls, Massachusetts, Mrs. Anne Sexton, a 32-year-old poet, turned from the typewriter to greet her two children on their return from school. It was a welcome interruption, but of interruptions per se Mrs. Sexton observed: "When some people call me and I say I've been reading a book, they just keep chattering away. But if I say I'm baking a cake, they apologize and hang up. Unfortunately, some educated women reach a point where a fallen angel-food cake is almost more important than a lost idea." ("Women of Talent" 94)

Vytas Valaitis's photograph of Sexton, which graces the cover of the hardback edition of *This Business of Words*, originally appeared on the second page of the *Newsweek* article. Sexton is at her desk and her bookshelves are only beginning to be filled. The caption reads, "Poet Anne Sexton at Radcliffe: Research for lost ideas" (97). Sexton's study provided both a private workspace and a location for crafting her public image, what Helle calls Sexton's "Photographic Self-Fashioning"in her contribution to this volume.[15]

Sexton's surroundings—which included her books, manuscripts, and the pieces of paper she affixed above her desk—informed her composition process. In her accounts of the evolution of her work, Sexton recounted her fragments' significance in her poems and in relation to her work as a whole. For instance, Saul Bellow sent Sexton a note on a page of his manuscript for *Herzog* (1964) that provided her epigraph to *Live or Die* (1966) (Figs. I.1

and I.2). Sexton endowed this gift with great significance and it provided a source of inspiration:

> in circling that and in sending it to me, Saul Bellow had given me a message about my whole life. . . . So I stuck that message up over my desk and it was a kind of hidden message. You don't know what these messages mean to you, yet you stick them up over your desk or re-member them or write them down and put them in your wallet. One day I was rereading a quote from Rimbaud that said "Anne, Anne, flee on your donkey," and I typed it out because it had my name in it and because I wanted to flee. I put it in my wallet, went to see my doctor, and . . . In the hospital, I started to write the poem, "Flee on Your Donkey," as though the message had come to me at just the right mo-ment. (NES 96)

Sexton's response is reminiscent of Bellow's own characters who would also provide less traditional academic models as she began auditing courses and teaching.

Sexton's reading of Bellow is emblematic of her unconventional approach to studying others' writing and her own. During one of Sexton's therapy ses-sions, she exclaimed to her doctor, "My copy of this damn book *Henderson* is all underlined: that is the way *I* feel, that is it!" (AS 162). Underlining sug-gests a form of emphasis that Sexton cannot put into words. Not long after Bellow's *Henderson the Rain King* (1959) was published, Sexton admitted that she "would rather read it than breathe" (SPL 102).[16] To Anthony Hecht she reflected: "I have been reading Bellow backwards . . . but it doesn't hurt, showing me how Henderson could ever be brought forth and from where."[17] Sexton's inclination to unpack Bellow's novel resembles her treatment of her own drafts:

> Often I keep my worksheets, so that once in a while when I get de-pressed and think that I'll never write again, I can go back and see how that poem came into being. You watch the work and you watch the miracle. You have to look back at all those bad words, bad metaphors, everything started wrong, and then see how it came into being, the slow progress of it, because you're always fighting to find out what it is that you want to say. (NES 73)

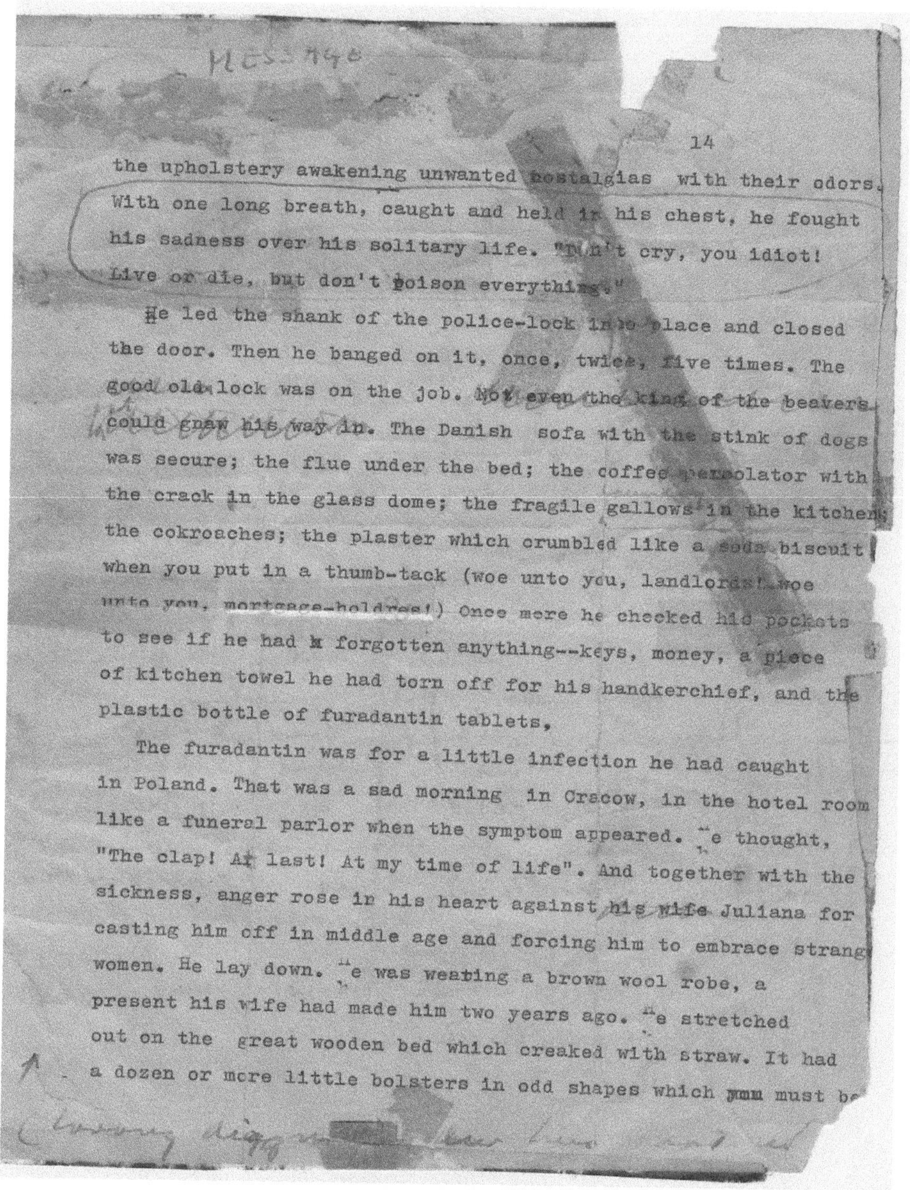

the upholstery awakening unwanted nostalgias with their odors. With one long breath, caught and held in his chest, he fought his sadness over his solitary life. "Don't cry, you idiot! Live or die, but don't poison everything."

He led the shank of the police-lock into place and closed the door. Then he banged on it, once, twice, five times. The good old lock was on the job. Not even the king of the beavers could gnaw his way in. The Danish sofa with the stink of dogs was secure; the flue under the bed; the coffee percolator with the crack in the glass dome; the fragile gallows in the kitchen; the cockroaches; the plaster which crumbled like a soda biscuit when you put in a thumb-tack (woe unto you, landlords! woe unto you, mortgage-holders!) Once more he checked his pockets to see if he had forgotten anything—keys, money, a piece of kitchen towel he had torn off for his handkerchief, and the plastic bottle of furadantin tablets.

The furadantin was for a little infection he had caught in Poland. That was a sad morning in Cracow, in the hotel room like a funeral parlor when the symptom appeared. He thought, "The clap! At last! At my time of life". And together with the sickness, anger rose in his heart against his wife Juliana for casting him off in middle age and forcing him to embrace strange women. He lay down. He was wearing a brown wool robe, a present his wife had made him two years ago. He stretched out on the great wooden bed which creaked with straw. It had a dozen or more little bolsters in odd shapes which you must be

FIGURE I.1. Saul Bellow letter to Anne Sexton, n.d. (Sexton Papers, box 18, folder 1).

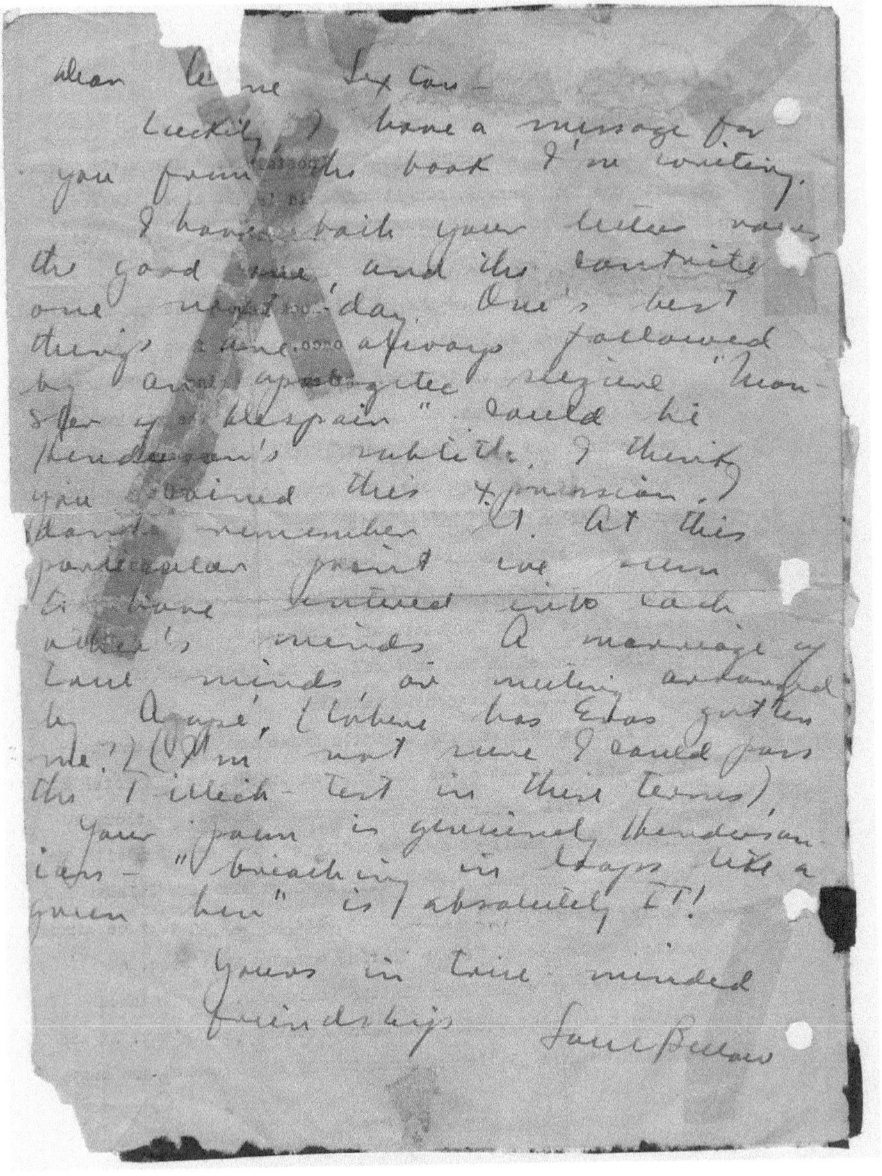
Dear Anne Sexton—

Luckily I have a message for you from the book I'm writing.

I have both your letters now, the good one and the contrite one mailed next day. One's best things are always followed by an apologetic reflex. "Monster of despair" could be Henderson's subtitle. I think you coined this expression? (I don't remember it.) At this particular point we seem to have entered into each other's minds. A marriage of true minds, or meeting arranged by Agape. (Where has Eros gotten to?) (I'm not sure I could pass the Tillich test in these terms).

Your poem is genuinely Hendersonian—"breaching in heaps like a green bee" is absolutely IT!

Yours in true minded friendship

Saul Bellow

FIGURE I.2. Verso of Bellow letter to Sexton (Sexton Papers, box 18, folder 1).

The focus that Sexton brought to her reading of Bellow reflects the fact that, in her estimation, he was "the great American writer of our generation."[18] Studying such a great figure reflects the magnitude of her aspirations and the effort she devoted to success.

After meeting Bellow in 1961, Sexton told an interviewer that she kept her copy of *Henderson the Rain King* in her "suitcase everywhere I traveled" (*NES* 95).[19] During their first encounter, Sexton "was overenthusiastic. I said, 'Oh, oh, you're Saul Bellow, I've wanted to meet you,' and he ran from the room. Very afraid" (95). Later, Sexton became self-conscious and asked Bellow's forgiveness:

> I was quite ashamed of my exuberance and then sometime, a year later, reading *Henderson the Rain King* over again, at three in the morning, I wrote Saul Bellow a fan letter about Henderson, saying . . . that I understood his position because Henderson was the one who had ruined life, who had blown up the frogs, made a mess out of everything. I drove to the mail box then and there! The next morning I wrote him a letter of apology. (95)[20]

Bellow responded on the verso of a page of his *Herzog* (1964) manuscript (Fig. I.2).[21] To Sexton's relief, Bellow praised her excitement: "I have both your letters now, the good one, and the contrite one the next day. One's best things are always followed by an apologetic seizure."[22] The overwhelming energy that filled Sexton's response to Bellow also became a factor in her academic persona.

As Sexton did not attend a university herself, teaching provided a source of anxiety. Bellow's novels introduced Sexton to less traditional literary personalities as she became more of a presence on college campuses. In *Henderson the Rain King*, Henderson responds to his reading with a combination of devotion and irreverence that resembles Sexton's response to her own. In the novel he admits, "I am a nervous and emotional reader. I hold a book up to my face and it takes only one good sentence to turn my brain into a volcano. . . . Anyway, I am the inspirational, and not the systematic, type" (*Henderson* 244). Sexton was also a reader without a clear curriculum. Henderson learns that "no rubric will fully hold you[,]" and this statement also speaks to the unexpected quality of Sexton's public and poetic personae (300).

Bellow's sarcastic treatment of academic conventions introduced Sexton to figures and failures that characterized the world she was navigating. In *Herzog,* for instance, there is "Asphalter . . . something of a marginal academic type without his Ph.D." (48). And Moses Herzog who "when he met his Philadelphia class in the morning, he could hardly see his lecture notes" (117). As Sexton traveled to universities to give readings and went on to teach, she became a more skillful reader of the roles of teacher, critic, student, and poet.

In her teaching notes for the final session of Sexton's course on her own poetry at Colgate University in 1972, "Anne on Anne," she returned to Bellow's inscription on the typescript page of *Herzog* that he had sent to her. Throughout her teaching notes, Sexton included answers in parentheses beside the questions she prepared to ask. In the process, she leaves critics with a document that records her close readings of her own poems. Near the close of the session, Sexton announced, "Now we come to the last poem ["Live"]. Saul Bellow marked his manuscript for me and he said 'With one long breath, caught and held in his chest, he fought his sadness over his solitary life. Don't cry, you idiot! Live or die, but don't poison everything. . . .' And I used part of that quote for my last poem 'Live.' What would you say the quotation meant? (don't foul up the world)" (*CL* 10, 15). Instead of elaborating on the quotation's significance, she turned the anecdote into a pedagogical exercise, asking her students to supply its meaning. She may have wanted to see and hear how the students would interpret the quotation. But her question also gestures toward the implication that there is one interpretation of a line, and she had performed this exercise in advance, leaving her answer in parentheses. If Sexton shared her gloss with the class, it would have also provided a form of parting advice that acknowledged Bellow's significance in her career.

◆   ◆   ◆

*This Business of Words* approaches Sexton's poetry from critical and creative perspectives. While any arrangement of essays precludes others, seeing the critical contributions together throws into relief common concerns, including the role of institutions, visual culture, space, and media. Reading the poets in sequence reveals a progression from seasoned to emerging voices grappling with Sexton's work and its impact on the field. Despite their separation, the essays in both sections speak to each other, reflecting their shared investment in such topics as performance, audience, professionalization, and gender. These intersections also suggest Sexton's relevance to readers and teachers of poetry at the present time.

The chapters of *This Business of Words* consider the spaces in which Sexton worked. In "'The house / of herself': Reading Place and Space in the Poetry of Anne Sexton," Jo Gill analyzes "poems that explicitly yoke space and time, that locate experience and the memory of it in specific places and, conversely, that use place and space as an index of particular temporal moments and thus as a productive route (I use the word advisedly) to understanding" (19). Reconsidering the role of domestic space in Sexton's writing, Gill provides new interpretations of poems like "You, Doctor Martin," arguing that "Recognizable signs of family, domesticity, and home are unsettlingly inverted; home becomes a spied-on 'nest'" (21). Sexton's home also became a site for taking professional photographs. In "Anne Sexton's Photographic Self-Fashioning," Anita Helle extends Judith Brown's articulation of a radiant sublime in modernist photography studies to reconsider Sexton's response to the medium. Helle proposes that "Against the broader continuum of modernist fascination with the aesthetic and technological potential of seeing through the camera lens, Sexton's art and its reception participate in the expropriation and reformulation of radiant technologized forms with sublime and aesthetic effects" (38). In addition to bringing into focus Sexton's role in crafting the images that accompanied her poetry volumes and advertised her readings, Helle sheds new light on the visual cultures that Sexton depicts in her work.

Several critics return to the institutions that shaped Sexton's poetry readings, psychiatric treatment, and cultivation of an audience. In "Anne Sexton's Institutional Voice," Kamran Javadizadeh examines the shifting role of the institution for Sexton and her contemporaries as they spent time in psychiatric and academic spaces. He argues "that poets like Plath, Lowell, and Sexton continue, rather than reject, key aspects of the institutional forms of modernism that they inherit, but that they do so, often, by writing poems in which they are themselves both the subjects and the objects of institutional scrutiny" (75). In "Reading, Voice, and Performance: 'The Freak Show' Revisited," Victoria Van Hyning takes Sexton's last reading at Goucher College in 1974 as a case study, considering Sexton's response to technology and the genre of poetry recordings. In "From the Podium to the Second Row: The Vanishing Feel of an Anne Sexton Reading," Christopher Grobe investigates the poetry of Sexton's male and female fans and the culture that arose around her poetry readings. Reproducing poems and contextualizing them with excerpts from Sexton's correspondence and his own exchanges with Sexton's fans, Grobe envisions and interprets the euphoria of Sexton's performances.

Following Grobe's treatment of poems that Sexton inspired, the poets in this collection address her artistic legacy. In "'Two Sweet Ladies': Anne Sexton and Sylvia Plath's Friendship and Mutual Influence," David Trinidad explores what lies behind the "irresistible glamour about their friendship" (155). Reviewing the existing accounts of Plath and Sexton's exchanges, he asks what their inconsistencies and omissions reflect about the poets' relationship. In "Are We Fake? Images of Anne Sexton, Twentieth-Century Woman/Poet," Kathleen Ossip considers the ways that readers, including herself, have responded to Sexton, resolving that "The wrapped package of Sexton's poems, both sparkling and rotten, her life story, her letters, and her comments on her poems, as well as captivating glimpses via photos and video, form her work: her myth" (180). Sexton's allure is also a subject of Jeffery Conway's "The Poet Has Collapsed: Coming to Terms with Anne Sexton's Late Poetics and Public Persona." Conway begins with the impact of Sexton's decadent performance style: "Great poets like Sexton allow themselves to let it all hang out—by wearing a striking Pucci-esque halter dress to a reading, by confessing secrets, and by letting whatever springs forth from her mind to land, unfiltered, right on the page (*splat*)" (196). Conway's sketch of Sexton's striking, unfiltered character complements Van Hyning's and Grobe's interpretations of her poetry readings. Conway also draws attention to the strength of Sexton's work, which often takes shape in its ability to shock readers.

Sexton's lasting appeal among readers, students, and poets is the focus of this book's final chapters. Sexton's skillful employment of the fairy tale genre is one of the most memorable and accessible aspects of her body of work. Jeanne Marie Beaumont, who edited a collection of poets' responses to the Brothers Grimm Fairy Tales, returns to Sexton's storytelling in "'The Speaker in This Case': Anne Sexton as Tale-Teller in *Transformations*." As poet and editor, Beaumont finds that "With each rereading [of *Transformations*], the deeper into the woods I am able to travel with them, not just as poems, but as markers for where Sexton was in her life and her craft as she wrote them, and as a particularly revealing document of mid-20th-century culture and its adult psyches, for they are nothing if not culturally and psychologically preoccupied" (218). Concluding the collection, in "Anne Sexton and the Wild Animal: An Exploration of the Bestiary Poems," Dorothea Lasky turns to Sexton's "Bestiary U.S.A." poems collected in *45 Mercy Street* (1976) to ask "how she took on animal imagery as masks to better infuse her lyrical *I* with wildness" (260). Lasky sees this impulse as part of what creates poetry. Her essay leaves readers with a sense of the spirit that continues to fuel artistic creation.

The "business of words" is changing, and access to Sexton's archival materials, the publications of her time, and the archives of her contemporaries alters the reading and teaching of her work. As contributions to this volume suggest, audio, visual, digital, and material resources will inspire further contextualization of Sexton's poetry. And like her protagonist in "The Ambition Bird," Sexton's words will continue to keep readers awake.

## Notes

1. The previous year, Mary-Elizabeth Murdock, head of the Sophia Smith Collection at Smith College, had expressed interest in Sexton's manuscripts. Letter, Murdock to Sexton, 21 Sept. 1971, Sexton Papers, box 26, folder 5. For further discussion of authors' archiving of their work see Chen.

2. See also Nelson's *Pursuing Privacy in Cold War America,* which interprets Sexton's poetry in relation to political and legal contexts.

3. See Helle regarding the Plath archive in *Feminist Studies* and Sexton's response to recording her poetry readings in Van Hyning's chapter of this collection, "Reading, Voice, and Performance: 'The Freak Show' Revisited."

4. CD-4, reel 4, 7 Feb. 1961, Audiotapes and papers of Anne Sexton, 1956–88, Schlesinger Library, Radcliffe Institute, Harvard University (*APAS*). See Skorczewski regarding the presence of the news and the background sounds in the tapes (xix).

5. CD-4, reel 4, 7 Feb. 1961, *APAS.*

6. CPI Inflation Calculator. United States Department of Labor. Web. 15 April 2016. <http://www.bls.gov/data/inflation_calculator.htm>. "Minimum Wage." The Official Website of the Attorney General of Massachusetts. Web. 15 April 2016. <http://www.mass.gov/ago/ doing-business-in-massachusetts/labor-laws -and-public-construction/wage-and-hour/minimum-wage.html>.

7. CD-3, reel 5, 14 Feb. 1961, *APAS.* CPI Inflation Calculator. United States Department of Labor. Web. 15 April 2016. <http://www.bls.gov/data/inflation

_calculator.htm>. Sexton's fee for readings increased over time. In a later response to an invitation from Smith College students, Sexton mentions that her fee is $1,000. Letter, Sexton to Jackie Shapiro, 13 July 1971, Sexton Papers, box 26, folder 5. $1,000 in 1971 is roughly $5,879.80 in 2016. CPI Inflation Calculator. United States Department of Labor. Web. 1 May 2016. <http://www.bls.gov/data/inflation_calculator.htm>.

8. See Paige Morgan's *Visible Prices*, a resource for assessing the value of products in British literature. Web. 15 April 2016. <http://www.paigemorgan.net/visibleprices/>. In addition, see Bryan Chitwood's work on contemporary poetry and economics. Lisa Stead observes in her introduction to *The Boundaries of the Literary Archive*, "the contemporary moment is experience a significant new stage in the archival turn, where issues of the digital make more insistent claims than ever on our understanding of, and interaction with, literary archives" (1).

9. For further consideration of fan culture, see Stead, "Letter Writing."

10. In a different context, Libbie Rifkin observes that she "seek[s] to loosen literary canonicity's grip on the analysis of reception by reconceiving the stakes of literary exchange in the narrower terms of the poetic career. A focus on career over canon enables an examination of institutions from the interested perspective of particular, historically situated individuals, and . . . it is also responsive to local material, ideological, and psychosocial demands" (6).

11. Skorczewski adds that Sexton's therapy tapes record her making "connections with academics and writers that would last throughout her lifetime" (xix).

12. Sexton discusses learning that she had received the Radcliffe Grant in CD-3, reel 23, 30 May 1961, *APAS*.

13. CD-3, reel 50, 17 Oct. 1961, *APAS*.

14. CD-3, reel 50, 17 Oct. 1961, *APAS*. Middlebrook brought this article to my attention (*AS* 150, 430n).

15. Rollie McKenna had previously photographed Sexton at her desk in what was probably the dining room of her house (the wallpaper is visible). McKenna's images appeared on the back cover of Sexton's second book of poetry *All My Pretty Ones* (1962).

16. Letter, Sexton to Hollis Summers, 16 March 1960. I presented an earlier version of this segment regarding Sexton's reading of Bellow at the American Literature Association Conference in 2010.

17. Letter, Sexton to Hecht, "July 26th I think" [probably 1961]. Anthony Hecht papers, 1894–2005. MSS 926. Stuart A. Rose Manuscript, Archives, and Rare Book Library, Emory University; hereafter cited in the text as Hecht Papers.

18. Letter, Sexton to Hecht, "Sat. morning" [probably 1961], Hecht Papers.

19. It was following her reading and annotating of Dostoevsky, Rilke, and

Kafka in Philip Rahv's course at Brandeis University in 1960 that Sexton may have underlined the copy of *Henderson* that she described to her therapist in 1961 (*AS* 128). While the copy of *Henderson* that Sexton carried is not housed with her library at the Ransom Center, it may have been among the books that she lost when her luggage was stolen while traveling in Europe in 1963 (*SPL* 184). Letter, Sexton to Hecht, 2 Oct. "all luggage stolen then," box 63, folder 36, Hecht Papers.

20. Sexton adds to Bellow's response in her account during the interview. See *NES* 96–97 and *AS* 161–62.

21. This was before the novel's success led to his placing of his *Adventures of Augie March* (1953) and *Henderson* manuscripts in the University of Chicago archive for tax purposes (Atlas 339).

22. Letter, Bellow to Sexton, n.d., Sexton Papers, box 18, folder 1. Sexton also repeats his response in her interview with the *Paris Review* (*NES* 95–96).

## Works Cited

Atlas, James. *Bellow: A Biography*. New York: Random House, 2000. Print.

Bellow, Saul. *Henderson the Rain King*. 1958. New York: Penguin, 1996. Print.

———. *Herzog*. 1964. New York: Penguin, 1991. Print.

Bryant, Marsha. *Women's Poetry and Popular Culture*. New York: Palgrave, 2011. Print.

Chen, Amy Hildreth. "Archival Bodies: Twentieth Century Literary Collections." PhD diss., Emory University, Spring 2013. Print.

Colburn, Stephen E., ed. *Anne Sexton: Telling the Tale*. Ann Arbor: U of Michigan P, 1988. Print.

Davison, Peter. *The Fading Smile: Poets in Boston, 1955–1960, From Robert Frost to Robert Lowell to Sylvia Plath*. 1994. New York: Norton, 1996. Print.

Gill, Jo. *Anne Sexton's Confessional Poetics*. Gainesville, FL: UP of Florida, 2007. Print.

Golden, Amanda. "Anne Sexton's Modern Library." *Collecting, Curating, and Researching Writers' Libraries: A Handbook*. Ed. Richard W. Oram and Joseph Nicholson. Rowman and Littlefield, 2014. 85–102. Print.

———. *Annotating Modernism: Marginalia and Pedagogy from Virginia Woolf to the Confessional Poets*. Routledge, Forthcoming. Print.

Helle, Anita, ed. *The Unraveling Archive: Essays on Sylvia Plath*. Ann Arbor: U of Michigan P, 2007. Print.

Hume George, Diana, ed. *Sexton: Selected Criticism*. Chicago: U of Chicago P, 1988. Print.

McClatchy, J. D., ed. *Anne Sexton: The Artist and Her Critics*. Bloomington: Indiana UP, 1978. Print.

McGowan, Philip. *Anne Sexton and Middle Generation Poetry: The Geography of Grief*. Westport, CT: Praeger Publishers, 2004. Print.

Middlebrook, Diane Wood. *Anne Sexton: A Biography*. 1991. New York: Random House, 1992. Print.

———. "Circle of Women Artists: Tillie Olsen and Anne Sexton at the Radcliffe Institute." *Listening to Silences: New Essays in Feminist Criticism*. Ed. Elaine Hedges and Shelley Fisher Fishkin. New York: Oxford UP, 1994. 17–22. Print.

———. "Diane Middlebrook's interview on Anne Sexton biography (Part 1)." *You Tube*. Web. 15 July 2014. <http://www.youtube.com/watch?v=-a-25dg9STc>.

———. "The Making of 'The Awful Rowing Toward God.'" *Rossetti to Sexton: Six Women Poets at Texas*. Ed. Dave Oliphant. Austin: Harry Ransom Center for Humanities Research, 1992. 223–35. Print.

Nelson, Deborah. *Pursuing Privacy in Cold War America*. New York: Columbia UP, 2002. Print.

Oliphant, Dave, ed. *Rossetti to Sexton: Six Women Poets at Texas*. Austin: Harry Ransom Center for Humanities Research, 1992. Print.

Rifkin, Libbie. *Career Moves: Olson, Creeley, Zukofsky, Berrigan, and the American Avant-Garde*. Madison: U of Wisconsin P, 2000. Print.

Salvio, Paula M. *Anne Sexton: Teacher of Weird Abundance*. Albany, NY: State U of New York P, 2007. Print.

Sexton, Linda Gray. Conversation with the author, 17 June 2013.

———. *Half in Love: Surviving the Legacy of Suicide*. Berkeley: Counterpoint Press, 2011. Kindle ed.

———. *Searching for Mercy Street: My Journey Back to My Mother, Anne Sexton*. New York: Little, Brown, 1994. Print.

Skorczewski, Dawn M. *An Accident of Hope: The Therapy Tapes of Anne Sexton*. New York: Routledge, 2012. Print.

Stead, Lisa. Introduction. *The Boundaries of the Literary Archive: Reclamation and Representation*. Ed. Carrie Smith and Lisa Stead. Farnham, Surrey: Ashgate, 2013. Print.

———. "Letter Writing, Cinemagoing, and Archive Ephemera." *The Boundaries of the Literary Archive: Reclamation and Representation*. Ed. Carrie Smith and Lisa Stead. Farnham, Surrey: Ashgate, 2013. 139–53. Print.

Wagner-Martin, Linda, ed. *Critical Essays on Anne Sexton*. Boston: G. K. Hall, 1989. Print.

"Women of Talent." *Newsweek*. 23 Oct.1961: 94–97. Print.

# ···1

## "The house / of herself"

Reading Place and Space in the Poetry of Anne Sexton

JO GILL

The work of confessional poet, Anne Sexton, the writer primarily known for her apparent transgression of the limits of personal privacy, has only belatedly been understood as having wider preoccupations and a deeper significance than her own troubled psyche. Deborah Nelson's *Pursuing Privacy in Cold War America* has situated her writing in relation to the contradictory impulses of the Cold War years; Philip McGowan's *Anne Sexton and Middle Generation Poetry* has read it in a midcentury literary context, my own *Anne Sexton's Confessional Poetics* has offered a new reading of Sexton and of the confessional movement in terms of the insights of Foucault and other poststructuralist thinkers, while Gillian White's *Lyric Shame* has presented a provocative re-reading of Sexton's place within the larger field of postwar poetics. What has not yet been proposed—although what is tacitly suggested by some of the studies above—is a critical analysis of Sexton's poetry that situates it spatially.

My original intention for the present essay was to examine Sexton's writing in terms of its negotiation and reworking of history. This remains, as will become clear, one part of my argument. But as my thinking about this project has developed, it soon became apparent—both for theoretical reasons and because of the imperatives of the poems themselves—that to think about history in isolation would be inadequate. In order to understand

Sexton's poetic engagement with the past, it is also necessary and fruitful, to consider her writing in relation to place and space.[1]

My argument in this respect is informed by the body of theoretical work that has emerged over the past several decades in the field of cultural geography. Cultural geography explores the relationships between space and time, the topographical and the temporal, and the ways in which each of these shapes and mediates the other. As important, it recognizes that subjectivity itself is constituted, understood, and played out in relation to both of these dimensions. Cultural geography is concerned, in Edward Soja's terms, with "the inherent spatiality of human life" (1). For Sara Blair, "spatiality" is best defined as the "affective and social experience of space" (544). This "spatial turn," as Soja terms it, prompts us to recognize "the simultaneity and inter-woven complexity of the social, the historical, *and the spatial*, their insepa-rability and often problematic interdependence" (14). Doreen Massey de-velops the point, arguing that "The social spaces through which we live do not only consist of physical things: of bricks and mortar, streets and bridges, mountains and sea-shore, and of what we make of these things. They consist also of those less tangible spaces we construct out of social interaction. The intimate social relations of the kitchen and the interaction from there to the backyard and the living room" (49). Such insights are particularly helpful in understanding the social experience of gender and evaluating the extent to which it is constituted in relation both to historical *and* to geographical circumstances. As we will see, this is an insight that underpins many of my readings of Sexton's work in the chapter that follows.

Central to these debates is an understanding that a geographical cri-tique—that is, one that attends to the spatial dimensions of existence—is *as* important as an understanding of historical context to our reading of lit-erary and cultural texts. The equivalence of these fields of enquiry is crucial. It is not that cultural geography has replaced history, but rather that cultural geography is able to complement, supplement, develop or critique histori-cist analysis, enabling both to better comprehend the temporal, spatial, ma-terial, social, and discursive conditions of subjectivity and, specifically in Sexton's case, its poetic representation.[2] Such methodologies demand, in Soja's terms, that we "shift the 'rhythm' of dialectical thinking from a tem-poral to a more spatial mode, from a linear or diachronic sequencing to the configurative simultaneities, the synchronies" (21). Poetry—as a form that operates simultaneously in time and in space—is particularly amenable to being viewed through this critical lens. The aim of this chapter is to find out what happens to our understanding of Sexton's work when we move away from a biographical, psychoanalytic, or poststructuralist reading, or even a purely historicist reading, and begin to think in this radically new way.

Sexton's poetry is rich with specific places (the suburban kitchen, the asylum or "summer hotel," the beach house) and with abstract spaces (the forest, the hall of mirrors, the stage set). And both, as I will argue, are inextricably associated with the retrospective gaze—a search back through time, a dredging of past memories, or the scrutiny of the "hauled up / notebooks" of life, in the words of "45 Mercy Street" (CP 484). In this chapter, I will address poems that explicitly yoke space and time, that locate experience and the memory of it in specific places, and, conversely, that use place and space as an index of particular temporal moments and thus as a productive route (I use the word advisedly) to understanding.

Sexton's first collection *To Bedlam and Part Way Back* (1960) is replete with topographical metaphors.[3] Numerous poems open with an explicit depiction of place. For example, the "nest of your real death" in the 1958 poem "Elizabeth Gone" (CP 8); the emphatic "Here, in front of the summer hotel" of "The Kite" (11); the opening line, "Oh down at the tavern" of "Portrait of an Old Woman on the College Tavern Wall" (18); the kitchen window and suburban street of "What's That" (25); the claustrophobic automobile interior in "The Road Back" (30); the "thin classroom," "window sill," and "plain chairs" that provide the setting for "Elegy in the Classroom" (32), and the "locked screens," "faded curtains," and "window sills" of the "best ward at Bedlam" in "Lullaby" (29) that is also, of course, the setting for "You, Doctor Martin," "Ringing the Bells," and numerous other poems in the collection. All make explicit use of particular places in order not only to set the scene but also to invoke aspects of experience and subjectivity. "Portrait of an Old Woman on the College Tavern Wall" itself emerged from a particular time and a specific place; Sexton derived a parable about isolation and identification from the convergence of the two. As she recalls in unpublished lecture notes (prepared for a series of talks she delivered at Colgate University in 1972 while holding the Crawshaw Chair in Literature): "I was sitting in a tavern in Antioch, Ohio. I was there for a writers' conference back in 1959. All the poets and teachers and prose writers were sitting around a table singing songs and drinking beer. We were very gay. We were very merry. Suddenly I felt I was an observer[. . . . ] I looked up and there was a portrait staring at me of the woman who originally owned the house[. . . . ] At that moment I entered her life. I applied the mask of her face. I looked out from the wall and with her tongue I spoke these words" (1).

Other poems in *To Bedlam* spell out their locations more subtly, as in the seaside setting of "Torn Down from Glory Daily" and "The Exorcists" or the rural landscape of "The Farmer's Wife," or signal the alienating un-certainties associated with placelessness. In "Kind Sir: These Woods," for example, the location, although apparently specific (on "*The* Island" [my emphasis]) is simultaneously imprecise and uncertain (*CP* 4). The speak-er's repeated attempts to pin down this particular place (it is on "The is-land," it is in "down Maine," it is in woodland "between Dingley Dell" and "Grandfather's Cottage") seem, finally, overdetermined as though to signal its elusiveness. The strangeness of the environment is rendered even more alien by images of "cold fog" that obscure what might otherwise have been a familiar landscape and by the sinister inversion of time such that, *Macbeth*-like, night seems like day and vice versa. Space here forms an apt metaphor for the speaker's own disturbed and uncertain mindset; her figurative loss of selfhood is anticipated, stimulated, and replicated in the poem's "strange" topography.

I have previously argued of "Kind Sir: These Woods," that it pictures a confessional speaker in the process of seeking out conditions commensu-rate with self-scrutiny. I would now add that the spatial dynamics of the poem offer a further possible way of reading—one that is also applicable to several of the other poems mentioned thus far. "Kind Sir: These Woods," like some of these others, describes the thrill—which is also the psychic risk—of dissociating oneself from and in space and time. It indicates the importance to the establishment of a stable subjectivity of a sense of one's geographical and temporal relationships and dares to contemplate the con-sequences of the loss of such foundations.

Other poems from the same period expose a similar and equally trou-bling rootlessness, or a search for place, which is often a metaphorical jour-ney into the past and a (usually thwarted) quest for a stable identity. "The Lost Ingredient," for example, opens with an imagined memory of "gentle ladies" seeking a cure for their nonspecific ailments in the salt waters of Atlantic City (*CP* 30). Moving forward (albeit not always smoothly, hence the strange chronology of the poem's opening words: "Almost yesterday"), the speaker records a journey "West" which is interrupted by "lost" minutes of driving time during each stop at a specific place, culminating in a visit to the casino at Reno. As the "gentle ladies" of stanza one wait, seemingly endlessly, for a cure that never comes, so, too, the speaker travels, apparently fruitlessly, in search of reassurance about her own psychic integrity. The journey across the American landscape, like the dredging of past memories and past narratives that is characteristic of the psychotherapeutic process, proves unable to deliver the coherent subjectivity sought. Instead the speaker finds herself caught in a temporal trap, or a kind of Möbius strip of time and place, where today and yesterday, here and there become indistinguishable, leaving her in the closing stanza tantalizingly out of reach of her destination.

Several poems of this period evoke the significance of travel to, across, or between particular locations—none of which, alone, provides the secure foothold sought by the speaker in order to ground her increasingly vulnerable subjectivity. In "You, Doctor Martin," the addressee himself straddles space and time and in so doing crosses the divide between the rational and the insane, the everyday and the exceptional. This is memorably realized as the walk from "breakfast to madness" (*CP* 3). His controlled and deliberate stroll is parodied in the next line by the speaker's uncontrolled rush ("I speed") to occupy the same space. The relentless immediacy of the present-tense verb forms ("You walk," "I speed," "We stand,") represents a troubling cessation of time as though in this strange space temporality is suspended. Recognizable signs of family, domesticity, and home are unsettlingly inverted; home becomes a spied-on "nest," the asylum dining room a regimented, institutionalized space where inmates eat "in rows," the bedrooms are defamiliarized as "separate boxes." The effect is uncanny. There is—there must be—a history here, a personal and social past that would explain the overwhelming present. But this is inferred only tentatively at the end of the poem as though it has been effaced by the immediacy of the experience of this particular place. "Once I was beautiful," the speaker wistfully recalls in the antepenultimate line, but now "I am myself." This self is firmly and explicitly located within the physical and metaphorical cage of the asylum, hence the closing metaphor of regimented stacks of moccasins, inert like the speaker, waiting on a "silent shelf."

"The Double Image," arguably Sexton's first major poem, similarly positions its speaker in transit across and between various places and spaces. The poem opens with the speaker and her young daughter standing, presumably by a domestic window, and watching as the "yellow leaves go queer" (CP 35). The experience seems as firmly located in time (hence the Fall setting and careful delineation of the speaker's and addressee's ages) as it is in space. If anything, and again like in "Kind Sir: These Woods," the many locations of the poem are overdetermined. The speaker is almost trying too hard to secure this experience in a context otherwise marked by uncertainty ("you'll never know"), loss (the "struck leaves letting go"), and the temptations of self-annihilation as experienced and represented by the "I" who, in section one, stanza two, confesses to herself, to her reader, and to her infant daughter, that she has twice attempted suicide. Indeed, the specificities of place and time become a paradoxical index of their elusiveness. And as the poem proceeds, it becomes clear that the speaker herself is in perpetual motion, unsettled, at home nowhere. She circles around her own home, her mother's house, and the mental asylum or "sealed hotel" just as she fleetingly experiments with the social identities of mother, daughter, and psychiatric patient. She is never able, quite, to settle into or to claim any of these locations or subjectivities as her own. What she sees and envies in her own child is the ability to live in her own skin, to *be* herself in time and, more specifically, in space or, as the final stanza puts it, to settle in the "house / of herself."

A slightly later poem, "Housewife," from Sexton's second collection, *All My Pretty Ones* (1962), offers a different and less affirmative perspective on a similar situation. As the poem's opening line rather flatly asserts: "Some women marry houses," thereby growing "another kind of skin" (CP 77). The poem anticipates Nancy Duncan's argument about the potential of the kinds of theoretical approaches outlined above, particularly when thinking about the ways in which the social experience of space inflects gender. "Feminists," she explains, "are presently exploring the far-reaching implications of a new epistemological viewpoint based on the idea of knowledge as embodied, engendered, and embedded in the material context of place and space" (1). The "knowledge" in Sexton's poem is the knowledge of suffering and of coercion; the female subject is trapped within rather than liberated by her environment. "Housewife" exaggerates and allegorizes the enforced identification with the home so characteristic of the experience of white middle-class women of Sexton's generation and culture.[4]

It would be a mistake, though, to read Sexton's description of such domestic spaces as always and inevitably oppressive. At times domesticity—a term that describes everyday duties taking place in the private domain—is indeed restricting (as, for example, in "Housewife") or banal ("Man and Wife") or grotesque ("The House" and "The Death Baby"). But elsewhere, the domestic sphere proves to be nurturing and productive. In "What's That," for example, the suburban interior (signified by line two's allusion to the "kitchen window" and a later reference to the "suburban street") becomes the fertile resting place for the speaker's muse that arrives unannounced, but nevertheless finds a welcome home (*CP* 25–26). Similarly, and from the same early period, "For John, Who Begs Me Not to Enquire Further" sees in the familiar spaces of home ("my kitchen") the source of creativity and, as important, of poetic dialogue. As the poem famously concludes, here setting up an explicit connection between place and subjectivity: "my kitchen, your kitchen, / my face, your face" (35).

In his influential study, *The Poetics of Space: The Classic Look at How We Experience Intimate Spaces*, Gaston Bachelard offers a suggestive reading of the subtle significations of space in a variety of representational modes. His particular interest is in the origin and operation of poetic images.[5] More specifically, his focus is on "images of *felicitous space*," or on the ways in which the poetic imagination ascribes particular meanings or "imagined values" to space. To narrow things down still further, Bachelard examines "the problem of the poetics of the house," addressing the ways in which "the house image" (and its various cognates including, among others, "the houses of things," "nests and shells," metaphors of "large and small," "house and universe," "open and closed") together constitute the "topography of our intimate being" (xxxv–xxxvi).

For Bachelard, spatial images from the most obvious invocations of domestic architecture through to more subtle signifiers (cupboards, corners, nests, shells) are revelations of a "psychic state" that "bespeak intimacy" (72); the unconscious, he suggests, is thus "housed." Sexton's early poem, "Elizabeth Gone" (from *To Bedlam and Part Way Back*) provides a startling illustration of this process. According to Bachelard, "nest and shell are two great images that reflect back their daydreams" (120). What I understand him to mean by this is that they crystallize profound human desires. In Sexton's poem, conversely and exponentially more interestingly, they signify her worst fears.

"Elizabeth Gone," through its title alone, signals an explicit and extreme loss. The "nest" in the poem, as the opening line reveals, is "the nest of your real death" (*CP* 8). The elegized object is emphatically "gone" (hence the title), but she is also simultaneously there, as indicated by the immediacy of address to an apostrophized "you." The poem's use of the metaphor of the nest thus invokes but then swiftly undermines the association with security and comfort identified by Bachelard as typical of its deployment. The "nest" in this case signifies not safety but regression to a baby-like state of dependency. The cocoon-like deathbed, while protective of and for Elizabeth, repels the speaker who describes the dying woman as being out of the reach or "print" of her "nervous fingers." The metaphor is characteristically ambiguous in that Elizabeth is beyond reach literally (she can no longer be touched) and figuratively (she can no longer be affected by the intimate revelations of this very text). As is so common in Sexton's work, there is an anxiety here about the ethical consequences of the process of writing, or of the damage that might be caused by her "print." The "nest" itself is transmuted in this the first part of the poem into a "human bed" (itself a curiously ambivalent image both of birth and of death) and from thence into a coffin or "crate." For Bachelard, images of boxes and cupboards signal the important "dialectics of inside and outside" (85). In Sexton's poem, the "crate" represents the ultimate dialectic—that between living and dead, the present and the "gone."

In the second section of the poem, the nest image is abandoned in favor of its analogue, the shell. Again, for Bachelard, the shell (especially the snail shell) connotes a place of safety, or the hermeticism of a self-contained domesticity. For Sexton, the image is altogether more troubling. The "ash and bony shells" that make up the addressee's relics represent not self-possession but its opposite. They contain nothing; they are empty vessels. Sheltering no life, they "Rattl[e] like stones," until they are finally thrown away. Thus Sexton inverts the nurturing, protective promise of this spatial metaphor. Having said this, for Bachelard, images of nests and shells represent, in part, the "sign of *return*" and, as he goes on to say, "human returning takes place in the great rhythm of human life, rhythm that reaches back across the years and, through the dream, combats all absence." In this sense, Sexton's appropriation of images of nests and shells in "Elizabeth Gone" allows her to return in memory—which is also in imagination—to the lost, mourned Elizabeth while also conceding the inevitability, in Bachelard's terms, of the "great rhythm" of life and death. Thus she acknowledges the immediate loss while situating it in a wider temporal context. The images, in enabling her to cradle or cocoon the memory, thereby allow her—in these words from the final stanza—to "let her go, let her go" and to resume her own life.

Sexton's rather later poem, the often-overlooked "Christmas Eve," from her third collection *Live or Die* (1966), invokes the intimate spaces of home to similarly unsettling effect. "Christmas Eve" depicts the speaker contemplating the loss of her mother on what we can only assume to be the first anniversary of the latter's death (CP 139). It situates the speaker alone within the family home, seeking therein some kind of refuge from the exigencies of the outside world—a world that is in the throes of social change. The cyclicality of the Christmas Eve setting functions as an index of the passing of time, bestowing an attenuated version of what Angus Fletcher identifies as "diurnal knowledge" (an awareness of cyclical and seasonal change and a reminder of the "natural order") (77, 91). The temporal setting is resonant in its immediacy. It gestures back to a succession of past Christmas Eves and implicitly anticipates those of the future. The latter may be replete with hope—in the terms of Siobhan Phillips's study of *The Poetics of the Everyday*, with the promise of "ceremonial renewal"—or, as seems more likely here, foreshadowed by loss (2).

In Sexton's poem, Christmas Eve is a time to lament the dead and to acknowledge their legacy to the living. The intimate space of the home, decorated with the familiar—if simultaneously uncanny—tree (the outside is, here, brought inside for display), becomes a space poignant with longing (CP 4). Like in Bachelard's *Poetics*, the house is "our corner of the world"; lit by Christmas bulbs, it "vigilantly waits" (34).[6] It offers something akin to communication with the lost, mourned mother whose absence from this domestic space is particularly marked. When set for the first time against the routines and trappings of the season, the illuminated home seems imbued with her presence; it "becomes human" (Bachelard 35).

Similarly intimate spaces are to be found in Sexton's second volume, *All My Pretty Ones* (1962), for example, in the October 1961 poem, "The Fortress" (CP 66–68). Written at a time of growing political tension (the disastrous events of the Bay of Pigs had taken place just six months earlier), the poem tests the limits of the supposedly safe spaces of home. Addressed to the young daughter, Linda, "The Fortress" seeks to weave around her a protective spell. Mother and daughter lie huddled on the bed under the pink comforter. The setting promises sanctuary, but even here safety cannot be guaranteed.[7] In stanza two, as the speaker anxiously touches the daughter's "brown mole"—a blemish inherited from her own face—she is forced to concede that this may be a mark of some canker within. In a scene that allegorizes her contemporary culture's wider fear of contamination (in ideological terms; the McCarthyite revulsion toward the enemy within, or the red-under-the-bed, and more literally, the pervasive effects of atomic fallout or other environmental toxins), she reveals how vulnerable are the boundaries between inside and out, private and public spaces, safety and danger.[8]

Throughout, the poem seeks a balance between the private domains of self, family, and home, and the wider—and insidious—pressures of nation and history. Stanza four must confess that the intimacy of home offers but a frail and insubstantial barrier against the larger imperatives of this place and time. The speaker is impelled to explain to her daughter that she can no longer protect her, that she will remain forever vulnerable even in adulthood and in "your own house on your own land" (CP 67). The poem's attempt at redemption, and at the restoration of the intimate bonds between mother and daughter, promises much. In the words of the final line, "I promise you love. Time will not take away that." Yet the sinister incursions of disease, poison, and fear in the preceding stanzas compromise the efficacy of the closing benediction. As stanza four had already warned, this may not be a promise that the speaker is empowered to keep.

In "The Fortress," as in several of the other poems discussed thus far, Sexton establishes a dialectic of inside and out. In poems such as "Flee on Your Donkey" (CP 97–105), from the 1966 collection Live or Die, it is not so much the specificity of either of these places that signifies as the relationship between and process of moving from one realm or dimension to another. These are evoked in terms of historical and spatial change and ultimately in terms of the tension (as articulated in the collection's title) between living and dying.

"Flee on Your Donkey," like "You, Doctor Martin" and a number of other asylum poems, examines the seductiveness of these suburban sanctuaries—particularly to the desperate and alienated who have no other port of call.[9] Starting in the past tense ("Because there was"), the poem rapidly moves into a kind of perpetual—and pathologized—present as signaled by repeated allusions to the diagnostic and therapeutic events of "Today" (CP 97, 98). The speaker is thus suspended in a liminal space; neither child nor adult, neither sick nor well, neither yesterday nor tomorrow. But then the narrative swings back again, further this time, into the speaker's childhood memories of home (and specifically of listening to radio shows such as *The Green Hornet* and *The Shadow*) and then forward into the present-day experience of "Now," and of the "*Dinn, Dinn, Dinn!*" of the asylum (99). The effect is vertiginous, as though neither space nor time can be brought into proper equilibrium. Out of this dialectical suspension between historical and spatial poles comes a new insight, a realization that the speaker must move beyond this place and the history it embodies in order ever to become well. The circumscription of her present condition stimulates a plaintive speculation as to what might have been: "I could have gone around the world twice / or had new children—all boys" (99). But it also prompts painful memories of other scenes of past constriction—of her dead mother and alcoholic father.

For the poem's speaker, the painful experiences of the past and of her troubled psyche are reified in images of particular places; the analyst's "office" (located more precisely still on "Marlborough Street"), the "snowy street" on which she once collapsed, and the barred windows of her present-day prison.[10] In order to break free of her long-lived psychological illness, she must escape the place that seems to exemplify it. As the magnificent final section of the poem avows, the speaker ("Anne") must take courage and flee, careering out on the donkey, "any old way you please!" (104).

The poems of Sexton's middle period, *Love Songs* (1969) and *Transformations* (1971), use space and time to rather different and often more attenuated and abstract effect. In *Love Songs*, places are rarely specifically described and the focus, as for example in "Mr. Mine," "Knee Song," or "Us," is often on the physical body, on sexuality, and on desire, rather than on particular events in concrete places. *Transformations* makes extensive use of imagined or fictionalized spaces such as the "dwarf house" in "Snow White and the Seven Dwarfs" and the "room full of straw" in which the miller's daughter spins her gold in "Rumpelstiltskin" (224, 233). Nevertheless, the effect of these often stylized settings is to expose the banality of the fairy tale ideal. The "rich man['s]" house in "Cinderella," for example (258), is revealed to be a place of deprivation for the rejected youngest daughter, a "marriage market" for the favored older two, and a place of despair—not unlike the suburban trap indicted by Betty Friedan in her 1963 *The Feminine Mystique*—for the supposedly contented married couple who are dismissed in the poem's sardonic conclusion as "Regular Bobbsey Twins." Likewise, in

"One-Eye, Two-Eyes, Three-Eyes," the family home is the site of corruption and violence.

"Red Riding Hood," the poem in the collection most explicitly concerned with the evocation of place, pictures the speaker constructing for herself an ideal home—"a summer house on Cape Ann. / A simple A-frame" (CP 269). The fantasy evoked here—and so dominant in the period—of taking possession of a newly built, well-equipped, single-family home, proves chimerical or worse.[11] The house is possessed (note the images of haunting and the specter of the mother, "that departed soul"), toxic (gas seeps in through the windows), and deeply disturbing (the image of the "smell" in the "electric kitchen" invokes the experience of Electro-Convulsive Therapy [ECT]). This preamble introduces the story of "Red Riding Hood," the young girl who is safe nowhere and at her most vulnerable in the place where she should be protected, her grandmother's cottage. The sense of threat is pervasive and is matched only in the collection's penultimate poem, "Hansel and Gretel," wherein the family home again proves to be malignant; the site of nurturance becomes one of rejection as the starving children are expelled by their despairing parents. The witch's cottage in the woods—or, in Sexton's vivid terms, a "rococo house," constructed entirely from food even up to its "chocolate chimney"—corrupts the children, turning them into scheming murderers (CP 288). In these poems, then, "home" does not signify in quite the way we might expect. Place determines experience and thereby subjectivity, and it determines, too, the rhetoric of the poems themselves which often play on our expectations of homely spaces the better to undermine them (a point to which we will return shortly when we examine the uncanny architecture of some of Sexton's late poems).

In Sexton's next and subsequent collections, for example in *The Book of Folly* (1972), the focus is on the intensities of personal relationships and psychological experience, both of which appear to be disconnected in space and time. "Mother and Daughter," for example, returns to the intimate and now severely compromised relationship between the generations seen first in "The Fortress" and "The Double Image." The specificities of time and space evoked in the earlier poems have now faded into the background. Where "The Fortress" is inspired by a particular moment in the whispered intimacy of the bedroom (speaker and daughter cuddle up under a pink quilt), in the later poem, "Mother and Daughter," there is a separation of subject and object. The mother declaims at one remove, denouncing her child and thereby consolidating both the distance between them and the larger processes of change and of loss that the poem emblematizes (305).

In other poems in this collection, places are figurative or nonspecific and often surreal. "Going Gone," for example, opens on an apocalyptic landscape, scattered with "walls and barns," with "black-eyed Susans" (the name of a flower, but also an image of violent abuse), with "circus tents," and "moon rockets" (311). The nightmarish vision of a subsequent poem, "The Red Shoes" (inspired, no doubt, by memories of Michael Powell and Emeric Pressburger's disturbing 1948 film of the same name) opens in similar style with the speaker pausing in a depopulated and derelict "dead city" to tie on her "red shoes" (315). Thus Sexton seeks to secure or ground her narratives; in each case it appears that the only fit locus for her despair is a dystopian wasteland.

Those poems that do move closer to home depict once-familiar spaces in what we might call "uncanny" terms. Sigmund Freud, in his essay on "The Uncanny," is preoccupied by the relationship between the familiar (the homely or *heimlich*) and the unfamiliar, or *unheimlich*. More properly, perhaps, he is concerned with the slipperiness of these terms and the mutability of the relationship between them; his interest lies in the indeterminacy of the borderlines, or the moment when the *heimlich* shades into the *unheimlich*, and vice versa. It is worth noting the inescapably spatial and temporal terms—of borderlines and moments—that I am necessarily deploying here.

Uncanny effects are produced as a consequence of some kind of slippage or error in the efficacy of the formative processes by which the infant child becomes a conscious subject. In brief, according to Freud's influential model of the human mind, during the oedipal stage the dependent (male) infant must learn the necessity of separating himself from his mother and of aligning himself with his father.[12] The infant does this under what he perceives as the threat of castration—a threat often metonymized in literature, such as in E. T. A. Hoffman's short story, "The Sandman," of which Freud's "The Uncanny" offers a sustained critique, in terms of damage to the eyes or the loss of sight. At the oedipal moment, certain otherwise psychically damaging desires and forces are pushed or repressed into a newly emergent space—the unconscious—where they can be retained under (usually) safe control. Only if the ego and superego (the conscious mind and a form of socially constructed conscience) momentarily drop their guard might brief, unexpected glimpses emerge of that which is usually kept under safe control. These moments are common in dreams, jokes, parapraxis, and in what Freud, after many attempts, defines as the "Uncanny." The uncanny "proceeds from something familiar which has been repressed" and manifests itself as "something repressed which *recurs*" [Freud's emphasis] (370, 363). It appears in a number of ways that vary over time and in different contexts; in other words, the uncanny is an effect rather than a formula. In his essay on the theme, Freud lists several possible examples of this effect including animism, automatism, the appearance of the double, involuntary action or repetition (what he was subsequently, in "Beyond the Pleasure Principle," to associate with the death drive), the fear of being buried alive (a fear to which many of Sexton's poems gesture [see, for example, "The Hoarder"]), and finally, as in Sexton's poem of this title, in silence.

In "The Silence," from Sexton's *The Book of Folly*, the once-familiar—and for the woman-writer, idealized and nurturing—"room of one's own" becomes a disturbing and uncanny space. It is, at one and the same time, familiar and unfamiliar as represented by images of a "whitewashed" room, bleached "chicken bones," and "pure garbage" (*CP* 318). The space distils the speaker's own sense of emptiness—her own evisceration. The room and the house are metaphors both for her sense of psychic unease and for her experience of feeling physically out of place. The inescapably architectural connotations of Freud's concept of the *unheimlich* or unhomely are brought vividly into focus in Sexton's poem; in other words, the disturbance in the speaker's sense of herself is absolutely rooted in her spatial dislocation. As Anthony Vidler proposes, here developing Freud's thought: "The theme of the uncanny serves to join architectural speculation on the peculiarly unstable nature of 'house and home' to more general reflection on the questions of social and individual estrangement, alienation, [and] exile" (ix).

Sexton's poem exemplifies the potential of such a perspective. The room of the poem's opening line is characterized by "the silence" of the title, effaced of distinguishing features, troubled by strange repetitions such as the dominance of the word white ("whitewashed," "white," "whiter"), and shadowed by signs of death ("chicken bones" seen fading to nothing in the cold light of the moon). In this alien, dislocated realm where the suburban home is transformed into a "rural station house," the speaker herself appropriates an uncanny form. In stanza two she is depicted as a blackness and a whiteness; features that—while polar opposites—seem strangely interchangeable (the hair is made "dark" by "white fire"). Allusions to "eyes" gesture both to the underlying fear of castration that subtends the early stages of the oedipal crisis and to the place of doubling and repetition in Freud's account, hence Sexton's metaphor of "twenty eyes" in line five of the second stanza. In the third stanza, the speaker's repressed desires emerge to shatter the surface silence. She "fill[s] the room" with language, her pen "leak[s]" blood, her words fly "zinging" into the atmosphere (CP 319). Yet it is silence, "always silence," that finally wins the day and that returns the speaker's words to her, emptied of meaning and power like a huge "baby mouth" (319).[13] The effect, again, is uncanny—the monstrous baby mouth forms a cruel, parodic double of the speaker's own voice and a signifier of the failure of her attempt to put her experience into language.

"The Room of My Life," from *The Awful Rowing Toward God* (1975) (CP 422) uses physical location to equally uncanny effect. "Here," as the poem opens, "in the room of my life," material objects cannot hold still. Architecture dominates the speaker; the room is anthropomorphized by reference to "the suffering brother" of its wooden walls, to lamps that keep "poking" at her, and to windows that seem to be "starving." The effect is disorientating to speaker and reader alike. Shorn of her moorings and unable to locate herself in relation to a physical setting that refuses to stay still (to a room that seems to transmute into an ocean-going vessel), the speaker is finally cast adrift. In this poem a fragmented subjectivity proves unable to achieve wholeness in part because of its dissociation in time (the poem speaks in an immediate present tense entirely disconnected from the past and the future) but primarily because of its disconnection in space. To extend the argument of Leigh Gilmore's important study, *Autobiographics: A Feminist Theory of Women's Self-Representation*, one can only begin to understand who one is by relating or triangulating oneself in terms of fixed points in the landscape or to cartographic representations of such loci. Without such reference points, the subject struggles to locate or articulate her own meaning (6–7). In "The Room of My Life," her own words are overwhelmed in the end by "the sea that bangs in my throat" (CP 422).

This profound disorientation—physical, chronological, and existential—is seen most obviously, perhaps, in the late and again little-studied poem, "45 Mercy Street," the first poem in the first part ("Beginning the Hegira") of the eponymous collection (CP 481–84). Here, memory is both temporal and spatial. The poem evokes and tests the condition of nostalgia, a concept that signals not only a desire to return to the past but also a yearning for lost places. More than this, as Wendy Wheeler proposes, nostalgia "both returns us to the affective images of the place (or places) in which we think we have been immediately present to ourselves in experience—to a sense of 'being-in-place'—and also connects us to other subjects" (98). In Sexton's poem, the nostalgia is felt particularly acutely even though—or, perhaps, precisely because—the place she seeks is phantasmagorical. "45 Mercy Street" is the object of a disordered imagination—and all the more vivid for that. Moreover, the "other subjects" (to quote Wheeler) who might provide some sense of home and thus of familiarity to herself are equally elusive or, worse still, malign.[14]

"45 Mercy Street" opens with the return of the repressed memory of a particular place, or of a set of emotions identified with place. The "Mercy Street" of the poem's title, even though it figures relentlessly in the speaker's dreams, or perhaps nightmares, tantalizingly cannot be found. The memory of this absent place is inextricably linked with the generations of family who previously lived there, with the "mother, grandmother, great-grandmother," and household help (CP 481).[15] And it also summons to the speaker's mind recollections of the family's repressed past history, as previously played out in this lost place, of alcoholism, insanity, oppression, and illegitimacy. The first-person speaker's search for self—or her attempt to find a coherent subjectivity—occurs against the topography of the lost "Mercy Street" home. Stripped of the familiar markers of normative, white middle-class identity in the postwar period—the "green Ford," the "house in the suburbs," and the "two little kids"—she is reduced to prowling the streets, "hold[ing] matches at the street signs" in a futile attempt to find what she is looking for (483, 482).

In a closing gesture born of frustration, the speaker abandons her search ("the street is unfindable" [483]) and concedes instead that she has only her own paltry resources to rely on. Unable to orientate herself in terms of geographical or historical markers, her only option is the painful one of constituting herself in writing or through the painful and difficult process of "haul[ing] up / notebooks" (484). Circumscribed by the exigencies of time (the "clumsy calendar" is likened to the formidable obstacle of a "cement wall"), the narration of a life seems, finally, like a poor or painful substitute for the lost objects of her search. Other poems in this collection, "Talking to Sheep," for example, similarly portray the failed quest for a stable and secure identity and posit the writing (and written) self as, at best, an ambivalent reward (484–86).

Only in the late poem, "There You Were," is Sexton able, at last, to bring subject, place, and time into productive and beneficent alignment (552–54). Like "The Consecrating Mother," (drafted some three months earlier in April 1974), the poem is addressed to Sexton's then-therapist, Barbara Schwartz (AS 395). After the chaos and despair of the poems in her preceding two or three collections, "There You Were" reaches some kind of reconciliation with the forces which had previously controlled and eluded her by turns. The poem speaks directly to its addressee (the "you" of the opening line), and, most unusually, jettisons the relentless "I" that by this time had come to dominate Sexton's verse. The speaking subject is coherent unto herself, at last. And this is primarily because she is able simultaneously to situate herself socially (that is, in implied dialogue with the poem's "you"), spatially ("There you were . . . surveying your own unpeopled beach"), and temporally (it is "7:00 A.M" on "that day").

The poem skillfully develops a sustained metaphor of self as a broken home, washed up on the shore, with the therapist/addressee pictured as the "carpenter" charged with "set[ting] it upright" (553). The sardonic tone of earlier poems such as "Housewife" that had played with similar tropes ("Some women marry houses. / It's another kind of skin" [CP 77]) is now muted, respectful, and carefully articulates the parallels between broken psyche and sea-tossed relic. The salvaging and restoration of the treasures of the speaker's (Sexton's) damaged architecture is a labor of love. The reconstruction progresses slowly over time. The metaphorical house/self (we recall the much admired daughter, "already loud in the house / of herself" in "The Double Image") gradually appropriates and learns to inhabit the space it needs until, at last, in the poem's closing lines it can stand solid and (tentatively) proud on its shored-up foundations, "cranky but firm" (554).

As Bachelard indicates in his introduction to The Poetics of Space, the poetic images that interest him (of houses, corners, cupboards, garrets, cellars, and, of relevance to the poem just discussed, of shells) are not in any direct or straightforward way related to past experience or the memory of it. The spatial metaphors that he observes have an "entity and dynamism" of their own, or are self-generating. The implication is that such figures give meaning to, rather than derive their meaning from, the past. "This relationship is not," as he goes on to say, "a causal one" (his emphasis). It is "in the opposite of causality, that is, in *reverberation* . . . that I think we find the real measure of the being of a poetic image" (xi). Another way of putting this—one that I would argue helps us to understand the relationship between time and space in Sexton's work—is that: "Through the brilliance of an image, the distant past resounds with echoes, and it is hard to know at what depth those echoes will reverberate and die away" (xvi). Bachelard's rhetoric is topological—even geological—and it is temporal. Time and space are to be understood as mutually constitutive, malleable, and contingent. Sexton's poetry is exemplary in this regard. History manifests itself or resonates in particular places (the asylum, the family home, the washed-up house) just as particular places reverberate and find their answering echoes in the past. And it is in relation to both that the poetic subject constitutes herself.

## Notes

1. In common with other thinkers in this field, I distinguish here between space (signifying an abstract, discursive concept) and place (a specific and material location) while also recognizing the interrelationship between and importance of both in Sexton's oeuvre.

2. The introduction to, and essays in, Read's edited collection *Architecturally Speaking: Practices of Art, Architecture and the Everyday* provide a useful overview of current debates: "For some time, the publishing of late modernism has been underpinned by geographical inquiry, while history has been superseded. Space, not time, has become the privileged domain. This volume recognizes this shift towards the spatial yet is critical of the valorization of space at the expense of the critical relations between temporality, built form and the performative dynamics of architecture within everyday life" (1).

3. Where relevant in the discussion that follows, I cite the name of the collection in which each poem was first published.

4. For more on this fascinating period of American culture, see Coontz, Cowan, May, and, for a compelling reading of the ways in which Sexton's contemporary, Sylvia Plath, negotiated the discourses of the period, see Bryant.

5. For reasons of space, it is not possible to explore Bachelard's argument in detail here; suffice it to say that *The Poetics of Space* differentiates between metaphors ("at the most . . . a fabricated image") and images proper, or "the pure product of absolute imagination" (74, 75).

6. Metaphors of lamplight, streetlight, and moonlight occur with surprising frequency in the poetry of the immediate postwar period—particularly in the

poetry of the suburbs—and help to situate the action in a liminal dawn or dusk timeframe, poised between night and day. See, for example, Wright's "A Girl in a Window," Schwartz's "I Did Not Know the Truth of Growing Trees," and Nemerov's "Blue Suburban."

7. The proliferation of the postwar American suburbs may be explained, in part, by widespread consensus about the wisdom of dispersing populations away from urban centers (Hine 43). See also Stilgoe 301.

8. See Nelson and Peel for interesting accounts of contemporary poetry in relation to Cold War discourses.

9. Faith in the restorative power of nature (and anxiety, conversely, about the damaging effects of the urban environment) was reified in the late nineteenth and early twentieth centuries by the building of asylums, hospitals, penitentiaries, and reform schools in the supposedly "safe" suburbs—well away from the physiological, psychological, and moral contamination of the city. Suburbia thus became, in Panetta's words, "a place of healing for the social casualties of the industrial-immigrant city" (62). Other contemporary suburban asylum poems include Justice's "On a Painting by Patient B of the Independence State Hospital for the Insane" and Louise Bogan's "Evening in the Sanatorium." See Gill, *Poetics of the American Suburbs*.

10. Sexton's comments on the poem in the lectures she gave at Colgate University while holding the Crawshaw Chair in Literature firmly locate it in actual events that took place between her then-therapist's two offices and the street outside and they also specify dates of drafting and revision: "That night and the next morning I wrote my first draft of the poem, a poem that would take me from June 1962 to June 1966 to complete" (7).

11. In the postwar period, antipathy toward older homes was such that, "a *Saturday Evening Post* survey in 1945 revealed that only 14% of the population would be satisfied to live in an apartment or 'used house'" (Baxandall and Ewen 87).

12. The model, as numerous critics have pointed out (and as Freud himself was to attempt to remedy by means of his subsequent identification of an "Electra Complex"), is centered on male experience. See Mitchell for a cogent account of debates in the field.

13. The concept of the uncanny provides a link between Freud's model of infantile development and his subsequent account of a fundamental death drive. The death instinct, he observes, "works in silence" (*Autobiographical* 105).

14. Massey cautions that "memory and the desire for communal identifications can cut both ways. They can be an aid to reactionary claims for a return (to something which of course never quite was, or which at least is open to dispute)" (52).

15. Bishop's well-known note of caution to Robert Lowell concerning Sexton's work anticipates the imagery of this poem: "That Anne Sexton I think still has a bit too much romanticism and what I think of as the 'our beautiful old silver' school of female writing which is really boasting about how 'nice' *we* were" (*Words* 333).

## Works Cited

Bachelard, Gaston. *The Poetics of Space: The Classic Look at How We Experience Intimate Places*. 1958. Fwd. John R. Stilgoe. Boston: Beacon Press, 1994. Print.

Baxandall, Rosalyn, and Elizabeth Ewen. *Picture Windows: How the Suburbs Happened*. New York: Basic Books, 2001. Print.

Bishop, Elizabeth, and Robert Lowell. *Words in Air: The Complete Correspondence*. Ed. Thomas Travisano with Saskia Hamilton. London: Faber and Faber, 2008. Print.

Blair, Sara. "Cultural Geography and the Place of the Literary." *American Literary History* 10.3 (1998): 544–67. Print.

Bogan, Louise. *Collected Poems*. London: Peter Owen, 1956. Print.

Bryant, Marsha. "Ariel's Kitchen: *Ladies Home Journal* and the Domestic Surreal." *The Unraveling Archive: Essays on Sylvia Plath*. Ed. Anita Helle. Ann Arbor: U of Michigan P, 2007. 211–35. Print.

Coontz, Stephanie. *The Way We Never Were: American Families and the Nostalgia Trap*. Rev. ed. New York: Basic Books, 2000. Print.

Cowan, Ruth Schwartz. *More Work for Mother: The Ironies of Household Technology from the Open Hearth to the Microwave*. New York: Basic Books, 1983. Print.

Duncan, Nancy, ed. *Body Space: Destabilizing Geographies of Gender and Sexuality*. London: Routledge, 1996. Print.

Fletcher, Angus. *A New Theory for American Poetry: Democracy, the Environment, and the Future of Imagination*. Cambridge, MA: Harvard UP, 2004. Print.

Freud, Sigmund. *An Autobiographical Study*. Trans. James Strachey. London: Hogarth, 1948. Print.

———. "Beyond the Pleasure Principle." *On Metapsychology*. Penguin Freud Library 11. Ed. Angela Richards and Albert Dickson. Harmondsworth: Penguin, 1984. 269–338. Print.

———. "The Uncanny." *Art and Literature*. Penguin Freud Library 14. Ed. and trans. James Strachey. Harmondsworth: Penguin, 1985. 335–76. Print.

Friedan, Betty. *The Feminine Mystique*. 1963. Harmondsworth: Pelican, 1982. Print.

Gill, Jo. *Anne Sexton's Confessional Poetics*. Gainesville, FL: UP of Florida, 2007. Print.

———. *The Poetics of the American Suburbs*. New York: Macmillan, 2013. Print.

Gilmore, Leigh. *Autobiographics: A Feminist Theory of Women's Self-Representation*. Ithaca: Cornell UP, 1994. Print.

Hine, Thomas. *Populuxe*. London: Bloomsbury, 1988. Print.

Justice, Donald. *Selected Poems*. London: Anvil Press, 1980. Print.

Massey, Doreen. "Space-time and the politics of location." *Architecturally Speaking: Practices of Art, Architecture and the Everyday*. Ed. Alan Read. London: Routledge, 2000. 49–61. Print.

May, Elaine Tyler. *Homeward Bound: American Families in the Cold War Era*. Rev. ed. New York: Basic Books, 1999. Print.

McGowan, Philip. *Anne Sexton and Middle Generation Poetry: The Geography of Grief*. London: Praeger, 2004. Print.

Mitchell, Juliet. *Psychoanalysis and Feminism: A Radical Reassessment of Freudian Psychoanalysis*. Harmondsworth: Penguin, 1990. Print.

Nelson, Deborah. *Pursuing Privacy in Cold War America*. New York: Columbia UP, 2002. Print.

Nemerov, Howard. *The Collected Poems of Howard Nemerov*. London: University of Chicago Press, 1977. Print.

Panetta, Roger. "The Rise of the Therapeutic Suburb: Child Care in Westchester County, New York, 1880–1920." *Redefining Suburban Studies: Searching for New Paradigms*. Ed. Daniel Rubey. Hofstra: National Center for Suburban Studies, 2009. 63–77. Print.

Peel, Robin. *Writing Back: Sylvia Plath and Cold War Politics*. London: Associated UP, 2002. Print.

Phillips, Siobhan. *The Poetics of the Everyday: Creative Repetition in Modern American Verse*. New York: Columbia UP, 2010. Print.

Read, Alan, ed. *Architecturally Speaking: Practices of Art, Architecture and the Everyday*. London and New York: Routledge, 2000. Print.

Rubey, Daniel, ed. *Redefining Suburban Studies: Searching for New Paradigms*. Hofstra: National Center for Suburban Studies, 2009. Print.

Schwartz, Delmore. *What Is to be Given: Selected Poems*. Introd. by Douglas Dunn. Manchester: Carcanet, 1976. Print.

Sexton, Anne. *The Complete Poems*. Boston: Houghton Mifflin, 1981. Print.

———. Colgate University lecture notes. Sexton Papers, box 16, folder 5.

Soja, Edward. *Third Space: Journeys to Los Angeles and Other Real-and-Imagined Places*. Oxford: Blackwell, 1996. Print.

Stilgoe, John R. *Borderland: Origins of the American Suburb, 1820–1939*. London: Yale UP, 1988. Print.

Vidler, Anthony. *The Architectural Uncanny: Essays in the Modern Unhomely*. Cambridge, MA: MIT P, 1992. Print.

Wheeler, Wendy. "Nostalgia Isn't Nasty: The Postmodernizing of Parliamentary Democracy." *Altered States: Postmodernism, Politics, Culture*. London: Lawrence and Wishart, 1994. Print.

White, Gillian. *Lyric Shame*. Cambridge, MA: Harvard UP, 2014. Print.

Wright, James. *Above the River: The Complete Poems*. Introd. by Donald Hall. 1990. Newcastle: Bloodaxe Books, 1992. Print.

# ···2

## Anne Sexton's Photographic Self-Fashioning

ANITA HELLE

The condition of Anne Sexton's poetry and its relationship to twentieth-century culture is audience, an affective and aesthetic matrix through which the borders of identity, celebrity, and the "business" of words were negotiated throughout her career. That Sexton's relationship to audience was invoked, absorbed, refracted, and deflected through photographic media positions her in the mainstream of midcentury poets in what Kiku Adatto terms the "age of the photo-op," definable as a form of "image-consciousness" that unfolded since the Second World War and resulted in heightened blurring of the artifactual and the real in literature, visual media, and (eventually) on the Internet (7). Against the broader continuum of modernist fascination with the aesthetic and technological potential of seeing through the camera lens, Sexton's art and its reception participate in the expropriation and reformulation of radiant technologized forms with sublime and aesthetic effects.[1]

Surprisingly, Sexton criticism has touched only briefly on the relationship between Sexton's photographic consciousness and her reception in the broader cultural contexts of modern glamour and celebrity studies. In *Anne Sexton's Confessional Poetics*, Jo Gill opens an important inquiry into Sexton's use of visual media with a broad premise drawn from classical semiotics and deconstruction: Gill argues that the visual sign in Sexton's poetic functions "in a manner similar to linguistic signs" and as a means by which truth, identity, and representation are interrogated (123). But photography also has a medium-specific history in modernist constructions of literary celebrity. Judith Brown, Jonathan Goldman, Jennifer Wicke, and many others have contributed to a rich scholarship on photography and affective production that offers new approaches to re-thinking and re-situating the relationship between bodies, images, affects, and publics.[2] This essay argues that several genres of photography at midcentury mediated conflicting cultural narratives of Sexton's art and personhood. Piecing together poems, correspondence, and photographic images from her archive, I provide context and readings of local instances of photographic self-fashioning in Sexton's media transactions through the photographic imaginary her poems construct.

At stake in the work of cross-referencing photographs and texts in Sexton's archive is the need for reassessing a critical tradition in which Sexton is too often seen as a poet more vulnerable than most to the temptations, volatility, seductiveness, and manipulations of media's glamour-making effects. Sexton has been seen as a much-photographed and preternaturally photogenic (or worse, "exhibitionist") subject who is evaluated, judged, and blamed for provoking a fascinated gaze (*CP* xxii). To be sure, a vocabulary of visual onslaught on personhood enters Sexton's poems and her photographic self-consciousness through hyperbolic imagery in which her speakers invoke, celebrate, and castigate the cultural fascination with what it means to be a "freak," a "monster," an asylum sideshow, and an illuminated body in the media spotlight. This image of her has been missing more careful attention to the relationship of vulnerability to agency, and of objectification to intentional uses of self-as-object; it has been missing attention to the author's awareness of voyeurism, and to the strange fascination and desire we find among midcentury image-based poets who are captivated by the surrealist possibilities of the exquisite corpse, the body-in-pieces as it evolves in relation to a media-fascinated gaze. These alternate perspectives call for more detailed attention to the layers of photographic reference in her poems and for repositioning photographic self-consciousness in wider cultural frames. By juxtaposing Sexton's work on the pose in family photographs with closer study of artifacts of literary celebrity and photographic encounters, this essay challenges the myths of her moral culpability and situates her constructions of glamour and celebrity not in victimhood, but in Sexton's shrewd awareness of connections between looking and writing.

The potential for reading across text and image in Sexton's case is enhanced by the wealth of photographic objects and visual documentary media available for study in the Anne Sexton Papers at the Harry Ransom Center for Humanities Research. This collection includes over 240 photographs drawn from memorabilia and from family albums, a scrapbook from her first year of marriage, photojournalistic artifacts, film footage from a National Educational Television (NET) production taken at her home, contact sheets from a photo-book commissioned during the last year of her life,[3] a modeling portfolio from her brief career in fashion at the Hart Modeling Agency, and correspondence with publishers, agents, and photographers (both portrait photographers and photojournalists). However, these remains are not just glorious contents waiting to be unboxed. The Anne Sexton archive is, in fact, a divided archive, with familial, professional, and commercial photographic prints and contact sheets boxed within the Harry Ransom Center photography collections and separated from tear sheets of print publications, manuscripts, and holographs in the collection of Sexton Papers. The photographic archive chronicles a richly videated life, but its visual contents have been acquired piecemeal and are catalogued neither chronologically or by subject or occasion, creating challenges for reading across photos and manuscripts. Moreover, because photographic images of Sexton the writer continue to proliferate as a visually powerful public affect, scholars can also glean insight from studying photographic evidence that lies outside official archives, in the circulation of posthumously digital photographic images on the Internet and in the blogosphere, which continue to render Sexton one of our postmillennial icons of literary "glam."

Deemed "glamorous" or not, photographs as objects and images are abundantly referenced in histories and autobiographical narratives of midcentury poets, distilling the modern quest for sensation and provoking cultural anxieties of authorship. Just as an earlier generation of modernists such as Virginia Woolf had used camera eye's metaphors to register the unsettling irruption of identity that ensued from the shock of viewing details that had been invisible without technological means, Thomas Travisano has argued that poets at midcentury reformulate the terms of photographic reference through auto-ethnographic representations of the self in its "own surviving artifacts" (67).

Essential to understanding Sexton's image-consciousness and the interpellation of photographic objects and images is a "grammar" of space and time as much as representational content and themes.[4] Film scholar Kaja Silverman has theorized and located central feature of this grammar in the bodily pose. The pose is the staging of the body in the picture, a staging that is also a cultural spacing and an agentive moment (even if imaginary) that is held in anticipation of what is to come, the seizure (or shudder) of the camera's click, before the image is frozen into time. For the viewer, the picture invariably exceeds the moment of the pose. The pose and its affects, conditioned by setting and by light, simultaneously create a space for the bodily imprint and disclose its margins. In the imaginary that a photograph represents for the viewer, the transformative power that attaches to the bodily pose comes about through its selection of (or departure from, in the case of what I refer to as "bad posing") an image already existing in a photographic archive of encoded poses.

In a well-known passage, Silverman notes that the radiance of form is the effect of the pose in the photographic imaginary, which constructs an entire environment of viewing and an appearance of expressive force:

> The representational force which the pose exerts is so great that it radiates outward, and transforms the space around the body and everything which comes into contact with it into an imaginary photograph. Indeed, the pose includes in itself every other feature of the photographic image which is relevant within the domain of subjectivity. (203)

At the threshold between artifact and audience, the blurring of real and imagined identities does not culminate in the revelation of the subject naturalistically in an unguarded moment—rather, its cultural narratives of posing encapsulate the contradictions of "life" produced in the media-saturated gaze.

Among Sexton's contemporaries, the tweaked smile in the photo-flash is a trope through which narratives and discourses of literary authorship and celebrity are contested and revised. Peter Davison's pointedly nostalgic memoir on the midcentury modern generation turns on the "fading smile" as a metaphor of nostalgia and authorial dis-ease. As the toweringly influential (and much photographed) first generation of modernists aged, and as a second generation of writers anxiously looked back from the other side of the camera, the idea of the poet threatened to diminish, in Roland Barthes's formulation, like a distantly shrinking figurine (146). Developing technologies and practices could compensate for or contribute to the anxiety of authorial extinction. One need look no further than the commodified world of literary anthologies to observe that John Malcom Brinnin and Bill

Read's photo-textual collaboration with Rosalie Thorne McKenna (Rollie McKenna) in *The Modern Poets: An American-British Anthology* (1963) represented a new synthesis of art and commerce, a pedagogical apparatus that assigned equivocal print value to the photographic signature, with full-page photographic portraits placed face to face with pages of printed poems.[5] The photographs evoke and attempt to naturalize the "real" image of writers at work, in their homes and studies or against backdrops suggestive of thematic content, while at the same time encouraging fascination with the interior lives and distinctive sensibilities of literary figures as celebrity "stars."

Sexton was in the vanguard in her awareness of changing literacies and shifting boundaries of word and image. Her public pedagogical imperatives were firmly articulated in 1974, when she responded to one of Al Poulin's editorial assistants for an anthology project, *Contemporary American Poetry*. In a vehemently worded letter, in which she establishes her authority as one who "has traveled widely throughout the U.S.A." and as one "in constant touch" with "just those people who would or would not purchase this anthology," she voiced concern about a proposed replacement of thumbnail-sized snapshots for full-page photos:

> I have grave, grave doubts about your planned format for the photographs—both student and teacher want to get a GOOD LOOK [*sic*] at the poet—why? Because poets to the average student ... come like little dwarves from Mars. It is important the pictures be full size, at least in most places, or they will seem just like those creatures from Mars.[6]

Few among Sexton's confessional contemporaries would be as public-minded in contemplating their radiant and ghostly second-skins.

The dependence of writers on publishing's visual apparatus is more starkly and grimly portrayed in Robert Lowell's sonnet, "Picture in *The Literary Life*, a scrapbook," which hints at extinction of the "authentic" self: "a mag photo, before I was *I*, or my books" (*Poems* 524). Here, Lowell satirizes the handiwork of Robert Phelps, co-founder of The Grove Press; Phelps, in a fashion that might appear to presage Facebook, had cut and pasted dust-jackets with authorial photos (including Lowell's) in new kind of product, a self-assembled canon of photos, gossip, and tidbits. "The Poet's Face," as Phelps first dubbed his creation, eventually became a popular literary coffee table book whose very title evokes the authorial body in bits and pieces: *The Literary Life: A Scrapbook Almanac of the Anglo-American Literary Scene* (1970). At another end of the spectrum from Sexton's equivocal embrace of the power and deception of photographs as integral to her business of words, Elizabeth Bishop professed disgust for the crass synthesis of art and commerce that rendered the photo-op a necessity for public dissemination of literary fame, in an interview lumping photojournalists with life insurance salesmen and funeral directors as the "worst forms of life" a successful writer had to contend with (Spires n.p.). By contrast to Lowell and Bishop, Sexton is exceptional for her equivocal embrace of the medium, and for her head-on confrontation with its contradictions. Her photographic encounters are remarkable as a site of the mixed desires that motivate the evolution of the poet-as-celebrity figure and of an artistic process complicated by glamour, spectacle, and bodily exposure.

It may be appropriate at this point to acknowledge that much of the criticism inspired by feminist and gender theory has addressed issues of photographic reference within in the framework of woman's persistent "looked-at-ness" (Mulvey 19). I take that looked-at-ness of gender as a relevant, but not exclusively overdetermining, feature of a feeling for photographs that emerges as an affective matrix in Sexton's work. Photographic reference in her case operates in more than the singular register dictated by her gendered cultural visibility. While mortality clings to the photograph, and, secondarily, modern glamour has been said to cling to the feminine (Brown 10),[7] cultural analysis of Sexton's photographic archive calls for more than the singular backward-looking memorial gaze and for a deeper contextualization of Sexton's culturally defined femininity—infamous for impressing viewers as "chic," as Maxine Kumin noted, "every inch the fashion model" (*AS* xix). Structural and poetic layered-ness of seeing and being seen within photographic transactions in a variety of material settings provides a framework for addressing Sexton's relationship to visual photographic media. In the double helix of a heightened reflexivity that photographs make available, the poetic act of saying "I" for Sexton doubles back (reflexively) on the "you" that is imaged reflexively as singular and/or collective object-to-be-seen, operating at an intra-subjective level as well as an inter-subjective projection (that is, in the signifier) in the photographic transaction. Photography, in other words, provides a transactional medium for the reflection of

the subject from a projected surface, with distinctive cultural power to ne-
gotiate affects and meaning in relation to its culturally contextualized forms.

### Smiling into the Camera: The Pose in the Family Photograph— Faces, Smiles, Teeth

> I was
> the girl of the chain letter,
> the girl full of talk of coffins and keyholes,
> the one of the telephone bills,
> the wrinkled photo and the lost connections. (CP 115)

Was photography one of Sexton's revisionary "black arts"? Does the
photograph operate as a mediumistic charm, materialized and mystified in
the transformative play of fascinated *looking,* like the enchantment of keys,
typewriter, her long fingers—another way of keeping imaginative resources
perpetually in view? It would seem so from early poems, elegies, and self-
elegies, wherein adult or aging speakers wistfully or angrily survey the past
through portraits and photographs drawn from a family album. In "O Ye
Tongues," a Roethke-like invocation of the infant's earliest symbol-making
capacities, Sexton places herself as an orphan with photographs ("two death
masks on the mantel" [CP 401]) born through the "grave of my mama's
belly into the commerce / of Boston" (CP 401). Integral as photography was
to her "business" of words (CP 12), the mask-making potential of the illumi-
nated image was also, in her surrealist imagination, always potentially a fig-
ure *for* death, an artifact to be imaginatively mobilized and transformed into
sublime illumination (a tiny translucent body transported into the "piece of
kindergarten called STAR" in "Rats Live on No Evil Star" [CP 360] or a mo-
ment of all-consuming rapture, as in "The Starry Night" [54]). In Sexton's
habit of embracing paradox, the photograph could also be an emblem of
frustration with stigmatization and dehumanization (as a deathly or frozen
"still" of the arrested moment).

There is nothing inherently glamourous about photographs of dead
family members inspected under the pressure of loss and mourning. But in
Sexton's early elegies and anti-elegies in *All My Pretty Ones* (1962), the dead
are radiant—smiling, posing, smirking, readily apostrophized, and more
glamorous in photos than through any other means (they are "boxes of

pictures of people I do not know" [*CP* 50]). Sexton was schooled in posing before the camera during a brief career as a fashion model, and poems such as "The Money Swing," after F. Scott Fitzgerald's "Babylon Revisited" (*CP* 487–88) evoke a family life in which "posing" with smiling countenance was a resource for managing calamity and crisis (holding a snapshot of her parents in her hand, she writes, "I know your smile will develop a boil" [*CP* 488]). Photographic images of great-aunt "Nana," fall from letters in the epistolary poem, "Some Foreign Letters"; the "Truth" that the "dead know" is captured as a "tiny smile" that purports to be a smirk, the photograph's play on the mask of death (*CP* 49). Although the speaker in "Some Foreign Letters" is reading *letters,* the letters are reframed in postcard-like images of a romantic heroine that follow in breathless succession, similar to images caught in staccato-like clicks of the camera. Later on, Sexton would invent a mystic writing pad assignment for her students that played on the theme of reviewing a strange photograph each time with a seizure of despair and astonishment: Diane Middlebrook notes, "'On the front page of the yellow pad,' she said, 'write CHERISH.' . . . 'Turn the page. Now write CAMERA. What can the camera cherish?' . . . 'Turn the page. Write LIES'" (qtd. in *AS* 386).[8] In "Elizabeth Gone," a poem that began with the title, "Three Lives of Mourning," one "life" begins as a wooden box, a coffin, another "life" begins in the deathbed, and a third "life" is initiated by viewing photographs of the dead ("Worksheets").

In drafts and holographs of Sexton's early manuscripts, she is often unsettled about titles, experimenting with a range: from titles that suggest or initiate the action of the poem musically or rhythmically ("Noon Walk on the Asylum Lawn") to the nominalist approach of many of her contemporaries ("The Bells," "The Starry Night") to titles such as "Self in 1958," "The House," ("Father, / an exact likeness, / his face bloated and pink," and "Mother, / with just the right gesture" [*CP* 72]), or "Mother and Jack and the Rain," which are more like album or scrapbook captions. Sexton's second collection, *All My Pretty Ones,* explores the paradoxes of death (lifeless depth) and life (life-filled depths) encoded in family photographs as souvenir objects and images. Poems of love and grief in which she portrays herself as the girl of the "wrinkled photo" at the end of a chain of missed and highly mediated connections registers her investment in visually mediated affects.

The title poem, "All My Pretty Ones," anticipates Sylvia Plath's "Daddy," in its motifs of vampirism, fascism, rage, longing, and, above all, in the use of a photographic image for re-possessing the past. Sexton's use of photo-graphic remains makes extensive use of personal artifacts (diaries, scrap-books, family photographs) as souvenir objects in a way that is similar to Plath's aggressively focused concentration on a single photograph of her father at the blackboard, "the picture I have of you," in "Daddy" (223). I use the term "souvenir" intentionally: Sexton's approach to constructing this appearance of truth in the title poem paradigmatically corresponds to the logic of the "souvenir" that, according to Susan Stewart, calls forth value when their exterior materiality of the photograph is a site of transmuta-tion into a more vivid, interior spectacle (137). Between these transforma-tive moments is a threshold, an interface of viewing; the work of Sexton's "All My Pretty Ones" takes place while the photograph is held in the hand ("I touch their cardboard faces" [CP 50]). Even when the illusion of the photograph's still surfaces cannot remake a face-to-face confrontation, re-encountering the materiality of the photograph releases passions—and a torrent of words: "Now I *fold* you down, *my* drunkard, *my* navigator, / *my* first lost keeper, to love or look at later" (CP 51; emphasis mine). The "first lost keeper" is the father who abusively incorporates the child into his own identity, but what is accomplished in claiming to "love" or to "look at later," is transmutation of feeling for photographs into a feeling for words.

What interests me about Sexton's penultimate stanza is what the action of the "fold" or "wrinkle" of paper makes possible, carrying the impress of sense and feeling across differing sense modalities, in order to shape an un-usual reckoning with poetic consolations in the final stanza. One modality of folded photograph is temporal: the fold of a photograph makes the past present, but with a difference—the speaker's age outstrips her father's in years; another modality is the material folding of the photograph's creases into lines of the poem on the page. The fold creates a continuum of exter-nal and internal space, extending the meaning from the "hoarded span" of words and years into the hoarded span of objects "shelved" around the desk, a life cluttered with photographs. The folding of the photograph prepares for its visual homologue, the "bent" contour of the poet's body folded over her desk (as we see her in many photographs outside the poem).

The final well-known lines of "All My Pretty Ones," "I outlive you, / bend down my strange face to yours and forgive you" (CP 51)reverse the image of the father's brutal dominion, by figuring dedication to writing informed by and infused with the visual image. It is the visualized text, in its written body, that forgives or gives back through its bonus of pleasure and that the speaker/poet finally looks upon with certitude that is not promised by filial "love." The closing assertion might have left us with a less complicated means of addressing grief and mourning, except that the poem does not propose to have transcended grief, but in some way to have put off closure indefinitely with the promise of repetitive "looking" and looking again.

The affective charge of visual culture was shaped for Sexton early on through the tactile relationship between hand, eye, word, and image in the making of scrapbooks and albums. The scrapbook, which may be read as a diary of Sexton's early married life, provides an example of the tactile borders of the affective and the visual.[9] One page on themes of early married love juxtaposes cutouts from advertisements (Swans Down Cake Mix) alongside scribbles of an early love poem, and images of matinee idols from films and plays (Rita Hayworth in *The Loves of Carmen,* Columbia Pictures, 1948, hints at pleasure in miming Hollywood starlets). The Gray family archives also include photographs referenced from family albums, many of which were later published in *Anne Sexton: Self-Portrait in Letters* (1977). Of photographs taken of Anne at an early age, Linda Gray Sexton notes an observance of decorum, tempered by something else: "Anne Sexton smiles out of childhood snapshots and portraits, but even so, her large green eyes convey the pain she would later put into words" (*SPL* 3).

Much has been said about the invitations that photographs issue when they bear the impress of familial features and settings.[10] Indeed, photographs anchor Sexton's acts of composition as they anchored the environments closest to her writing. Stills from the National Educational Television film of the poet in her study with her typewriter shows that spaces around her desk and bookshelves are plentiful with posted quotes and photographs among the "pals of her desk" (Kevles; *NES* 7). Several photographs can be identified above Sexton's desk in an early photograph by Rollie McKenna from 40 Clearwater Road. One of them, a portrait photograph in a filigreed frame, is presumably of her great-aunt Anna Dingley, and it repeats in later pictures of 14 Black Oak Road. As a poet who figured herself as a suburban American housewife, Sexton gained confidence in her art, she admitted, by watching the televised image of I. A. Richards, lecturing on the sonnet (*AS* 42). When she sought to solidify her relationship to W. D. Snodgrass, she requested a photograph to serve as inspiration at her desk (*SPL* 96).

Given the importance of Sexton's photographic consciousness to the deep structural play of looking and writing, seeing and being seen, it is not surprising that, as Sexton's celebrity grew, her photographic imaginary is recharged with skeptical intensity and sporadic moments of reflexivity. Whereas earlier poems look to photographs as opportunities to incorporate and reconfigure interior life, or to critique familial ideologies, later poems more often open up a space of reflection on reflection.[11] By contrast to an early poem, "Letter Written on a Ferry While Crossing Long Island Sound," where entering paradise is represented as a blissful yielding to the "gauzy" blur of light and shadow at the edge of ordinary vision (*"good news, good news"* [CP 184]), the late poems more uncomfortably confront the blurring of the artifactual and the real. Even a reader who has never set foot in Sexton's archives will notice that "Ms. Dog," in "Hurry Up Please It's Time," seems to riff on celebrity, real or imagined stills from readings and book jackets: "Once I hung around in my woolly tank suit[.] ... Now I am clothed in gold air with / one dozen haloes glistening on my skin" (CP 391); or, "Who's that at the podium / in black and white, / blurting into the mike? / Ms. Dog. / Is she spilling her guts? You bet. / Otherwise they cough" (CP 387). Indeed, later poems re-assemble a mosaic-like history of a saint's life in pictures. The persona of "Ms. God" ("Ms. Dog" as palindrome)—offers a loosely constructed phantasmagoric body of celebrity appearances, across the fractured spheres of media and publics, and underscores the necessity of constant feeding and consumption, represented by food imagery.[12]

Two late poems, "The Room of My Life" (CP 422) and "The Witch's Life" (CP 423) can be read as companion pieces, two versions on a common theme of looking back on a "life" through the perspective of celebrity relics. "The Witch's Life" has nothing of the braggadocio we find in the earlier signature poem, "Her Kind" (CP 15–16), where the speaker takes the presence of her "face in a book" (I take "in" to literalize the presence of the book jacket cover) as an emblem of her poetic powers of enchantment and daringly engages in flagrant and inflammatory acts of self-exposure. "The Witch's Life" begins with a recollected frame, the memory of an isolate female figure "peering" from a second story window and suspended in time as in a photograph. From behind vaguely diaphanous curtains, now "wrinkled," she sometimes bursts forth, yelling at those who are watching (from below), "Get out of my life!" (CP 423). The witch in the opening lines of this poem is a setup for the second part of the poem, where the speaker reflects that the body she has made for herself through the made-up witch-y persona is not her own body, quite, but a presence turned to caricature (or a mock-glamorous presence), with "shoes turn[ed] up like a jester's" and hair in "clumps" (423).

Looking and looking again is not always a blessed deferral, since the material remainder evokes both desire and loss. In both poems, shame and embarrassment threaten to surface as the things of her world—the oft-photographed study, the typewriter, the ashtray, the glasses—take on animate, distorted, and videated shapes: the "forty-eight keys of the typewriter / each an eyeball that is never shut" (422) or the heart, "blow[n] . . . up like a zeppelin" (423), another radiant spectacle of outsized proportion. The endings of both poems strive rhythmically and imagistically for an affirmative conclusion by reviving emblems of a charismatic talent, her "basket of fire" in "The Witch's Life" (424) and the "sea that bangs in my throat," in "The Room of My Life" (422), but the forms of closure are more subdued than poetically confident. The witch is seated, holding the basket, not "standing" in her whirligig cart, sparks licking her thighs. In "The Witch's Life," the idiopathic myth of genius is up for grabs, since "Only my books anoint me, / and a few friends, / those who reach into my veins" (423). The phantasmagoric image of seeing from great visionary heights (the view from the witch's cart in "Her Kind") at the end of "The Witch's Life" is now a dissolving image of "climbing the primordial climb" of success, a "dream within a dream" (423) fading off. "The Room of My Life" is overtly concerned with the fading accoutrements of glamour: surrounded by the detritus of the celebrity writer's life, the speaker reflects on "anointing" and "gilding" of celebrity with money and goods: "the books, each a contestant in a beauty contest," "the gold rug / a conversation of heels and toes," and "the lights / poking at me" (422). Every moment, the speaker complains, "I feed the world out there" (422). Retracing the theme of a glamour fascinating and yet disavowed, the speaker finds herself in depthless depths, where "nothing is just what it seems to be. / My objects dream and wear new costumes" (422).

A baby doll or an artificially illuminated seraphim (from *seraph*, to "burn") may also be taken as avatars of ghostly celebrity, ready-made images that have passed through technologized processes into ghastly, surreal radiance. In "The Death Baby" sequence, we find cast-off images in the modernist idiom of Eliot and Frost, different ways of dying or knowing death, oddly mixing organic and inorganic semblances, each of which carries the potential for shame and exposure. "Death baby" dies by ice ("ice baby," turned into a radiant cube, with "tears" as "two glass beads," a colored "Popsicle" [or "Pop-sickle"?] in the incandescent glow of the refrigerator); by dismemberment in a stockyard, an open spectacle of slaughter ("I was at the dogs' party. / I was their bone. . . . They loved me until / I was gone" [CP 354–55]); and by fire (the Dy-dee Doll "melts" under the radiant heat of the sun lamp [CP 355]).

The second of the six-part "Death Baby" sequence, titled "The Dy-dee Doll," looks back to the snapshot images of "Self in 1958," where "They" who are looking, "think I am me!" while "I" appear as a surreal synthesis, a "black angel," with "nylon legs, luminous arms, / and some advertised clothes" (CP 155). The Dy-dee doll, a blue-eyed avatar of the speaker, can be matched with the image of the "Almost Human Doll," advertised in *Life* magazine in 1937,[13] a doll with china-blue eyes, and pursed lips; she wets and drinks and comes with a wardrobe for every day of the week, and she appears in several poems. The "glass eye" and "ice" eye of the doll baby that "stares back" seems no longer a human creation, quite, but an artifact of the negative sublime. The speaker goes back at it. As the glass eye, ice eye artifacts of still surfaces stare back at her, the meanings of "star" and "stare" merge into the degraded image of being one stared at and staring back with incantatory spells. The "I" of the speaker in the poem confronts the "eyes" that stare, each stabbing line an ice-y and murderous linguistic pick:

> Glass eye, ice eye,
> primordial eye,
> lava eye,
> pin eye,
> break eye,
> how you stare back! (CP 358)

Another late image plucked from the family album, "Baby Picture" continues the theme of prying open ("peeling") the cool aestheticized celluloid surface from within. "Baby Picture" does not so much make a point about an actual child as it does about the artistic process of seeing behind the smiling imaginary represented by the photographic pose of the child—and then considering how looking at photographs could in any way be churned into creative work. In "Baby Picture," the photographic referent is apparent from the beginning, and as in the early poems, the palindromic structure works back in time from "picture" to "baby." At the same time, the poem makes ingenious use of decay in the surface material of the photograph as a metaphor of "aging without sound" (*CP* 362); there is an accurate description of the way that photographic surfaces disintegrate and brown into discoloration; there is also a fertile synthesis of celluloid and mold, organic and inorganic images, a process which matches the peristaltic oozing of "sweets" in the final stanza, as part of a cycle of creation. The wordplay on "smiling" pose and the lying smile ("smile lies") sets up the dilemma in the first stanza, the speaker's interrogation of the surface of the picture, which cannot itself talk back because the child is "stilled" into the frame (*CP* 363). Because the photograph cannot speak, the poet must, by "opening" up the smiling countenance, giving the pose a mouth for words ("I open the mouth / and my teeth are an angry army" [363]). The six times reiterated "I" opens each time onto a differently distasteful bodily spectacle of bad posing—veins, mouth, eyes, hair, dress, bowels. In this poem, the still surfaces of the photographed image cover over dung, rot, feces, all of which must be further broken down to fructify in the poem's warm yeast.

### Seeing through Glamour: "Some inner person never seen before"

July 21, 1970
Dear Rollie,
Thank you so much for sending me the proofs not only because they showed that my teeth looked all right (and I really didn't think they would) but because they are just wonderful pictures. There I am in that wonderful white room in the white wicker chair in a white dress with my black beads and black hair. It's fascinating. I had no way of knowing that day when I dressed that I was going to be ensconced in a white room. I will surely take one of these pictures for the back of my next book. I am not finished with the book yet but when I am I will contact you. I will either pick AS 699B, No. 17–18 or 11A-12. You are a real artist and have a knack of catching some essence that your subject is not aware of—some inner person . . . never seen before.
Best Wishes, A Sexton[14]

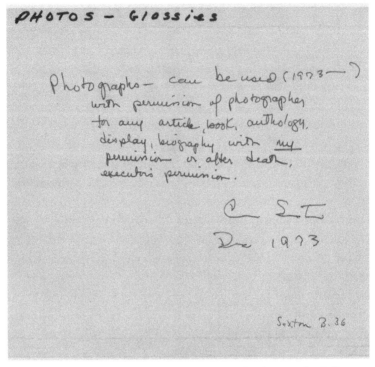

FIGURE 2.1. Anne Sexton (Anne Sexton Literary File, Photography Collection, container PH: LH, Sexton A, box 1, accession no. 981:0061:0001n=0010, Harry Ransom Center, University of Texas at Austin).

Fascinated, enveloped, absorbed by the light-and-dark enigma of photography's reversible and spectacular effects, Sexton could be as engrossed and sometimes transported by her own ghostly radiance in photographs as she was by images in family pictures. The Sexton Papers contains one manila folder of particular interest to the glamour and fatality of her life in photographs, assembled and inscribed in Sexton's hand as she began to make arrangements for disposition of her estate: "Photographs—can be used (1973— ) with permission of photographer for any article, book, anthology, display, biography with my permission—or after death, executor's permission" (Fig. 2.1).[15] In this photographic folder, she left her own exquisite corpse which has yet to be assembled.[16] The archival record of photographs and correspondence tells us that *she had a hand in it*—a hand in the record of her own photographic celebrity and in pictorial narratives she arranged for herself and others as a "photogenic" subject. I use the term photogenic in the traditional sense, denoting a subject likely to take "good pictures"—whatever that may mean—as well as in the sense of in Sexton's case, photo-gen*etic*, capable of generating multiple narratives that fascinate and disturb.

Between 1966–69, the years of the Pulitzer Prize, the filming of the National Educational Television *USA: Poetry* series, a *Look* magazine feature, and the much-videated moonshot, which generated a Sexton poem for the *Boston Globe*, Sexton enjoyed a growing relationship with photojournalists and photographers that could be at times, cooperative, collaborative, and mutually contesting. She shaped her own celebrity glamour initially around, the "middle-aged witch, me" (*CP* 223), alternately an enchantress or a clairvoyant presence, and when that failed, resorts to being a "bad poser," one who worked against typologies of expected glamour codes. In the NET film outtakes, she vies with the camera ("Does the camera *love* me?" she toys with the cameraman as a scene is being prepared, eyes tilted upward; in the next breath, elongating and playing on vowel sounds, "I am a *monster*," eyes casting down).[17]

With the success of her first two books, Sexton and her publishers actively responded to stepped-up inquiries from news organizations, popular magazines, and literary presses. Sexton's literary agents and her editors at Houghton Mifflin played mediating roles in the selection of photographers and sometimes of images to represent her literary persona, but there is also evidence that Sexton often directed the photo shoots as if they were stage plays in her ongoing bildungsroman. She transformed her relationships with several photographic journalists and portrait photographers, keeping up intimate, detailed correspondence with them—a task more her routinely left to publicists. Just as Sexton had excelled in recruiting poet-mentors such as Snodgrass while she was still an apprentice-poet, and just as she built an affinity system of poets and artistic collaborators to assist her public presentations, she rendered those who were present in the creation of public photographs as intimate allies and witnesses in acts of composition and the contradictions that her celebrity entailed.

Photo shoots with Rollie McKenna, who composed the book jacket portrait for *Transformations* (1972), and had been earlier enlisted for the Malcolm Brinnin anthology, exemplify the pattern of successful recruitment that memoirists such as Peter Davison have associated with Sexton's pattern of dependency on others, but which might also be seen as relational strengths. Whatever the photographer may have thought about the pictures (and we do not have McKenna's side of this exchange), from Sexton's side, the poet coaxed affection and admiration, conferring upon the photographer the authority of "true artist" and co-creator. Between 1962 and 1974, the list of photographers who took pictures of Sexton reads like a who's who of the leading photojournalists of her era, including high profile photojournalists best known for political subjects, such as Gwendolyn Stewart and Ted Polumbaum. She also welcomed portrait photographers into her home—McKenna, Rhoda Nathans, Elsa Dorfman, Ann Phillips, and Arthur Furst in connection with publishing projects—and her correspondence indicates she often sought to convert them to fellow artists and travelers. Unique to Sexton's photographic archive are photographers who have contributed perceptive criticism: Gwendolyn Stewart, for example, has created a website in which she comments on the "duality" of the pose that Sexton struck: "Cover the top part of the picture; look at the legs tortuously twisted together. . . . Now cover the bottom half of the photograph, and look at the arms and radiant face" (Stewart).

The idea that the photographic encounter might be transformed into a kind of co-creation emerges most sharply in Sexton's correspondence with Rhoda Nathans, who took pictures of Sexton between August-September 1974. Little is known about Nathans aside from the fact that she advertised in the *Village Voice* and in *New York Magazine*; in New York, she exhibited her prints of celebrity artists such as Merce Cunningham, John Cage, Howard Fast, as well as Claude Brown, Jack Dempsey, and Katharine Hepburn at Nikon House in the 1970s.[18] Nathans was also known in left-democratic circles for her prints of activist feminist and civil rights figures such as Dorothy Kenyon, William O. Douglas, and Helen Gahagan Douglas of the International Peace and Freedom Movement. It may have aided Nathans's cause that, in the letter of introduction requesting photographs of Sexton for a book of portraits Nathans was assembling, she had conveyed greetings from Muriel Rukeyser. In a 1972 letter, Sexton acknowledges the gift of Rukeyser's *The Speed of Darkness* and notes that she cherishes the memory of Rukeyser's "good face" from a photograph (*SPL* 322). In her letter of introduction, Nathans demonstrated her knowledge of contemporary poetry by evoking the language of Rukeyser's poems—the "rivers of the mind" and the "fragments that make a person what he is."[19] Furthermore, Nathans brought an orientation to the photographic portrait that may have

FIGURE 2.2. Anne Sexton photographic portrait by Rhoda Nathans, 1974 (Anne Sexton Literary File, Photography Collection, container PH: LH, Sexton A, box 3, accession no. 981:0089:0092, Harry Ransom Center, University of Texas at Austin).

resonated with Sexton's concerns as she anticipated publication of poems in *The Awful Rowing Toward God* (1975). When Nathans explains to Sexton what her approach to the photo shoot might be, it is not the sculpted form or the perfectly coiffed image she is after: rather, she writes that she has been trying to use the photographic medium with "spontaneity and hopefully with compassion" and to "record the faces of man and woman without contrivance—to distill, from the rivers of the mind some of the fragments that make a person what he is . . . somehow [to] convey the price one must pay for being a very HUMAN [*sic*] being."[20]

The Nathans photographs (unpublished) in the archives are stagy, theatricalized performances that reflect a collaboration between the photographer and her subject. They are revealing of a moment in which Sexton enlists a photographer to work with her against the aesthetics of routinized glamour in its most deathly, static guises. In one of the sequences (Fig. 2.2), Nathans sets up a single window or doorway or fence through or against which the poet is posed as an object of voyeuristic fascination; in this pose, Sexton looks *back*, peeping through a pane of glass inside the architecture of a double wood frame.[21] Glass beads and pearls from Sexton's earlier photographs are replaced by the pendant necklace, a gift from Lois Ames, seen in later photographs: "Don't let the bastards win." This may be a case of bad posing in the sense of disrupting an archive of expected poses for the confessional poet who, in "Making a Living," more properly floats in a sea of "God's littlest light bulbs," while eating his "whole past" and being spit out (CP 350). The playful self-image captured in the Nathans photographs echoes images captured by Anne Wilder's camera from 1965, where Sexton mockingly imitates the glamour pose of starlets such as Jean Harlow, her torso set at an angle against a pale stone and staring up into the camera.[22] The camera angle by itself intimates fascination with an aestheticized, deathly femininity, but the coloring of the photograph—greens, browns, grays, as well as its depth and detail—roughen up and work against extreme glamour codes. The roughness of the flagstone background contrasts with the smoothness of silk shantung of Orientalized bedroom lingerie; by contrast to the conventional "somnambulant" image evoked by the half-closed eyes of Harlow, Sexton's eyes are penetratingly open, awake, staring back (Fig. 2.3).[23] In September 1974, when Sexton selected a photograph by the fence among those she wanted to keep, she and Nathans exchanged several letters, mutually affectionate in tone. In one of them Sexton pronounced the photographs a "marvel,"

FIGURE 2.3. Anne Sexton, 1965. (Anne Sexton Literary File, Photography Collection, container PH: LH, Sexton A, box 3, accession no. 981:0089:0060, Harry Ransom Center, University of Texas at Austin).

and she notes that she'd like to use them in a book she was planning to publish. By the time she had prints of the Nathans photographs in hand, Sexton had also shared a poem (unidentified) with Nathans, who echoes back, "your poem, my poem, a marvel."[24]

The December 1968 *Look* magazine feature story on Sexton, "Through bedlam's door with Anne Sexton," with nine published photographs from several rolls of film shot at Sexton's home that summer, was as much a milestone in *Look* magazine's treatment of midcentury writers as it was a moment of innovation in the videated narrative of Sexton's "life" in photographs (t39–t40, t44). The photojournalist was well-known Boston-based freelancer Ted Polumbaum. The hallmark of Polumbaum's early and late photographs of Sexton is the high-contrast focus on light around the body (with white shifts, or white blouses Sexton preferred) and ominously shaded or backlit surrounds, contributing to the aura of mystery and enchantment. As usual, there was a female intermediary for the *Look* feature, journalist Barbara Kevles, at the time a production assistant at CBS. Kevles and Sexton became friendly, since Kevles was working on a *Paris Review* interview at the same time: questions for the *Paris Review* interview were drafted and exchanged between the two as the *Look* feature was being assembled, which gave Sexton numerous opportunities to watch the magazine operation at close hand and to inform the final *Look* text, while Kevles provides the "insider's view" of someone who has "come to know her better" than the theme of a just-escaped madwoman might suggest (*Look* t39). The irony of this photojournalistic narrative is that, on the eve of releasing *Love Poems* (1969), a book with poems about marital betrayals, the photos of Kayo Sexton and Anne Sexton tête-à-tête (in the manner of Listerine commercial in the same issue), largely re-install the poet into a more comfortable narrative of family and marriage.

But the juxtaposition of published and unpublished Polumbaum prints for *Look* is still interesting for what it suggests about the problem of exposing and containing the nonrational aspects of Sexton's creative life. In 1965, *Look's* editor, Pat Carbine, had commissioned a piece on Paul Engle and the Iowa Writers' Workshop, the first foray into representing the new fashion of the creative writing workshop for a pictorially driven middlebrow publication aimed largely at middle-class women and lifestyle interests (in the 1960s, the magazine regularly advertised inflatable backyard swimming pools). In the Engle piece, the Iowa model of the creative writing workshop is presented as a service to the nation, as warmly persuasive and productive as agri-business (see Harris 95–97). The feature on Sexton, coming three years later, articulates the growing gap between the narrative arc of expectation for the creative life of a high-achieving, sexually alluring woman, and the narrative expectation shaped by marriage and family life. These gaps are articulated in a controversy over a decision about two conflicting image-concepts that the editorial offices and the photographer struggled to reconcile, one characterized as a "visual/symbolic" narrative, and another as a chronological "documentary" of a poet's emergence. Correspondence with Kevles reveals that, for a while, as controversy raged in the editorial offices, Sexton and Kevles thought the article might be cut. In a three-hour meeting between Kevles and the editor, the crux of the dilemma emerged as needing to choose between the "visual-symbolic," approach and what was termed the "documentary" approach.[25] At least one set of unpublished prints in the archives gives us a look at what the "visual-symbolic" consisted of: objects and images from Sexton's poems are portrayed as "found" objects in

FIGURE 2.4. Anne Sexton by Ted Polumbaum, photographer's proof, 1967 (Anne Sexton Literary File, Photography Collection, container PH: LH, Sexton A, box 1, accession no. 957:0009:0023, Harry Ransom Center, University of Texas at Austin).

still-life domestic arrangements. In one image, the portraits of Sexton and her mother from "The Double Image" were scenically arranged in a dim-lit attic space, shown amid open cardboard boxes and stored clothing; another photo shows a simple table arrangement with a single flower stem in a glass vase, a bowl of sugar, and multiple bottles of prescription pills stacked on top of each other and tilting precariously. The published sequence favors a compromise approach grounded in 1950s family romance of charmed domesticity, stringing together images of Anne and Kayo, the children, with one close-cropped view of Anne in the swimming pool, and only a few scattered pictorial images that correspond to themes from particular poems.

In a letter to Houghton Mifflin, it is clear that Sexton demurred over publication of the erotically charged swimming pool sequence—as well she might have. The extended reel of unpublished swimming pool photographs in the archive, show Anne provocatively posing, stretching out her body in a swim, and splashing playfully, gripping the side of the pool all hands and knees, or emerging in a dazzling display of radiant water droplets magnifying light around the body (Fig. 2.4).[26] The photographic technique, as well as the poses, display striking similarity to Lawrence Schiller's photographs of Marilyn Monroe's nude swim in her controversial last film, *Something's*

*Got to Give,* which had been published in 1962 in *Life.*[27] Sexton notes of the photograph: "Fifty percent of my friends like it cropped, and fifty like it uncropped. I've told Ted Polumbaum to send you a bill."[28] In the final compromise, only a tightly cropped photograph from the swimming pool sequence was used.

The unpublished swimming pool sequence is also interesting when juxtaposed with a quotation from Kayo that likens the ideal state of marriage to a "calm sea" (*Look* 40t) and with a Sexton poem, "The Nude Swim," which appears a year later in *Love Poems.* In "The Nude Swim" a husband and wife have plunged into the waters of an "unknown grotto" (*CP* 183). The poem centers on two different modes of signification: one based on "posing" in erotic self-display and playfully narcissistic identification through a visual image which functions as a screen and another on "pointing." In the performing mode, the speaker engaged in playful eroticism with a lover overtly enjoys comparing herself to "Matisse's *Red Odalisque,*" likely a reference to one of a series of Henri Matisse's paintings, *Odalisque in Red Culottes* (1921). The speaker in the poem asserts that, like the odalisque, she takes pleasure from spreading her body out in the buoyancy of water as "on a divan," imaginatively posing with the weight of her body impossibly "floating" on one elbow. But when the lover in the poem points, "Look! Your eyes / are seacolor. Look! Your eyes / are skycolor," the speaker's eyes "shut down as if they were / suddenly ashamed" (*CP* 184).

Middlebrook's biography details the later struggle Sexton had with her publishers over wishing a Gwendolyn Stewart photo to appear on the dust jacket of *The Death Notebooks* (1974), "my advertisement for myself," and the extent to which she usurped the publicist's role in fashioning the billet for the 1974 Sanders Theatre reading at Harvard (*AS* 389). Even beyond these episodes, the archive provides evidence that in the last year of her life Sexton was shaping a new turn in her videated history through increasing intervention with her publishers on which images should represent her "across these big United States."[29] Arthur Furst, whose posthumously published photographs in *Anne Sexton: The Last Summer* have been the subject of some literary commentary, was not the only photographer whom Sexton invited in. The contact sheets from an Ann Phillips photo shoot (also unpublished) can be read as a short film in which Sexton's vivid gifts for conversation are displayed, and the settings evoke scenes and images from late poems (she is photographed with Dalmatians, against the stained-glass window of a chapel, and in her living room). Sexton annotated the back of the Phillips contact sheet prints, which otherwise betray no air of crisis, "½ hour before leaving my husband," continuing the pattern of managing an alternative life in photographs.[30]

In her later photographs, Sexton appears to have been especially interested in the potential of the portrait genre, with its traditional focus on character and personality. A story told by Cambridge photographer Elsa Dorfman of a sunny summer day photographing Sexton at her Weston home for a special issue of a *Fiction* magazine in 1974 confirms her interest in portrait photography—Dorfman was a well-known portrait photographer at the time—and registers Sexton's preoccupations at the time.[31] The story Dorfman tells is that upon her arrival, Sexton first toured the photographer around the house, pointing to a photograph of Sylvia Plath, which had apparently been positioned on the mantelpiece and which Dorfman speculates was set up for this occasion (2).[32] Dorfman remembers that Sexton was "very interested in photography" and "knew how to respond to a camera" (2). Sexton made a point of saying she had had her hair done for the occasion, and the tour involved pointing "to her every honorary degree—it was "BU [Boston University] this and BU that." She "seemed to love her kitchen, and showed me a framed advertisement for her father's business" (Dorfman interview). Even more notably, Dorfman recalls, in a later published memoir, on this occasion, "Anne talked about Sylvia Plath a lot during the [photographic] session, and seemed fond of and competitive with her. I really wanted to place her next to the mantel, but didn't" ("Portrait" 2). Instead Dorfman, who describes her photographic "MO" as being "passionate about letting a person talk and let[ting] her be" (1), followed Sexton's lead in taking the head-and-shoulders portrait at the typewriter beneath the bookshelves. The resulting photograph is a tightly framed head and shoulders portrait, "Anne Sexton at home." It evokes the photographic uncanny, with a double image, another photograph on a bookshelf shadowing one side of the picture next to Sexton's face.

## The Digital Afterlife of Sexton's Photographs: "The Very Model of a Modern Model-Poet"

Since the millennium, arrangements of Sexton photographs on Tumblr, Flickr, and in blogs and editorials have shaped new histories and narratives in the reception of her photogenic literary celebrity and its relationship to American culture. In these precincts, echoes of Sexton's divided legacy continue to be felt in explorations of art and desire, portals through which cultural constructs of aestheticized glamour and literary celebrity continue to haunt notions of art and personhood. The judgmental legacy continues to center on Sexton's reputed celebrity glamour, raising affective, ethical, and aesthetic questions about her management of the business of images as well as words: it was or was not admirable of Sexton to have contributed to her own celebrity by posing in this or that way; it is or is not significant that her personal appearance is linked to her tragic death; it is or is not proper to or valid to equate literary celebrity with artistic achievement. In the pixel play that is facilitated by the mash-up and re-mix of digital images, many of the photographs that represented Sexton are re-assembled around bits of her life in pictures.

In the slang of the urban dictionary, "'glam' is about femme girls and femme boys and girls who look like femme boys and boys who look like butch girls."[33] But "glam" is apparently still about beauty, about embodiment, about dying to be beautiful, and about exclusive categories of the aesthetic in public circulation and their culturally shocking or anesthetizing affects. A controversy about race, glamour, aesthetics, beauty, and skin privilege that erupted in the online *Lambda Literary* in 2012 and continued in various postings has come to be known as the "beauty-gate" scandal in some quarters of the postconfessional queer poetry scene. "Beauty-gate," as C. Dale Young dubbed it,[34] was touched off by Michael Klein's *Ploughshares* interview with Texan gay/Latino poet Eduardo C. Corral (the first gay Latino poet to win the Yale Younger Poets Prize), in which Corral comments on being an outsider in the New York City gay poetry scene. The controversy centered on these sentences of Corral's interview: "Beauty is on my mind these days. The queer poetry community in New York City is full of beautiful people, which makes me an outsider[.] . . . I'm disappointed in many of my queer peers[.] . . . So many of them value looks over talent" (qtd. in "Five for Eduardo C. Corral").

Corral's interview does not invoke the glamour of Anne Sexton, but subsequent commentators signposted Sexton's photographic image as the frame for "beauty-gate's" debates about style versus substance, the terrors and dangers of literary celebrity in a postconfessional age, and for beauty of "her kind"—whatever this may mean—as exemplary in Western culture. A full-length photographic image of Sexton from the aftermath of the Saunders poetry reading at Harvard serves as the headnote of James Fitzpatrick's op-ed commentary, "Anne Sexton, Aesthetics, and the Economy of Beauty." For those familiar with Sexton's biography, the photograph is familiar: it shows her in accustomed garb for poetry readings, seated, in a plunging dark jersey blouse, unbuttoned at the top, bedecked with jewelry and cigarette, the long swirling skirt fallen open and wrapped around her legs, with strappy sandals—and a distinctly "smirking" pose before the camera. However potentially campy Sexton's pose (also contestable), there is nothing too campy about Fitzpatrick's editorial commentary. It begins nonironically by invoking Maxine Kumin's well-known comment remarking on her friend's appearance years ago at their first meeting in 1957, "looking every inch the fashion model" [with] . . . "French perfume, high heels, matching lip and fingernail gloss . . . all intimidating sophistications" (CP xix). Fitzpatrick goes on to recollect that he "fell in love" with that Sexton through the photographs on her book covers. He is up to something else, a defense of personal "beauty" as intimately linked to professional craft, a conflation of poetic accomplishment with the representation of literary celebrity and a certain feminine body "beautiful." Fitzpatrick is openly admiring of Sexton not only as a "poet beautiful enough to be a model but also, in fact, something more and different—the "very model of a modern model-poet" ("Aesthetics"). He laments that, while it might be unfortunate that Corral has felt excluded in gay poetry circles because of his appearance (by implication darker, chubbier against the "beauty" of Anne's whiter, shinier, thinner visage), there would be something equally unfortunate in Corral's attitude, "the devaluation of something important to me—namely fashion and beauty." Fitzpatrick concludes that, "I'm afraid such an attitude [referring to Corral's attitude] sets up a false dichotomy: looks or talent, style or substance. I refuse to settle for one or the other. Silly as it may sound, I want to be beautiful and I want to write beautiful poems" ("Aesthetics").

What Anne Anlin Cheng calls "hidden grief" of the cultural sort that might more plainly expose both race and gender as constructions that imprison both marginal and dominant subjects in haunted relations of melancholic identification and loss are obscured in Fitzpatrick's editorial. Fitzpatrick's op-ed, like many that followed it, sought to extricate or reposition the Sexton narrative as the story of the "very model of the model poet" who dies for beauty, as if beauty, fashionableness, and glamour are inherent to Sexton's nature, thereby re-casting her image as that of an iconic fashion queen. In these commentaries, Sexton's beauty comes off as a different kind of pure cultural product than in the 1970s, but a pure product nonetheless—the bodily pose readily equated with its imaginary cultural effects. In "How to Survive in NYC: Two Young Gay Poet Versions," another blog in the swirling "beauty-gate" muddle begins with a still image of Sexton in her study drawn from the NET film, re-captioned: "Anne Sexton is back and ready for her close-up"; that blog concludes with a swimsuit photograph of Sexton from her fashion model days and a caption that reads, "Those fifteen minutes as a model have finally paid off!"[35]

But what exactly is the identity of "the very model of the model-poet"? Surely it is not the identity of Anne Sexton, the person or poet who made a successful career of fashioning a double image—and uncanny interrogation of the photographic real—in pictures and in words. In "beauty-gate," the signifier (photograph of a fashion model) has come to take the place of the signified (model-poet). We are in the realm of the simulacrum, Baudrillard's figure for the airless real in which each image is seen as an adequate replacement for the next. We are not in the realm of Sexton in "Snow White and the Seven Dwarfs," where what is important about "beauty" is dwelling in an awareness of cultural contradiction: "Beauty is a simple passion, / but, oh my friends, in the end / you will dance the fire dance in iron shoes" (CP 225).

As beauty-gate has played out in the blogosphere, other poets of color, queer and straight, have continued to invoke the problematic of looking at Sexton through the lens of skin, class, and gender privilege, and have occasionally also shattered the simulacrum of glamorized beauty. Saeed Jones, in "All the Pretty Ones" blog post reflects that, "When I look at pictures of her, I don't see glamour. I see a woman who wrote, 'Once I was beautiful. Now I am myself. . . .'" Saeed continues: "There is nothing wrong with beauty. I certainly am quite fond of it, but we are doing ourselves no favors by pretending that beauty is what we are really talking about[.] . . . It's in praise of a certain brand of glamour that, more often than not in Western culture, is married to both race and class privilege."[36] Italian-Caribbean American poet Kara Candito, in "I'm a Rabbit and This Is My Owl: On Beauty and the Female Poet's Body," returns to "beauty-gate," playing on Sexton's "The Awful Rowing Toward God" in "The Awful Rowing Toward Prosperity." Candito returns to a familiar theme, Sexton's economy of the aesthetic as a phenomenon of late capitalist advertising, with gender and glamour twin features of commodified desire in the marketing of feminine beauty products. Borrowing from the Pantene commercial from the 1980s ("Don't hate me for being beautiful") Candito argues that the double bind of the female poet in relation to beauty is inevitable: "For female poets, it's hate me because I probably already hate myself for trying or not trying to be beautiful."

◆ ◆ ◆

There is, of course, no "final" photograph of Anne Sexton's abundant life in pictures. In the open hybridized spaces of digital culture, where no one takes the time that scholars in this volume have taken to secure copyright permission, the screen's radiant glow never goes dark, and many photographs are orphaned to sensation. Nevertheless, I would return to the real-time archival pursuit and to its future perfect sense, to reconsider the use value of piecing together archival evidence of poems and the photographs Sexton's readers love to look at. To claim that Sexton "understood photography" is to note her familiarity with photography's various genres, with light sources, poses, effects to be gained by distances and close-ups, cropping, and the expectations of transport that different audiences brought to multiform public spheres of visibility. Sexton, unlike many of her contemporaries, accepted the fractured nature of the modern media sphere and the inevitability of misrecognition—and she managed it. Scholarship on her videated life continues to explode the myth that positions confessional poets in a binary of retreat and resistance from modern media effects or susceptibility to its frivolously manufactured illusions. Sexton is an especially apt figure for continuing the project that Judith Brown has begun, in analyzing how the "glamour spectrum" of modernism in the media-saturated gaze returns the etymological associations of *glamour* to earlier meanings of *enchantment* and to its educated roots in *gramarye*, the cognate of grammar (Brown 9–10)—that is, to *her* business of words as a critical lens. A best case scenario for Sexton studies is that scholars will continue to be interested in the abundant links between memory and invention that her real and imagined engagements with photographs propose and that trouble us still.

## Notes

1. In modern criticism, light effects associated with photography's representational force are readily assimilated to negative and positive poles of the aesthetic sublime. A genealogy of such references would include James Agee's attribution of the camera's "cruel radiance" as an essential "weapon" against the violence of culture in everyday life (James Agee and Walker Evans, *Let Us Now Praise Famous Men* [Boston: Houghton Mifflin, 1960], 11). Judith Brown in *Glamour in Six Dimensions: Modernism and the Radiance of Form* proposes that light sources in modern radiant technologized forms can be read across word and image (8–11): Virginia Woolf's "luminous halo" (160) makes innovative use of the new arts of photography through a language of stopped time that is intrinsic to glamour-effects and the encoding of desire (81–87). Marjorie Perloff in *Radical Artifice* argues precisely that language poetry of the 1980s resists the "radiance" of modern media, an argument I suggest is qualified by image-bearing poets such as Sexton, who effect a compromise-formation.

2. Voyaging into the relatively uncharted archival territory of Sexton's photographs, the essay benefitted from Marsha Bryant's encouragement, long before a word was written, and from Amanda Golden's careful reading along the way. For research support and permissions, I am grateful to the Harry Ransom Center for Humanities Research for support from the Marlene Nathan Meyerson Photography Fellowship (2011–12) and to Linda Briscoe-Meyers, curator of the photography collection. See also Judith Brown, whose thinking on the relationship of affect to glamour's sublime effects, while focused on early modernist figures, has particular relevance to my argument about Sexton. See also Trotter and the *PMLA* special issue, "Celebrity, Fame, Notoriety," 126.4 (Oct. 2011).

3. See Furst. Sexton invited Arthur Furst into her home in April 1974 to take pictures commissioned by Houghton Mifflin for Al Poulin's modern poetry anthology; they developed a friendship, and she also encouraged him to mentor her daughter Joy in her budding interests in photography. Furst's photobook, *Anne Sexton: The Last Summer,* was posthumously published with the cooperation of Linda Gray Sexton; it includes letters, manuscripts, and additional photographs from Sexton's archive.

4. For example, see Judith Brown's discussion of the "grammar of time" in photography's expressive potential and its past-conditional would-have-been sense; the oscillation of the representational power of the pose with the "shock" of the arrested moment instigates repetition at the level of desire and loss, a theory that partially explains the psychoanalytic dynamics of Sexton's feelings of fascination/repulsion with being one photographed (17, 87). For a discussion of

desire, loss, and traumatic events in twentieth-century poetry and photography, see also Prosser.

5. Rosalie Thorne McKenna, known as Rollie, photographed Anne Sexton on her screen porch for this appearance in the company of the moderns. While Sexton was building relationships with photographers who came into her study and her home, support for publishing poetry in the larger houses was dropping off. In a 1976 interview with Robert Penn Warren, he commented that only he and Robert Frost were among the few poets still "earning a living" from royalties for poetry books. In the same period (1968–74), a number of publishers, including Houghton Mifflin, were responding to diminished audiences for academic poetry by turning to mass-marketing of literary anthologies, in new formats. In Donald Hall's era, the best literary anthologies were "quiet" productions in their layout and design; a flashier style of marketing characterizes the transnational anthologies of the 1970s. "The documentary portraits are of interest in themselves," Read wrote in his preface (ix), making the details important while leaving it to viewers to peer within the frame and to see just what meaning to make of them.

6. Letter, Sexton to Cathy Musello, 14 Apr. 1974, Sexton Papers.

7. The connection drawn by Judith Brown is that the glamour of the cigarette, with its "sleek machine-age" aesthetic, visibly conjoins modernist aesthetics, the effeminate cosmopolitanism of the dandy, and fascination with death (4).

8. Williams in "Sexton in the Classroom" notes a similar "back-door technique" (98) of working with objects and opposing valences to generate images: "In the course of picturing what an object was not, one would often discover an unusual image that the object actually was" (98).

9. Pages from Sexton's scrapbook can be found at <http://www.poetryfoundation.org/article/182446>.

10. See Hirsch xxiv. Hirsch notably argues that poses in family photographs seldom represent naturalized familial groupings; rather, they must be taken as representations of the dominant ideologies of family life in film, advertising, and television (xvi).

11. For reasons of limited space, I do not have the opportunity here to trace the temporal and visual links between Sexton's suspended "trance" moments and the arrested vision of photographic fascination.

12. Wicke provides a provocative analogy to the mediated celebrity face as a reversal of *sparagmos* of maenadic ritual, in which the authorial celebrity body is dismembered and reassembled through media consumption that is figured through the collective meal in "Epilogue: Celebrity's Face Book." Wicke's analysis has implications for further readings of food imagery in the "Ms. God" persona in late poems, a subject I do not have space to pursue fully. Wicke's emphasis on

modernism (via George Bernard Shaw) as a transitional phase in which celebrity passes through a zone allied with literature's traditional function as social magic (1133–34) is consistent with my argument about Sexton, who unlike many of her contemporaries, insisted on a magic-laden discourse.

13. Effanbee Doll Co.'s "Dy-Dee Doll" is also a glamour-puss, as featured in a 22 Nov. 1937 *Life* magazine issue: see web. July 2014, <http://www.dollsmagazine.com/antique-vintage-dolls/41-effanbees-darlying-dy-dee.html>.

14. Letter, Sexton to McKenna, 21 July 1970, Sexton Papers, box 22, folder 6. The Rollie McKenna correspondence in the Anne Sexton Papers highlights Sexton's photographic consciousness by detailing scene, staging, transformative effects and atmospheres that photographs create.

15. Anne Sexton Photography Collection, Harry Ransom Center for Humanities Research, Anne Sexton, folder, 981:0061:0001; hereafter cited in the text as Sexton Photography Collection.

16. As an example of the problem with the broken archive, the contents of this folder have been distributed throughout the photographic archive, so we do not know which images Sexton may have intentionally included.

17. *Anne Sexton*, Richard O. Moore, dir., *USA: Poetry*. The uncut version of the NET program can be viewed at the New York Public Library Archives and Manuscripts.

18. Unlike the majority of Sexton's photographers, Rhoda Nathans (1937–97) worked outside the photojournalistic circuit and advertised a private studio portrait business. Sexton photographs may have been included in Nathans's Nikon House exhibit: see *New York Magazine*, 19 Dec. 1977: 43.

19. Letter, Nathans to Sexton, Sexton Papers, box 23, folder 3.

20. Letter, Sexton to Nathans, Sexton Papers, box 23, folder 3. This is one of two letters acknowledging receipt of the photographs.

21. Harry Ransom Center for Humanities Research, University of Texas at Austin, Anne Sexton Photographic Portrait, 1974, Ted Polumbaum, Location: PH: LH, Sexton A, box 3, 981:0089:0092.

22. Letter, Anne Wilder to Anne Sexton, 17 July 1965, Sexton Papers, box 43, folder 7. See Judith Brown's discussion of the Harlow photograph in *Glamour*, 5–7. This photograph, reproduced in Brown's study (6) appears to be a plastic overlay on a stone surface.

23. Harry Ransom Center for Humanities Research, University of Texas at Austin, Anne Sexton Literary File collection, n.d., location: PH: LH, Sexton A, box 3, 981:0089:0060.

24. Letter, Nathans to Sexton, Sexton Papers, box 23, folder 3. The title of the poem is not identified in the letter.

25. Letter, Kevles to Sexton, 13 July 1968, Sexton Papers. Kevles, who took the lead role in writing the photojournalist script, relays the substance of editorial meetings not witnessed by Sexton, and characterizes the tensions around two different approaches to photographic representations.

26. Ted Polumbaum/Newseum Collection, Harry Ransom Center for Humanities Research, University of Texas at Austin, Anne Sexton, Photographer's Proof, 1967, Ted Polumbaum, Location: PH: LH, Sexton A, box 3, 957:0009:0001–0023. Ted Polumbaum (1924–2001) was also conscripted by the Sterling Lord Agency to do several book jacket photographs, including one which would later appear on the cover of *The Collected Poems.*

27. See Schiller. On the swimming pool photograph as an artistic and commercial genre, see Cornell.

28. Letter, Sexton to Diane Darvin at *Look* magazine, 9 Oct. 1968, Sexton Papers.

29. Letter, Richard B. McAdoo to Sexton, 20 Sept. 1973, Sexton Papers. McAdoo was director of Houghton Mifflin's mass-market trade division until 1981. The involvement of a high-level executive in the day-to-day details of marketing Sexton is one indication of the publisher's watchful interest in her appeal to an audience in an era when major publishing houses were cutting back on publishing volumes of poetry from all but the most commercially successful artists.

30. Sexton Photography Collection, Ann Phillips contact sheets, box 3, 981:0089:0095. The photography collection includes several pages of contact sheets featuring Sexton alone, and Sexton and Kathleen Spivack in animated conversation (viewed together, they almost make a short film). Spivack details this several-hour photoshoot with *Newsweek* photographer Ann Phillips and reproduces one of the contact sheets from the session (59–61). According to Spivack, Sexton "gloried" in the photoshoot; the presence of the camera unleashed a torrent of words and the presence of the camera "visibly enlarged" (60) Sexton's performance. Sexton used the occasion of being photographed to confide intimate details of her marriage (Spivack 59–61). Ironically, the archival contact sheet is also annotated (verso) by Sexton, noting that the pictures were taken the day she left Kayo. Spivack's account suggests the presence of the camera may have instigated a mimesis of the confessional process, which rendered the photographer complicit, both "numbed" and "dazed" (61).

31. E-mail with Elsa Dorfman, 9 Mar. 2015. The photograph was taken in conjunction with an interview with Charles Balliro that appeared in *Fiction* magazine (1974) shortly after Sexton's death.

32. Dorfman recalls it was a book jacket photo. Interview. Oct. 15, 2010.

33. Web. June 2014, <www.urbandictionary.com>. "Glam" is a derivation of "glamourous," in the widely acknowledged dictionary of twenty-first century slang, where the term is also linked to the 1970s Glam Movement, queer subcultures, camp, advertising, and ostentatious sartorial display. Earlier meanings of "glamour," according to *New Fowler's Modern English Usage* (3rd ed., ed. R. W. Burchfield [Oxford: Oxford UP, 2007] 1) trace the literary etymology of "glamour" to the verbal realm of "grammar" or "gramarye," which carried the association of the occult, magic, learning, and necromancy from English and Scottish Romantic literature. The term then passes into usage in the 1930s as an attribute of modern personhood, "a delusive or alluring charm" or "physical allure" (qtd. in Brown 9–10).

34. "Beauty-Gate, Synchronicity, and History," web. June 2015. Jory Mikelson discusses the 26 May 2012 essay by Dale Young: <http://jorymickelson.blogspot.com/2012/05/beauty-gate-synchronicity-and-history.html>.

35. John Gallagher, "Nothing to Say and Saying It," web. June 2014, <http://jjgallaher.blogspot.com/2012/05/how-to-survive-in-nyc-two-young-gay.html>.

36. Web. 24 May 2012, <http://www.lambdaliterary.org/features/oped/05/24/all-the-pretty-ones/#sthash.ssDWyU4A.dpuf>, accessed 2014. In this essay-length blog, poet and literary editor at *BuzzFeed* Saeed Jones responds to the Fitzgerald-Corral debate and extends questions about the "politics of beauty" for women poets of Sexton's generation to current tensions between New York's gay and lesbian feminist communities, noting that few gay male poets attended Adrienne Rich's memorial reading at Columbia in the spring of 2012 (wasn't Rich "beautiful enough?" Saeed wonders.) 25 June 2014.

## Works Cited

Adatto, Kiku. *Picture Perfect: Life in the Age of the Photo Op*. New York: Princeton UP, 2008. Print.

Barthes, Roland. "The Death of the Author." *Image—Music—Text*. Trans. Stephen Heath. New York: Hill and Wang, 1977. Print.

Baudrillard, Jean. *Simulacra and Simulation*. Trans. Sheila Faira Glaser. Ann Arbor: U of Michigan P, 1995. Print.

Brinnin, John Malcolm, and Bill Read, eds. *The Modern Poets: A British-American Anthology*. New York: McGraw Hill, 1963. Print

Brown, Judith. *Glamour in Six Dimensions: Modernism and the Radiance of Form*. Ithaca: Cornell UP, 2009. Print.

Candito, Kara. "I'm a Rabbit and This Is My Owl: On Beauty and the Female Poet's Body." Web. 18 June 2014. <http://karacandito.com/im-a-rabbit-and-this-is-my-owl-on-beauty-and-the-female-poets-body/>.

Cheng, Anne Anlin. *The Melancholy of Race: Psychoanalysis, Assimilation, and Hidden Grief.* New York: Oxford UP 2001. Print.

Cornell, Daniell, ed. *Backyard Oasis: The Swimming Pool in Southern California Photography 1945–1982.* Palm Springs: Prestel, 2012. Print.

Davison, Peter. *The Fading Smile: Poets of Boston from Robert Frost to Robert Lowell to Sylvia Plath.* New York: Knopf, 1994. Print.

Dorfman, Elsa. "Portrait of the Portrait Photographer." *The Journal of New England Photography* 2 (Winter 1981): 1–14. Print.

Fitzpatrick, James. "Anne Sexton, Aesthetics, and the Economy of Beauty." *Lamda Literary.* 23 May 2012. Web. 6 Nov. 2015. <http://www.lambdaliterary.org/sandbox/features/oped/05/23/anne-sexton-aesthetics-the-economy-of-beauty/>.

Furst, Arthur. *Anne Sexton: The Last Summer.* New York: St. Martin's Press, 2000. Print.

Gill, Jo. *Anne Sexton's Confessional Poetics.* Gainesville: UP of Florida, 2007. Print.

Goldman, Jonathan. *Modernism Is the Literature of Celebrity.* Austin: U of Texas P, 2012. Print.

Harris, T. George. "Paul Engle: poet-grower to the world," *Look* 29.11 (1 June 1965): 95–97. Print.

Helle, Anita. E-mail from Elsa Dorfman, 9 Mar. 2015.

———. Interview with Elsa Dorfman. 9 Sept. 2010. E-mail.

Hirsch, Marianne, ed., *Family Frames: Photography, Narrative, Postmemory.* New York: CreateSpace Independent Publishing Platform, 2012. Print.

Kevles, Barbara. "Through bedlam's door with Anne Sexton," *Look* 32.25 (10 Dec. 1968): t39–t40, t44. Print.

Klein, Michael. "Five for Eduardo C. Corral." *Ploughshares* Blog. 16 May 2012. Web. June 2014. <http://blog.pshares.org/index.php/five-for-eduardo-c-corral/>.

Klein, Richard. *Cigarettes Are Sublime.* Durham: Duke UP, 1993. Print.

Lowell, Robert. *Collected Poems.* Ed. Frank Bidart and David Gewander. New York: Farrar, Straus and Giroux, 2004. Print.

Mulvey, Laura. "Visual Pleasure and Narrative Cinema." *Screen* 16 (1975): 6–18. Print.

Moore, Richard O., dir. *Anne Sexton, USA: Poetry.* San Francisco, 1966. Video.

Plath, Sylvia. *Collected Poems.* Ed. Ted Hughes. New York: Harper and Row, 1981. Print.

Perloff, Marjorie. *Radical Artifice: Writing Poetry in the Age of Media.* U of Chicago P, 1991.

Phelps, Robert and Peter Deane. *The Literary Life: A Scrapbook Almanac of the Anglo-American Literary Scene: 1900-1950.* Chatto & Windus, 1970.

Prosser, Jay. *Light in a Dark Room: Poetry and Photography.* Minneapolis: U of Minnesota P, 2005. Print.

Schiller, Lawrence. *Marilyn and Me: A Photographer's Memoir.* New York: Nan A. Talese, 2012. Print.

Sexton, Anne. "Worksheets for 'Elizabeth Gone.'" *Anne Sexton: The Artist and Her Critics,* ed. J. D. McClatchy. Bloomington: Indiana UP, 1978. 51–73. Print.

Silverman, Kaja. *Threshold of the Visible World.* New York: Routledge, 1996. Print.

Spires, Elizabeth. Interview. "The Art of Poetry, No. 27." *Paris Review* 80 (1981). Web.

24 July 2014. <https://www.theparisreview.org/interviews/3229/the-art-of-poetry-no-27>.

Spivack, Kathleen. *With Robert Lowell and His Circle: Sylvia Plath, Anne Sexton, Elizabeth Bishop, Stanley Kunitz, and Others*. Northeastern UP, 2012. Print.

Stewart, Gwendolyn. "Anne Sexton." Web. 24 July 2014. <http://www.gwendolynstewart.com/sexton.html>.

Stewart, Susan. *On Longing: Narratives of the Miniature, the Gigantic, the Souvenir, and the Collection*. Baltimore: Johns Hopkins UP, 1992. Print.

Travisano, Thomas. *Midcentury Quartet: Bishop, Lowell, Jarrell, Berryman, and the Making of a Postmodern Aesthetic*. Charlottesville: U of Virginia P, 1999. Print.

Trotter, David. *Literature in the First Media Age: Britain Between the Wars*. Cambridge: Harvard UP, 2013. Print.

Wicke, Jennifer. "Epilogue: Celebrity's Face Book." Spec. issue of *PMLA* 126.4 (Oct. 2011): 1133–35. Print.

Williams, Polly C. "Sexton in the Classroom." *Anne Sexton: The Artist and Her Critics*. Ed. J. D. McClatchy. Bloomington: Indiana UP, 1978. 96–101. Print.

Woolf, Virginia. "Modern Fiction." *The Essays of Virginia Woolf: Volume. 4, 1925–1928*. Ed. Andrew McNellie, London: Hogarth Press, 1986. Print.

# ···3

## Anne Sexton's Institutional Voice

KAMRAN JAVADIZADEH

I am learning leaps and boundaries.
Anne Sexton to W. D. Snodgrass, 11 January 1959 (*SPL* 48).

Having just recorded a group of new poems, including several for which she is, today, most well-known, Sylvia Plath was asked by the British Council in late 1962 to explain the choice of subject matter in her recent work. She answered by gazing back across the Atlantic, to the writing of two of her contemporaries:

> I've been very excited by what I feel is the new breakthrough that came with, say, Robert Lowell's *Life Studies*, this intense breakthrough into very serious, very personal, emotional experience which I feel has been partly taboo. Robert Lowell's poems about his experience in a mental hospital, for example, interested me very much. . . . I think particularly the poetess Anne Sexton, who writes about her experiences as a mother, as a mother who has had a nervous breakdown, is an extremely emotional and feeling young woman and her poems are wonderfully craftsman-like poems and yet they have a kind of emotional and psychological depth which I think is something perhaps quite new, quite exciting. (Plath)

This story about breakthrough (and the sort of breakdown that both precipitated and provided material for it) was one that Lowell had told, as well.

A year earlier, in his *Paris Review* interview, Lowell complained about what he felt to be the current "Alexandrian age" in poetry: "Poets of my generation and particularly younger ones have gotten terribly proficient at these forms. . . . Yet the writing seems divorced from the culture. . . . It's become a craft, purely a craft, and there must be some breakthrough back into life" (*Prose* 244).

With respect to this breakthrough narrative, Lowell's career, in particular, is paradigmatic. The opening documents in Lowell's published correspondence are, tellingly, two curiously aggressive letters of application to Ezra Pound, written in 1936, when Lowell, as a Harvard freshman, had decided that he wished to leave the university with which his family was so closely associated and to come to study instead with the great modernist in Italy (*Letters* 3–6). Pound, evidently, declined Lowell's request; in any case, Lowell found his modernist tutors, just a year later, in the American South and then at Kenyon College, when he left Harvard to study with Allen Tate and John Crowe Ransom. Lowell's early reputation was built upon the scaffolding of his association with modernism and the New Criticism. His early work, at least through *The Mills of the Kavanaughs* (1951), was seen as exemplifying the dedication to the kind of densely crafted, impersonal technique that those related movements championed.

What changed everything for Lowell, according to this breakthrough narrative, was his experience of mental breakdown at some point in the 1950s. That breakdown (coupled, in most accounts, with a reading tour in California, in which Lowell rubbed elbows with the Beats) led to a loosening of Lowell's craft, and a turn, fundamentally, from the impersonal poetics of modernism to the personal poetry of *Life Studies* (1959). Here, for instance, is how Adam Kirsch describes the poets of Lowell's generation: "what unites them as a group is that each eventually rebelled against the New Critical understanding of poetry. In their very different ways, they attempted to break free of the styles and subjects that Modernism had considered suitable" (xiv). Charles Altieri, ostensibly in the same spirit as Kirsch, puts the case simply: "Robert Lowell was at one time a poster boy for the New Critics. . . . But his career took a radical turn with *Life Studies*" (*Art* 159–60).

This essay offers a critique and revisionary account of the breakthrough narrative, with Anne Sexton serving as its central example.[1] To be fair,

Altieri himself (though he does not mention Sexton) qualifies his narrative of breakthrough when, still writing about Lowell and his peers, he claims, "these writers in different ways developed the possibility that modernist attitudes towards sensation could be extended to include how we appear to ourselves" (Art 163). If a crucial aspect of the breakthrough narrative is that the poet makes a radical turn away from "objective" content and toward autobiography, then Altieri suggests a way in which we can both acknowledge the poet's renewed interest in his own life and at the same time preserve the possibility that certain legacies of modernist and New Critical poetics might still condition his deployment of autobiography. Put another way, my contention here (and throughout the larger project from which this essay is drawn) is that poets like Plath, Lowell, and Sexton continue, rather than reject, key aspects of the institutional forms of modernism that they inherit, but that they do so, often, by writing poems in which they are themselves both the subjects and the objects of institutional scrutiny.

I mean "institutional" in a few related senses. In the first place, the cultural productions of modernism, as Lawrence Rainey and others have shown, were, from the beginning, dependent on and embedded within a set of "shared institutional structures," which connected "works to readerships, or readerships to particular social structures" (6, 4). Moreover, as a certain strand of modernism (call it the Eliot-New Critical nexus) evolved over the first half of the twentieth century, it increasingly became "institutional" in the sense that it found a home in university curricula (and its practitioners in the ranks of university faculty) and became invested in aligning itself with and defending certain conceptions of literary tradition. But then I also have what might seem to be a quite different sense of the "institutional" in mind, one that was well known by all of the poets whom I have named so far. The mythological name Sexton gives to *this* institution is "Bedlam." Whether St. Elizabeths Hospital, where Ezra Pound was more or less incarcerated for thirteen years, McLean Hospital, where Plath and Lowell both were patients, or Westwood Lodge, where Sexton was hospitalized for depression, postwar poetry is replete with stories—both in the lives of the poets and in the poems they wrote—of psychiatric institutionalization. Both university and psychiatric hospital can be understood as versions of what Michel Foucault, in *Discipline and Punish*, calls "disciplinary institutions" (139), or of what Erving Goffman, in *Asylums*, calls "total institutions" (4), which is to say that, for all of their obvious differences, both university and psychiatric hospital are engaged in disciplining their residents into certain norms of behavior.

In Sexton's case, as I will show here, that discipline has left its record in her voice, which has learned to value coherence and completion (even or especially when the ostensible message carried by that voice is one of incoherence and madness), and which is reconciled to its embeddedness in impersonal social arrangements (even or especially when it makes claims for its uniquely personal individuation). What I am calling Sexton's "institutional voice" is, in this sense, conditioned both by a literary-academic culture that values formal complexity and an Eliotic relationship to "tradition" and by a kind of analogue in the therapeutic imperative that the wayward patient find her way back, via the thread of her own discourse, into the stability of its socially sanctioned space in the nuclear family.

Sexton understood this disciplinary intersection well enough to describe herself wryly, in "The Double Image," as a "graduate of the mental cases" (CP 39). While she was fond of pointing out that she never graduated from college, Sexton was not entirely an outsider to academic culture. What Plath neglected to mention to the British Council, when she cited the influential examples of Lowell and Sexton, was that the three poets had regularly gathered, three years earlier, around a seminar table at Boston University, and that their more or less contemporary "breakthrough[s] back into life" were, in very real and literal ways, mediated through that classroom and others like it. This essay will go on to argue that what Sexton learned in Lowell's classroom was not how to write a personal poem but rather how to write an institutional one. What Sexton found in Lowell's classroom was a disciplinary space in some ways not unlike the one that she had encountered in Westwood Lodge. My epigraph for this essay comes from one of Sexton's descriptions of Lowell's seminar. Her "breakthrough," such as it was, consisted not simply in her "leaps" beyond the "disciplinary institutions" that she entered, but in internalizing the "boundaries" that those institutions drew, and in crafting a kind of poem in which those institutional dramas could be restaged.

### Graduate of the Mental Cases

When, in 1960, the year in which her first book, *To Bedlam and Part Way Back*, was published, Anne Sexton made an audio recording of "The Double Image," she began by observing that it was "a very personal poem." One can hardly disagree. The poem describes, among other things, Sexton's estrangement from her baby daughter, her suicide attempts and hospitalizations, and her mother's death from cancer. Its lines do little to hide their autobiographical sources, instead encouraging their reader to equate speaker and poet with simple declaratives of date ("I am thirty this November") and place ("I came to my mother's house in Gloucester, / Massachusetts") (*CP* 35, 37). If what it means for a poem to be "personal" is that it grants its reader access to and focuses its attention on intimate knowledge about the poet's life, then "The Double Image" must be "personal."

And yet the kind of knowledge that "The Double Image" offers is not always so clear. Here, in the concluding lines of the poem's first stanza, Sexton addresses her three-year-old daughter during a late-autumn storm:

> I tell you what you'll never really know:
> all the medical hypothesis
> that explained my brain will never be as true as these
> struck leaves letting go. (*CP* 35)

The reader, who is invited to occupy the vantage point of the child, is being told not that she is about to learn something that she *has* never known or otherwise *would* never know, but rather that she is about to be told something that she *will* never know, not even after, that is, Sexton has told her. Put another way, what follows the colon in the quotation above is, evidently, *tellable* but not *knowable*. How can it be one and not the other? If we understand the addressee here to be a three-year-old child, then perhaps we can say that any number of statements could be heard but not understood (not "really," as the quotation's first line importantly qualifies). But the lines suggest a further kind of unknowability, one that results from replacing the intelligible but after all inadequate language of medical diagnosis with the opacity of the apt poetic image. That image, of "struck leaves letting go," is both "true" and resistant to our apprehension. Perhaps it describes Sexton's experience of mental illness as one of disconnection, but it also serves as a figure for the alienation of the "I" who writes the poem from the "you" who reads it. The speaker of the poem is no more connected, at this moment, to her reader than those "struck leaves" are to the branches from which they once grew. I will turn, by the end of this section, to a reading of "The Double Image"; for now, I cite these lines as a characteristic example of Sexton's tendency to be both personal and impersonal at once, to grant us access to the truth about her, but to preserve that truth as something that cannot "really" be known.

The paradox that I am identifying here is drawn out in some of the most astute recent scholarship on Sexton. Jo Gill, for example, adapting a term from Linda Hutcheon, locates in Sexton's early poetry a "sophisticated and self-reflexive textual narcissism" (35). According to Gill, what is often mistaken (especially by readers who wish to disparage Sexton in particular and confessional poetry in general) as "the apparent self-absorption of Anne Sexton (poet)" is better understood as the *text's* "catoptric" investment in itself (35, 45). Gill argues that Sexton's early poetry is, in that sense, more like the "radical" or "postmodern" kind of poetry in favor of which it has been devalued than is generally acknowledged, inasmuch as the self in Sexton's poetry is not simply revealed or expressed but textually constructed. For Gill, the "I" in Sexton's early poems emerges out of a linguistic process that depends upon free play and reflexivity, and a poem like "The Double Image," which is one of her central examples, "offer[s] no necessary access to reality" (45). Gill's reading of the poem concludes with a powerful and revisionary account of its final two lines, which once again address the poet's young daughter ("And this was my worst guilt; you could not cure / nor soothe it. I made you to find me" [CP 42]):

> the real interest lies in the confession not that the speaker made the daughter biologically but that she has constructed the daughter in the poem textually. . . . the ultimate referent of "double image" is the poem itself and the strategies which it employs in its construction and its aestheticization of relationships, experience, and subjectivity. The "worst guilt" to which the speaker refers pertains to her fabrication and manipulation of the mother/daughter relationship in order to construct this very poem and thereby to create or found—and emphatically not to reflect—her singular identity as a poet: "to find me."
> (47)

Despite all of the "personal" material that the poem appears to work through, its very conception of the nature of personhood as an essentially linguistic construction suggests Sexton's underlying commitment, according to Gill, to a postmodern poetics of textual indeterminacy (191).

Gill's privileging of the textual and indeterminate over the biological and personal is just the kind of move against which Christopher Grobe, in a still more recent essay, wants to push back. Grobe holds that "mid-century traditions of elocution and oral interpretation . . . contribute to that style of poetry—and of subjectivity—called confessional" (216). He argues for a critical methodology that would add to the close reading of poetic texts an equivalently close attention to the archive of the performances of those texts (especially for the confessional poets, who themselves attested to the centrality of oral performance in the development of their poetics), precisely so as to ground our readings of textual free play in the embodied particularities of performance. Grobe cites Sexton's interest in the acting theories of Konstantin Stanislavsky in an attempt to historicize Sexton's belief, articulated in a 1962 essay on "Some Foreign Letters," that a break or tremble in her voice during the public reading of a poem "signals that the boundaries between past and present, textual record and lived experience, privacy and publicity are breaking down" (226).

According to Grobe, just such a breakdown occurred during a 1964 reading of "The Double Image," a poem whose dizzying configuration of subject positions collapses into the (itself multiple, but singularly embodied) self who speaks from the stage. In a recording of that reading, we can hear Sexton's voice break when she reaches the lines, "Today, my small child, Joyce, / love your self's self where it lives." For Grobe, "This sentimental line, punctuated by the 'failure' of a breaking voice, is an injunction to herself, as much as to Joyce—and 'where it lives,' at that instant, is on the stage of the YM-YWHA Poetry Center in New York City" (228). Although Grobe might share Gill's view that, read as a primarily textual entity, the self in "The Double Image" is indeterminate and unknowable, he argues that when we lift our eyes from the page and fix our critical attention, instead, onto the stage, the "I" who speaks becomes singular and personal. As he puts it, "the logic of performed identity does not lead to performative free play but in fact offers a pathway out of a textually induced free play" (227–28).

If Gill maintains, on the one hand, that the self on display in "The Double Image" is a fundamentally literary construction and characterized by all of the indeterminacy of Sexton's verbal play, and if Grobe, on the other hand, attending to the archival record of Sexton's body in performance, points us down "a pathway out of a textually induced free play" and toward Sexton's personal particularity, then what I am arguing for, in this essay, is, in Sexton's terms, a pathway "part way back." I posit that the classroom is just such a space, one poised between Gill's page and Grobe's stage.[2] When we consider the role played by Lowell's Boston University workshop in shaping "The Double Image," we begin to see more clearly how that poem, like much of Sexton's early work, can seem both personal and impersonal at once, and, moreover, how it achieves its particular effects by being impersonal *about* material we have generally understood as personal.

Sexton would have found this curious configuration at work in the Lowell workshop. For his students, Lowell's classroom could, at times, seem like a purely textual and impersonal space, one in which students' poems were, more often than not, distributed anonymously and discussed in relation to examples drawn from literary history.[3] But then Lowell's classes (like all classes, to be sure) were also quite clearly stages for what Goffman, in the same year, had termed "the legitimate performances of everyday life" (*Presentation* 73). And while we have traditionally treated them as opposed terms, I am arguing, with respect to "The Double Image," that "text" and "performance" are better understood as referring to mutually engaged modes of poetic production.[4] The dynamic interaction between text and performance is precisely what makes the classroom the kind of disciplinary institution that I am claiming it is.

Early on in *The Presentation of Self in Everyday Life*, Goffman describes a significant consequence of his book's basic claim, that we are all, in a sense, actors who "act better than we know how" (74):

> When an actor takes on an established social role, usually he finds that a particular front has already been established for it. Whether his acquisition of the role was primarily motivated by a desire to perform the given task or by a desire to maintain the corresponding front, the actor will find that he must do both. (27)

Goffman's insight here illuminates what I take to be Sexton's productive predicament in Lowell's class. Her acquisition of the role of student-poet in Lowell's classroom, whether motivated by a desire to "perform the given task" of learning how to write better poems (as we have every reason to assume it was) or by the desire to maintain the "established social role" of the student-poet in Lowell's orbit, would compel her, ultimately, to do both. The consequences of that doubled obligation can be read in the lines of "The Double Image."

Consider Sexton's account, sent in a letter to W. D. Snodgrass, of the day when the class turned its attention to what was, at that point, her most ambitious poem: "Then last tuesday Lowell did the complete 'Double Image' in class and what's more he made ME read it. I was quite unprepared but he was adamant—I *had* to read it out loud" (*SPL* 65). Once it has been inserted into the familiar discursive economy of the workshop, Sexton's "very personal" poem becomes something over which she has considerably less control. In her idiom, it was Lowell, not she, who "did" the poem in class. The fact that she registers surprise at being singled out even to *read* the poem ("what's more he made ME read it") suggests not only that, within the culture of the workshop, authors bore no necessary connection to their texts but also that, as in this case, Lowell could exert his power as leader of the seminar to establish that kind of personal connection, post hoc, between poet and poem, voice and text. Citing Foucault's claim that "confession" is a "technique . . . for producing truth," Gill writes that, for Sexton as for Foucault, "confession is generated and sustained not by the profundity of need or strength of compulsion of the author, but by the discursive relationship between speaker, text, and reader—penitent, confession, and confessor" (17). Here, that relational model, in which *every* confession is, to some extent, a *forced* confession, takes a kind of literal form: "I was quite unprepared but he was adamant—I *had* to read it out loud." Whatever Lowell's reasons for requiring this oral performance, the effect of his insistence was to create a lasting identification, for those in the room, between the "I" of the poem and its author.

Kathleen Spivack, another member of the workshop, remembers the occasion vividly: "When Lowell passed out copies of Anne's poem 'The Double Image' and asked her to read it aloud, Anne read it feelingly in her hoarse terrific voice" (28). For Spivack—and surely for other members of the workshop—Sexton's "feeling" performance grounded the text of her poem in the particularity of her identity, bodied forth metonymically by "her hoarse terrific voice." Spivack also notes that the kind of personal identification with the poem so insistently enforced by Lowell's injunction to Sexton to read her poem aloud was a common, if usually less obvious, pedagogical tactic: "Slyly, Lowell would flush out the unfortunate author. Passing out those smeary carbon copies with a seemingly tentative bend of the head, a kindly smile, he would somehow get the author to confess ownership" (48).

Lowell's authority over a student's poem extended also to his ability to establish its textual genealogy. If his injunction to Sexton to read her poem out loud enforced a personal connection between poet and poem, his habit of embedding a student's poem within a notional library of prior texts and disciplines could make those poems seem impersonal even to their own authors. Snodgrass, who studied with Lowell at the Iowa Writers' Workshop in 1953, provides the following account:

> When Lowell "did" your poem, said one student, it was as if a muscle-bound octopus came and sat down on it. Then, deliberately, it would stretch out one tentacle and haul in mythology, a second for sociology, a third for classical literature, others for religion, history, psychology. Meantime, you sat there thinking, "This man *is* as mad as they said; none of this has anything to do with my poor, little poem!" Then he began tying these disciplines, one by one, into your text; you saw that it *did* have to do, had almost everything to do, with your poem. ("Mentors" 126–27)

If you were a student in Lowell's classroom, you would be unseated from your position of privileged access to your poem. In your stead would sit Lowell, the "muscle-bound octopus," who would perform the Eliotic work of situating your poem in an idiosyncratically defined literary (and academic) tradition. Lowell knows your poem better than you do. And what he knows is that it's *not* yours, not simply. Lowell, according to Snodgrass, does not so much establish the connections between the student's poem and a broad range of other texts as he reveals, instead, that those connections have been present all along.

Sexton was, for her part, quite self-conscious about one of those connections in particular. In the same letter to Snodgrass in which she described Lowell's treatment of her poem in class, she broached the uncomfortable topic of her poem's debt to Snodgrass, offering an admission and a defense that I wish to quote at some length:

When you do read ... ["The Double Image"], *and please wait until it comes out in ... [The Hudson Review]* ... it will remind you, in its like ways, of "Heart's Needle" because there was some experience so alike; the letting go of the child; the visits of the child[.] ... But in main, now that I can be objective about it—I do not feel it is an imitation of your great poem[.] ... (I was afraid it was, you know).... But it ain't really. It is much more twisted, less objective, more caught up in its own sickness—and then, it resolves like a story. I can never add nor subtract to it.—Does this seem odd to write you about this???? Maybe I do because I think you don't want to read it because you love me and don't want to find me copying you with my own like sick inventions pasted over your true poem[.] ... And if you feel that I have, when you do read it, I can only say that when I read your poem, that first time, leafing through the anthology, and it walked out at me and grew like a bone inside my heart. So, if the bone shows, it will only add to your fame and fortune. Now that it and even you are a kind of terrible part of me—I do not know how to disorganize myself. I have grown into this. No way back. No way at all. (*SPL* 65–66)

Against the charge of imitation (which, she concedes, was once her own fear), Sexton offers two related defenses. First of all, she insists that, despite their obvious similarities, the poems are different. Hers is "more twisted, less objective, more caught up in its own sickness" than "Heart's Needle." Essentially, this line of defense amounts to Sexton's insistence that "The Double Image" is indeed a personal poem (and perhaps more intensely personal than "Heart's Needle"), that its determining source has been not Snodgrass's poem (or, for that matter, any other poem), but rather the stuff of her own life. The fact that the poems resemble each other so closely is attributable, she suggests, simply to the coincidence that she and Snodgrass have had "experience so alike."

Her second line of defense concedes more without relinquishing the premises upon which that first defense had been mounted. For of course it is not simply the case that Sexton's poem resembles Snodgrass's in terms of their choice of subject matter ("the letting go of the child; the visits of the child"). Formally, too, "The Double Image" seems to have been modeled on "Heart's Needle": both poems arrange their numbered sections into an episodic narrative; in both poems, each of those numbered sections features its own recurring stanzaic pattern; and both poems, finally, balance their formality with a tone that seems always on the verge of sentimentality. Given all of this, how can Sexton rightly claim that hers is a personal poem, rather than a direct imitation of "Heart's Needle"? How can "The Double Image" both be personal, which is to say authentically grounded in Sexton's lived experience, *and* be so clearly indebted to "Heart's Needle"?

The answer, according to Sexton, is that "Heart's Needle" has itself become part of her. Her metaphor for her first reading of Snodgrass's poem is simultaneously organic and strained: "it walked out at me and grew like a bone inside my heart." If Sexton is willing—eager, even—to concede the influence of Snodgrass's poem, it is because she can tell a story about that influence that is built upon the premise of a personal poetics. Snodgrass and his poem are, to Sexton, interchangeable terms here, and they have lodged themselves at the "heart" of Sexton's being in a manner that is at once uncomfortable (rather like a fishbone in one's throat) and irreversible (inasmuch as both "bone" and "heart" are ways of referring to what is fundamental in the body).

In a letter to Snodgrass written a month earlier, Sexton made this point even more simply: "It is too late to turn you out of my heart. Part of you lives here" (58). The "heart" is, of course, one of the governing images of "Heart's Needle"; in twice borrowing that metaphorical language to describe the transformative nature of her encounter with the poem, Sexton is, ipso facto, demonstrating the truth of her claim. And this, for Sexton, is what poetry can and should do; in another letter to Snodgrass, she would write: "What I'm trying to say is that, I think a poem that can do that to people, make them see themselves through yourself, is valid . . . not unseemly, not too personal, but worth it!" (63).

When we contrast these ready admissions of Snodgrass's influence on "The Double Image" with her statements about Lowell's influence, however, we see a rather different dynamic at work. When an interviewer for the *Hudson Review* (the journal in which "The Double Image" had first been published) asked about Lowell's influence as a poet (rather than as a teacher), Sexton demurred:

Actually, this is a terrible thing to admit, but I had not read any of his poetry when I studied with him. I did not go to college, and when I was studying with him I was so innocent as not to have read any of his poems, and his *Life Studies* had not come out at the time. They came out after I had finished studying with him. So they didn't influence me at all, because I hadn't seen them. If anything influenced me it was W. D. Snodgrass's *Heart's Needle*. (*NES* 78–79)

In her memoir about the Lowell seminar, Sexton had struck a similar note, pithily distinguishing herself from the "graduates" who were her classmates by claiming, "I was the only one in that room who hadn't read *Lord Weary's Castle*" (*NES* 3). A few things emerge from Sexton's disavowals of Lowell's influence (particularly when contrasted with her claiming of Snodgrass). The Lowell whom Sexton first met in the fall of 1958 was not yet the "personal" poet of *Life Studies*, at least not in print. His reputation still rested largely on a decade-old literary sensation (*Lord Weary's Castle* was published in 1946 and was awarded the Pulitzer in 1947) whose surrounding publicity—for all of the book's poetic accomplishments—almost always mentioned its author's famous family name and the approval of an older generation of modernists. This was still, in other words, a poet of the establishment, the not-yet-broken-through figure whom Altieri and others have described as a "poster boy for the New Critics" (*Art* 159). Or so Sexton would consistently imply. Asked by her *Paris Review* interviewer whether Lowell read her poems before or after he published *Life Studies*, Sexton was once again clear:

> Before. I sent him the poems in the summer; the following spring *Life Studies* came out. Everyone says I was influenced by Robert Lowell's revelation of madness in that book, but I was writing *To Bedlam and Part Way Back*, the story of my madness, before *Life Studies* was published. I showed my poems to Mr. Lowell as he was working on his book. Perhaps I even influenced him. I have never asked him. But stranger things have happened. (*NES* 90)

If Sexton was eager to acknowledge Snodgrass's influence because to do so was consistent with her faith in a personal poetics, then Lowell, whom Sexton described as "formal in a rather awkward New England sense" (*NES* 3–4), needed to be held off at arm's length because what he represented to Sexton was an impersonal, academic culture, which she approached always as an outsider.

Where Sexton *did* credit Lowell's influence, it was not as poet but as critic and editor. Consider the following lengthy parenthetical aside, written in a letter to Snodgrass upon receiving his comments on her poem "The Division of Parts" in the summer of 1959:

> (tho I WISH you wouldn't keep telling me it suffers from Lowell's voice or your voice when, of course, I'm so sure that I haven't borrowed anyone's voice. Or, at least, sure about the Lowell influence. I've been so careful not to read his work. If anything, [I] have been influenced by his critical sense, his teaching—you know, just sitting in class and keeping my big ears clean and open. And YOU told me to. And I did[.] . . . Jesus, I'm a defensive creature! and in manicy moments I say to myself, I'm better than Lowell!—How is *that* for poetic conceit. !!! You know, De, I never WANTED to take a course from him because I always heard he had such mixed imagery[.] . . . These were *my* faults and I didn't want to be influenced by my own weaknesses. But, when you told me you had studied with him[.] . . . Still, I'm damn glad I did. He taught me great. It was as easy as filling an empty vase. After all, I didn't know a damn thing about any poetry really. 2 years ago I had never heard of any poet but Edna St. Vincent . . . and now do know how to walk through lots of people's poetry and pick and pick over . . . god, is this still an aside.)))))) (*SPL* 79–80)

The fact that Sexton concludes this "aside" with six consecutive parentheses indicates both her eagerness to shelve the issue, to confine her consideration of Lowell's influence to a grammatically subordinate position, and her recognition ("Jesus, I'm a defensive creature!") that Lowell occupies an anxious and not easily contained place in her own sense of her poetic development. The "care" that Sexton has taken not to be infected, as it were, by Lowell's "work" finds its epistolary analogue in her attempt to restrict her remarks on that threatening influence to a parenthetical aside—and the length of that aside suggests that, careful as Sexton has been, she has felt Lowell's influence after all. According to Sexton, that influence consists in "his critical sense, his teaching," which has left her now able "to walk through lots of people's poetry and pick and pick over."

And while, in the letter, Sexton opposes this kind of influence to the matter of "voice," in her essay about Lowell's classroom, she would claim that his actual voice meant more to her than his words:

His voice was soft and low. It seems to me that people remember the voice of the teacher they loved long after they have forgotten what he said. At least, I have noticed this among poets and their teachers. Mr. Lowell's reverence for John Crowe Ransom's voice was something I wouldn't understand until today as I find myself remembering Lowell's voice and the way *he* would read a poem. (*NES* 4)

Lowell's "soft and low" voice becomes the vehicle for his exacting critical sense; it is allied in Sexton's genealogy with the voice of the New Critic who was (with the possible exception of Allen Tate) Lowell's most influential teacher. In that sense, the "reverence" identified here by Sexton of each successive generation of students for its teacher's voice might be understood as the historical dissemination of institutional discipline. That is, Sexton places herself in a tradition of poets who are also always teachers, so that the line between those two vocations is necessarily blurred. (Blurred, too, in New Critical pedagogical practice, is the line between the teacher's literal *reading* of the poem out loud in class and the authoritative "reading"—as "interpretation"—of the poem that his pedagogy is designed to inculcate.)[5]

About Lowell's value as a teacher, Sexton wrote: "He works with a cold chisel with no more mercy than a dentist. He gets out the decay" (*NES* 4). Compare that estimation of Lowell's tough love to lines that Sexton would no doubt have also had in mind, lines written by Snodgrass in "Heart's Needle" to a daughter whose Halloween visit to her father has recently ended: "for days / I crave sweets when you leave and know / they rot my teeth. Indeed our sweet / foods leave us cavities" (*Heart's Needle* 55). If, in Snodgrass, Sexton finds the sweetness of the personal, then she seems to know well enough to seek out the disciplinary dentistry of Lowell as an impersonal corrective in the New Critical (and modernist) tradition.

Keeping in mind the notion that, within this Ransom-Lowell line of succession claimed by Sexton, the poet is also always both critic and teacher, it should come as no surprise that Lowell's critical influence on Sexton would bleed over into her poetry—that the two strands would not be quite as easily separable as Sexton would have us believe. The editorial voice telling Sexton "what to leave out," the voice of New Critical impersonality, represents to Lowell and Sexton both not just an editorial disposition but also a disciplinary poetics (*NES* 5). For all of her insistence that she had no exposure to Lowell's *Life Studies* poems in the workshop, we know from contemporary accounts that Sexton is quite likely to have read a handful of them in draft form. Spivack notes that, during class, "Lowell shared his doubts about the personal direction such poetry was taking, reading drafts of some of his poems in *Life Studies* aloud, such as 'Waking in the Blue'" (28). That poem, according to Ian Hamilton, Lowell's biographer, was begun in January 1958, several months before Sexton applied to Lowell's workshop (244–49). "Skunk Hour," perhaps the most well known of the *Life Studies* poems, was completed in October 1957 (233–34). Both poems inform "The Double Image."

Although Sexton would consistently position herself as someone "who had never been to college," and while "The Double Image" contains no direct depictions of academic life, the poem does make metaphorical use of academic discourse. This is Sexton, describing her discharge from hospital:

> I checked out for the last time
> on the first of May;
> graduate of the mental cases,
> with my analyst's okay,
> my complete book of rhymes,
> my typewriter and my suitcases. (*CP* 39)

Here we have an example of the "mixed imagery" that Sexton had acknowledged to Snodgrass as a "fault" she feared she had in common with Lowell. The hospital is both a "hotel" (a joking euphemism that she used in the poem and in life), from which she could check out, and, it seems, a "school," from which she could graduate in May, as though in cap and gown.[6] Recalling Goffman's definition of the "total institution" as "a place of residence and work where a large number of like-situated individuals, cut off from the wider society for an appreciable period of time, together lead an enclosed, formally administered round of life," we can understand how hospital, hotel, and university might align in Sexton's imagination (*Asylums* xiii). Hospital and university, in particular, satisfy not only the formal but also the functional definition of Goffman's "total institution"; both can be understood as "forcing houses for changing persons; each is a natural experiment on what can be done to the self" (12). As Sexton conflates them here, the hospital is like the university in that both are disciplinary institutions, whose professional staffs are empowered ("my analyst's okay") with policing the subject into conformity with their norms and standards. When we remember that this poem began with an image of disconnection, of "struck leaves letting go," the speaker's "complete book of rhymes" now appears as a metonym for those norms: linguistic coherence, connection, and completion.[7] Goffman's "place of residence and work" sends its former resident out into the world equipped once again with the props ("my typewriter and my suitcases") for both.

As I have suggested, Sexton had a ready model for this kind of depiction of the psychiatric hospital as university in Lowell's "Waking in the Blue." Throughout his poem, which is based on one of Lowell's hospitalizations in McLean, the institutional setting of the hospital is conflated ironically with the vestiges of academia. All of the poem's characters—from the "night attendant," described as "a B.U. sophomore," to Lowell's fellow patients, "Stanley," who was "once a Harvard all-American fullback," and "Bobbie," identified by reference to his Harvard final club and year, "Porcellian '29"— are known via their relationships to universities (*Poems* 183). Near the end of the poem, Lowell's speaker, in terms that would be echoed in the above passage from "The Double Image," proudly reports:

> Cock of the walk,
> I strut in my turtle-necked French sailor's jersey
> before the metal shaving mirrors,
> and see the shaky future grow familiar
> in the pinched, indigenous faces
> of these thoroughbred mental cases,
> twice my age and half my weight. (*Poems* 184)

Lowell's speaker, like Sexton's, sees himself as one among a company of "mental cases," which is one of the primary effects of the institution: the "personal," which is to say individuated, subject who enters the institution is conditioned by its strictures to play, however imperfectly, the role that it supplies (this is what follows from having been reduced discursively to the status of the "mental case").

What we learn when we consider either poem in this light is that neither is in any simple sense "personal." Rather, both dramatize the entry of the presumably personal subject into the impersonal institution, demonstrating, as Lowell writes in "Home After Three Months Away" (a poem that grew out of the same drafts that produced "Waking in the Blue"), that the therapeutic benefits of institutionalization have come with the associated costs of feeling "frizzled, stale and small" (*Poems* 186). For Sexton, this drama of institutionalization serves not only as one of the stories that "The Double Image" tells but also as the story she repeatedly told of being Lowell's student (and therefore of the circumstances in which the poem was completed). "If you have enough natural energy," Sexton wrote about Lowell, "he can show you how to chain it in" (*NES* 5). Or again, as she phrased it in a letter to Snodgrass, from Lowell she was "learning leaps and boundaries" (*SPL* 48).

Even when we set aside the thorny question of who influenced whom, when we view "The Double Image" alongside Lowell's "Home After Three Months Away" and Snodgrass's "Heart's Needle," a striking family resemblance emerges, a period poem in triptych: the wayward poet, who finds him or herself in a state of radical separation from the nuclear family (a separation that is made to seem both symptom and cause of illness), follows a thread of sentimentalized direct address back to a scene of reconciliation (however provisional or attenuated) with a young daughter. That daughter, in turn, serves as synecdoche for what the poet and the culture alike understand as health—and for what Lee Edelman, in *No Future* (2004), has termed "the familiar narrativity of reproductive futurism," in which the "Child . . . marks the fetishistic fixation of heteronormativity: an erotic investment in the rigid sameness of identity" (17, 21). "And you are still my daughter," writes Snodgrass in the final line of "Heart's Needle"—"still," that is, even after the poem's painful evocations of the personal dislocations that follow divorce (62). Lowell's speaker, granted a temporary leave from McLean and its collection of "mental cases," finds himself, in "Home After Three Months Away," so close to his daughter and the futurity that gathers in her that, he says, "Our noses rub" (*Poems* 185). To be sure, for both Snodgrass and Lowell (and for Sexton, as I will continue to argue), the return to the family circle is fraught with instability and doubt, but the narrative is, nevertheless, the familiar one of familial return.

Within "The Double Image," the "boundaries" that the speaker has learned as "graduate of the mental cases" extend into the rhythms of her daily routines, which are recognizable as preserving the safety of postwar domesticity. Home from the hospital, and having "learned life / back into my own / seven rooms," the speaker tells us, for example, that she "answered the phone, / served cocktails as a wife / should" (*CP* 39). That last enjambment suggests, first of all, that Sexton is performing a life that she must seem, to those around her, simply to be living, as though "wife" were a role that she appeared "as" and not a kind of person who she in fact *was*. But then the "should" that follows the line break makes clear that Sexton's performance "as a wife," far from being freely chosen, is behavior compelled by the normative demands of the "life" she has "learned" to live. To the daughter from whom she remains separated, Sexton writes: "And you came each / weekend. But I lie. / You seldom came" (39). Once again the poem establishes a set of polite expectations only to reveal, in its next breath, that life falls short of them. And just as the poem's rhyme scheme imposes the promise of a regular structure that the irregularities of the speaker's "natural" language is compelled, for all its irregularities, to fulfill, the "learned life" establishes its own set of expectations that Sexton's path, however wayward, must inevitably bend toward. The story that "The Double Image" tells is of the endurance of institutionalized, impersonal form and of its capacity to make meaningful the personal lives that reside within it.

Alienated from both her daughter and her mother, the poem's speaker nevertheless returns, throughout the poem, to the identity-forming power of those relationships. As she tells her daughter in the poem's shocking last words, "I made you to find me" (42). Gill, we remember, maintains that this is a confession about linguistic rather than biological construction— and as proof, thereby, of the poem's fundamental postmodernity. Without disputing the validity of Gill's insight, I read this last line as a distillation of the basic truth on offer throughout "The Double Image," that the personal cannot be known except insofar as it is embedded in a network of social relations that begin, in a sense, with the family and that extend outward into the kinds of arrangements that I, following Goffman, have been calling "total institutions."

Upon "graduating" from "Bedlam," the speaker returns not only to her daughter but also, as a daughter herself, to her mother. Her journey back to her mother's home occasions a memory that at once fixes her identity as her mother's daughter and reveals that even that identity has always been a kind of impersonal performance:

That October day we went
to Gloucester the red hills
reminded me of the dry red fur fox

coat I played in as a child; stock-still
like a bear or a tent,
like a great cave laughing or a red fur fox. (*CP* 40)

The journey to visit her mother recalls an earlier approach to that maternal figure, a memory of dressing in her mother's clothes. Of course, in this particular case, mother's clothes are, in some crucial sense, not really even hers; the coat, as Sexton's versification reminds us, belonged originally to the "red fur fox." Poetry is, in this way, like the fashion industry, a form of culture, a way of making things human. The clever enjambment between the stanza's third and fourth lines linguistically makes the "red fur fox" into a "coat" just as surely as the industry produced the piece of clothing. To play at being mother, in both the past and present of this poem, is to appropriate a costume of foxy cunning while leaving blank any certain knowledge of what lies within. Even as the hills connect the speaker to her mother via this attenuated memory of childhood play, they also call to mind the earlier description of the surgical treatment of her mother's breast cancer— "They carved her sweet hills out / and still I couldn't answer"—and point again, thereby, to the hollowing out of connection between mother and daughter (38).

Whether or not she had it in mind, Sexton's image recalls another description of autumn foliage from Lowell's "Skunk Hour." That poem's speaker declares, "The season's ill," and offers up, apparently as proof, the following description of the Maine landscape: "A red fox stain covers Blue Hill" (*Poems* 191). Lowell would insist that he chose the image primarily because of its ability to conjure the particular hue of a New England autumn—but then also because the line had "sinister and askew suggestions" (*Prose* 229). By the end of "Skunk Hour," after Lowell has described a night of voyeuristic cruising, he confesses to an even more radical crisis: "I myself am hell; / nobody's here—// only skunks, that search / in the moonlight for a bite to eat" (*Poems* 192). The foxes, absent from the poem and having left behind only their "sinister" trace, prefigure the evacuation of the poet's very self from his dramatic monologue. In their—and in his—place, comes "a mother skunk with her column of kittens," creatures of will but of only a very dim kind of consciousness. Ultimately, self-representation throughout *Life Studies* looks something like this: the "Robert Lowell" who speaks and populates the poems is, in the words of Lawrence Kramer, "as empty as his descriptions are full." Kramer goes on: "Robert Lowell is not the speaking subject of his life history; he is only one of its many objects" (87).

So, too, is the "Anne Sexton" of "The Double Image" primarily the object rather than the subject of her self-descriptions. The poem's governing image, which gives it its title and recurs in all but its first and last sections, is of an act of self-representation executed by proxy: "I had my portrait / done instead" (CP 37). The painting of the poet, like the verbal representation of the poet within the poem, is presumably as "personal" as any portrait. And yet it is executed impersonally and displayed opposite another portrait, of the mother who could of course also claim to be the poet's creator, on a wall of the house in which she feels only precariously at home. Just so, the poet who found herself in the disciplinary space of Lowell's classroom could only claim to be "part way back" from Bedlam.

## A Straight and Good Road

Even if, as she conceded in the midst of that lengthy and defensive parenthetical aside to Snodgrass, Sexton "had never heard of any poet but Edna St. Vincent" before her late entry into academic culture and Lowell's classroom, we can be certain that she would not have left that year of study without one very specific counterexample to the romantic Millay in mind.[8] Spivack, again, provides a useful window into the seminar:

> No one was able to escape Lowell's classes without being convinced that Elizabeth Bishop was one of the best American poets writing. They were friends, and he respected her fine, exacting poetry, with its perfect mastery of form and attention to detail. Reading her poems taught us all that poetry demands accuracy of observation, even of the smallest things. (49)

In this part of the essay, I will argue first of all that what Bishop represented to Sexton was another disciplinary model, another avatar of institutionalized modernism.

By looking at Sexton's "Ringing the Bells," a poem that was drafted during a three-day hospitalization at Westwood Lodge in January 1959, in relation to the poem on which it was modeled, Bishop's "Visits to St. Elizabeths," we will see that what Sexton learned from Bishop, cognate with what she had learned from Lowell, was a kind of late modernist institutional poetics. Personal and impersonal at once, Sexton's poem features a self that is subject to and contingent on the disciplinary forces of the hospital in which it resides and that, at the same time, stands with and assumes the subject position of that same institution (itself imagined as a formal arrangement not unlike a poem). If my discussion of "The Double Image" demonstrated that the classroom functioned in Sexton's poetic development analogously to the way the madhouse functioned in the life represented within her poem, my discussion of "Ringing the Bells" will show that Sexton herself always understood "Bedlam" as a particular kind of classroom.

Sexton thought well enough of Bishop to have Houghton Mifflin send her copies of *To Bedlam and Part Way Back*, when it was published in 1960, and *All My Pretty Ones*, when it was published in 1962. According to Diane Middlebrook, the second book elicited a direct response from Bishop:

> Bishop was also asked for a blurb, but she wrote to Sexton instead. In *Bedlam*, she said, "You began right off . . . speaking in an authentic voice of your own; this is very rare and has saved you a great deal of time!" Tactfully suppressing reservations she had earlier expressed to Lowell, Bishop found the poems of *Pretty Ones* equally authentic, "harrowing, awful, very real—and very good." (174)

Although Middlebrook is right to claim that Bishop had expressed reservations about Sexton in letters to Lowell, even with him those reservations were mixed with a particular sort of praise: "I like some of her really mad ones best; those that sound as though she'd written them all at once. I think she must really have been in what Lota called the other day the 'Luna Bin'" (*Words in Air* 327). In both cases, what Bishop singles out for praise is the authenticity of Sexton's voice, particularly when that authenticity is matched with material that is "harrowing." Bishop admires the poems that bear the markers of spontaneous utterance, poems that testify to their origins in states of mental affliction and physical confinement precisely because, it seems, those "really mad" states have a way of producing poetry that is, correspondingly, "very real."

But if Bishop admired Sexton's voice for its "harrowing, awful" authenticity, Sexton, conversely, sought Bishop's approval because of what she understood as the more established poet's discipline and sanity. This much is evident from Sexton's response to Bishop's letter of praise for *All My Pretty Ones*. In fact, Sexton wrote not one but two letters in response to Bishop's encouragement.[9] In the first, Sexton offers her "sincere admiration" for what she calls "the clear speech" of Bishop's poetry, in which there is "never a wrong word." Having already mailed that first letter, Sexton grew worried, as she explained in a second letter to Bishop, composed that same evening, that the note she had struck was "sincere but formal seeming." Sexton's second letter, riddled with false starts, typos, and effusions of feeling that, in Sexton's own words, marked it as "a fan letter," risked (again in Sexton's words) sounding "foolishly sincere" precisely because the foolishness of Sexton's feeling for Bishop was a necessary part of its truth.

Sexton's ellipses, for instance, multiply in the second letter, which contains twice as many ellipses (34) as periods marking full stops (17). These ellipses signify failures of meaning: when she tells Bishop, "your letter was something of a mark to me . . . a goal" and "I keep looking to your poems for a kind of sanity and beauty . . . you stretch out like a straight and good road showing me where to head for," Bishop serves in Sexton's prose for the syntactical completion that Sexton herself cannot achieve, for the "straight and good road" from which Sexton is, even while she writes those words, taking errant detours. And if Bishop, as Sexton suggests, represents sanity, then, to the extent that Sexton falls short of or diverges from her model, Sexton verbally performs just the kind of "really mad," "authentic" utterance that had initially captured Bishop's attention. And the model provided by Bishop (notionally as a figure of what a poet might be, and more literally, as we will see, in terms of supplying a source text for one of Sexton's poems) thus functions as a kind of normative institution within which Sexton's pathology can be read as the madness of the proverbial bedlamite.

By the time she wrote her "fan letter" to Bishop, Sexton had already written, and Bishop had presumably already read, "Ringing the Bells," which Sexton had described to Snodgrass as "another 'bedlam poem'" (*SPL* 54). The poem's first word declares, however ambiguously, the derivativeness of what follows:

    And this is the way they ring
    the bells in Bedlam

and this is the bell-lady
who comes each Tuesday morning
to give us a music lesson (*CP* 28)

The pun is irresistible, which is, after all, to the point: the poem must have "rung a bell" for Bishop, who, two years before Sexton wrote "Ringing the Bells," had published her poem about Ezra Pound, "Visits to St. Elizabeths," in the Spring 1957 issue of *Partisan Review*.[10] Bishop's poem, modeled on the nursery rhyme "The House That Jack Built," begins, "This is the house of Bedlam. // This is the man / that lies in the house of Bedlam" (*Poems, Prose, and Letters* 127). The formal similarities are striking, beginning especially with Sexton's addition to Bishop's first word: we move from Bishop's "This" to Sexton's "And this," which suggests its status as a response without explicitly declaring its antecedent.[11]

As Susan Schweik has recently argued, Sexton's voice in this poem is "of a person subjected to repetition." Citing the way the poem's opening lines recall the rhythm of the conductor's "and one / and two / and," Schweik compares the metrical dynamic at work in "Ringing the Bells" to "what Max Cavitch, writing about the poetry of slavery, calls the 'history of subjectivation through rhythm'" (Schweik 24; Cavitch 95–96). If, in Bishop, Sexton had found "a straight and good road showing me where to head for," then here it seems we can see the younger poet following that path in quite literal and exacting terms. Bishop, by this measure, might very well be taken to be the figure behind Sexton's "bell-lady / who comes each Tuesday morning / to give us a music lesson."

One wonders if this is the kind of poem Bishop had in mind when she wrote to Lowell, "I like some of her really mad ones best; those that sound as [though] she'd written them all at once" (*Words in Air* 327). While Sexton seems rather explicitly to be responding to Bishop's poem about Pound, and while Sexton's poem shares an anaphoric structure with Bishop's and a setting in "Bedlam," Sexton's poem departs radically from the most prominent formal feature of Bishop's. "Visits to St. Elizabeths" borrows its form, as previously noted, from the nursery rhyme "The House that Jack Built," and it develops its "mad" feeling from seeming to be in the grip of a self-generating, overwrought form.

To read "Visits to St. Elizabeths" is to feel, along with the poem's speaker, a loss of agency; the form of the poem itself seems to exert a kind of disciplinary control over its reader. As stanza builds on stanza, always we are left with an image of the "man / that lies in the house of Bedlam," and, in every stanza, that "man," Bishop's version of Pound, earns a new epithet. He is, sequentially, "tragic," "talkative," "honored," "old, brave," "cranky," "cruel," "busy," "tedious," "the poet," and, finally, "wretched" (127–29). The accumulating lines of each stanza, which surround this "man" with a growing cast of bedlamites who seem drawn from Pound's mind, provide the logic that functions to characterize Pound thusly; the poem's institutional logic suggests that the architecture and social arrangements of the space in which Pound "lies" determine the nature of the self who is there made visible.

Apart from this all, it seems, stands our speaker, herself a kind of saintly Elizabeth. Contra the poem's terrifying encounter with madness is its insistence, intimated through more than one channel, that the speaker (and perhaps, with her, the reader) is clinging to some last measure of self-determination. The poem's title, for one thing, implies that its speaker is not herself a patient but rather a kindly visitor to the "wretched man." She thus can lay claim to some measure of sanity against which the ghastly madness of Bedlam can be measured. The poem's anaphoric structure, which always begins its descriptions by declaring, "This is" or "These are," implies the image of a speaker who can stand apart from the things she describes, and point them out to her reader, as though with extended arm.

Even in her choice of relative pronoun, when she insists on using "that" rather than "who" to describe "the man / *that* lies in the house of Bedlam" (*Poems, Prose, and Letters* 127; emphasis added), argues Schweik, "we can locate the poem's aversion to its subject" (20). While Bishop gives her poem a title that suggests the possibility that she identified with the scene at Bedlam, the poem deploys a host of strategies to keep what seems threatening about its institutional power at bay. Or rather, since her name is to be found in the name of the institution rather than among its collection of bedlamites, it might be more accurate to say that Bishop identifies more strongly with the institution itself than with the subjects whom ("that," the speaker would disdainfully say) it houses.

Sexton's speaker, of course, is a patient and not a visitor to Bedlam, and *her* poem's form produces what perhaps even Bishop would have judged a more primary or direct experience of madness. For the poem *does* "sound as though she'd written [it] all at once": gone are Bishop's stanzas, modeled on those of the nursery rhyme; gone, too, with one notable exception, is the syntactical rhythm of Bishop's often short, declarative sentences. Instead, until its last three words, Sexton's poem winds through its short lines in the single breath of a run-on sentence. The first two lines, "And this is the way they ring / the bells in Bedlam," announce that the discourse of this poem has been produced from a position deeply embedded within the madhouse—the crucial word becomes the second line's penultimate "in," which is to be opposed to Bishop's more indirect visits "to" Bedlam (CP 28). The speaker, then, herself a patient, is subject to the power of the institution in a way that Bishop's speaker never was.

And though I have said that Sexton's discourse is primary in the sense of originating from madness rather than describing or confining it, that categorical position, the fact of her madness, makes her, paradoxically, always a secondary sort of figure within her own poem, a predicament that maps neatly onto Sexton's belated, secondary relationship to Bishop. As I suggested above, one might go so far as to say that Bishop is in the poem, after all: "and this is the bell-lady / who comes each Tuesday morning / to give us a music lesson." The "bell-lady," an institutionally authorized visitor to Bedlam, appears again at poem's end: "and this is always my bell responding / to my hand that responds to the lady / who points at me, E flat" (29). The speaker's very agency has been removed—"bell" responds to "hand" at the order of "the lady" in a kind of Pavlovian series of behaviors. Bishop's "sanity," as Sexton saw it, can be detected as well in the bell-lady's calm authority. Directed at the mad younger poet, it seems to demand a "flat" performance in response.

The institutional structure on display within the hospital scene in "Ringing the Bells" is credited by the poem's own logic with having created the madness it polices:

> and because the attendants make you go
> and because we mind by instinct,
> like bees caught in the wrong hive,
> we are the circle of crazy ladies
> who sit in the lounge of the mental house
> and smile at the smiling woman
> who passes us each a bell. (28)

The authority invested by the institution in the "attendants" is the formal cause of the assembly of this "circle of crazy ladies" among whose ranks Sexton sits, undifferentiated.

Differentiation comes soon enough, as Sexton turns to the patients who sit beside her:

and this is the gray dress next to me
who grumbles as if it were special
to be old, to be old,
and this is the small hunched squirrel girl
on the other side of me
who picks at the hairs over her lip,
who picks at the hairs over her lip all day. (28)

The speaker's disdain for her fellow patients, who are, as Schweik puts it, "objectified . . . animalized and enfreaked" (25), tellingly recalls her attitude toward her classmates in Lowell's workshop, as she described them to Snodgrass: "The class just sits there like little doggies waggling their heads at his every statement" (*SPL* 49). Those students are likewise "animalized," satirized by Sexton for their servile deference to Lowell's authority.

But just as she would come to value that same authority as a form of discipline that could "chain . . . in" her natural "energy," so too does the speaker of "Ringing the Bells" accede to the institutional power of Bedlam (and to the authority invested in Bishop). The poem ends with a note of skepticism about the therapeutic benefit of the "music lesson," but without any doubt about the efficaciousness of its power: "and although we are no better for it, / they tell you to go. And you do" (*CP* 29). Sexton's "we" has become a "you," a pronoun that serves at once as a proxy for the "I" who is altogether absent from the poem and for the reader who enters its institutional architecture.

## Notes

1. The earliest and most sustained critical articulation of the "breakthrough narrative" is Breslin's *From Modern to Contemporary*. I am hardly the first to resist this account. To my mind, the strongest critiques of the breakthrough narrative have been made by Hammer, in the final chapter of his *Hart Crane and Allen Tate* (211–32) and by Longenbach, in the first chapter of his *Modern Poetry after*

*Modernism* (3–21). See also Travisano's response to Longenbach in his *Midcentury Quartet* (302n13) as well as Altieri's quite lengthy footnote, also in response to Longenbach and in defense of Breslin, in his *Postmodernisms Now* (82–84n).

2. I am, in this sense, arguing for the surprising centrality, in Sexton's early work, of what Hammer, writing about Plath, has termed "the culture of the school" ("Plath's Lives" 66).

3. In her recently published memoir of Lowell, Spivack provides an anecdote that illustrates this impersonal side to Lowell's classes: "it was not until years later, when I met Roger Rosenblatt . . . that I realized we had sat opposite each other for an entire year, without identifying ourselves. But eight years later, we could still remember each other's poems and Lowell's devastating comments about them" (91).

4. There has, for some time, been a call from within the field of performance studies for complicating this traditional opposition between "text" and "performance." Grobe's essay, cited above, is one such effort; within that essay, he cites Peggy Phelan's call for the study of "the intimacy of the connection between literature and performance" (Grobe 216; Phelan 946). Phelan's injunction recalls Worthen's earlier claim that "no simple opposition between text and performance . . . will be sufficient to capture the rich, contradictory, incommensurable ways that they engage one another" (20).

5. My thanks to Christopher Grobe, who made this observation upon reading a draft of this essay.

6. Alex Beam, in *Gracefully Insane*, his history of McLean Hospital (where Plath, Lowell, and—eventually—Sexton herself would be patients), cites another example of Sexton's linguistic conflation of the psychiatric hospital and the academy: "I want a scholarship to McLean" (146).

7. For another view of the relationship between rhyme and the construction of the self in Sexton's poetry, see the final chapter of Mutlu Konuk Blasing's *Lyric Poetry*. Blasing investigates Sexton's belief that rhyme, specifically, and form, in general, are aligned with the superego, evade the controlling dishonesty of the ego, and allow access, thereby, to "linguistic truth" (181).

8. Sexton's claim about her ignorance of all modern poets but Millay is belied by one of Spivack's memories: "'Who is your favorite poet?' asked Robert Lowell. Anne's favorite was William Carlos Williams, a strange choice when considered against the kind of personal poetry she was to share with the class" (54).

9. The fact that Bishop saved those letters, now housed among Bishop's papers at Vassar, may suggest that she thought more highly of Sexton than we have come to believe. Letter, Sexton to Bishop, 26 Sept. 1962, Elizabeth Bishop Papers, box 18, folder 4, Archives and Special Collections Library, Vassar College Libraries.

10. Among the 756 titles collected in the Anne Sexton library at the Harry Ransom Center are two issues of *Partisan Review*. One of those is indeed the Spring 1957, number, containing Bishop's "Visits to St. Elizabeths." The poem had originally appeared a year earlier in a special issue of the Italian journal *Nuova Corrente*. See Francesco Rognoni's "'A World of Books Gone Flat': Elizabeth Bishop's Visits to St. Elizabeths" for a detailed account of the poem's publication history, including Rognoni's thoughts on the variations between the *Nuova Corrente* and *Partisan Review* versions. The text of the poem in *Partisan Review* is identical to the one in *Questions of Travel* (1965), which was the poem's first book publication. For another reading of the relationship between Bishop's poem and Sexton's, see Wegs.

11. Bishop's, of course, is the surest candidate, but we might also remember that the *Cantos*, the central work of Bishop's subject in "Visits to St. Elizabeths," itself begins with the word, "And."

## Works Cited

Altieri, Charles. *The Art of Twentieth-Century American Poetry: Modernism and After*. Malden, MA: Blackwell, 2006. Print.

——. *Postmodernisms Now: Essays on Contemporaneity in the Arts*. University Park, PA: Pennsylvania State UP, 1998. Print.

Beam, Alex. *Gracefully Insane: Life and Death Inside America's Premier Mental Hospital*. New York: Public Affairs, 2001. Print.

Bishop, Elizabeth. *Poems, Prose, and Letters*. Ed. Robert Giroux and Lloyd Schwartz. New York: Library of America, 2008. Print.

——. *Words in Air: The Complete Correspondence between Elizabeth Bishop and Robert Lowell*. Ed. Thomas Travisano with Saskia Hamilton. New York: Farrar, Straus and Giroux, 2008. Print.

Blasing, Mutlu Konuk. *Lyric Poetry: The Pain and the Pleasure of Words*. Princeton: Princeton UP, 2007. Print.

Breslin, James E. B. *From Modern to Contemporary: American Poetry, 1945–1965*. Chicago: U of Chicago P, 1984. Print.

Cavitch, Max. "Slavery and Its Metrics." *The Cambridge Companion to Nineteenth-Century American Poetry*. Ed. Kerry Larson. New York: Cambridge UP, 2011. Print.

Edelman, Lee. *No Future: Queer Theory and the Death Drive*. Durham, NC: Duke UP, 2004. Print.

Foucault, Michel. *Discipline and Punish: The Birth of the Prison*. Trans. Alan Sheridan. New York: Pantheon, 1978. Print.

Gill, Jo. *Anne Sexton's Confessional Poetics*. Gainesville: UP of Florida, 2007. Print.

Goffman, Erving. *Asylums: Essays on the Social Situation of Mental Patients and Other Inmates*. New York: Random House, 1961. Print.

———. *The Presentation of Self in Everyday Life*. New York: Random House, 1959. Print.

Grobe, Christopher. "The Breath of the Poem: Confessional Print/Performance circa 1959." *PMLA* 127.2 (2012): 215–30. Print.

Hamilton, Ian. *Robert Lowell: A Biography*. New York: Random House, 1982.

Hammer, Langdon. *Hart Crane and Allen Tate: Janus-Faced Modernism*. Princeton: Princeton UP, 1993. Print.

———. "Plath's Lives." *Representations* 75 (Summer 2001): 61–88. Print.

Kirsch, Adam. *The Wounded Surgeon: Confession and Transformation in Six American Poets*. New York: Norton, 2005. Print.

Kramer, Lawrence. "Freud and the Skunks: Genre and Language in *Life Studies*." *Robert Lowell: Essays on the Poetry*. Ed. Stephen Gould Axelrod and Helen Deese. Cambridge: Cambridge UP, 1986. Print.

Longenbach, James. *Modern Poetry after Modernism*. New York: Oxford UP, 1997. Print.

Lowell, Robert. *Collected Poems*. Ed. Frank Bidart and David Gewanter. New York: Farrar, Straus and Giroux, 2003. Print.

———. *Collected Prose*. Ed. Robert Giroux. New York: Farrar, Straus and Giroux, 1987. Print.

———. *The Letters of Robert Lowell*. Ed. Saskia Hamilton. New York: Farrar, Straus and Giroux, 2005. Print.

Middlebrook, Diane. *Anne Sexton: A Biography*. Boston: Houghton Mifflin, 1991. Print.

Phelan, Peggy. "'Just Want to Say': Performance and Literature, Jackson and Poirier." *PMLA* 125.4 (2010): 942–47. Print.

Plath, Sylvia. Interview by Peter Orr. *Youtube.com*. N.p., n.d. Web. 15 April 2016. <https://www.youtube.com/watch?v=g2lMsVpRh5c>.

Rainey, Lawrence. *Institutions of Modernism: Literary Elites and Public Culture*. New Haven: Yale UP, 1998. Print.

Rognoni, Francesco. "'A World of Books Gone Flat': Elizabeth Bishop's Visits to St. Elizabeths." *Elizabeth Bishop in the 21st Century: Reading the New Editions*. Ed. Angus Cleghorn, Bethany Hicok, and Thomas Travisano. Charlottesville: U of Virginia P, 2012. Print.

Schweik, Susan. "Modernist Eugenics and Post-Modern Poetics." Disability and Modernism. Penn English Department. University of Pennsylvania. 15 Mar. 2013. Lecture.

Sexton, Anne. Letters to Bishop. 26 Sept. 1962. Elizabeth Bishop Papers, box 18, folder 4. Archives and Special Collections Library, Vassar College Libraries.

———. *The Complete Poems*. Boston: Houghton Mifflin, 1981. Print.

———. *No Evil Star: Selected Essays, Interviews, and Prose*. Ed. Steven E. Colburn. Ann Arbor: U of Michigan P, 1985. Print.

———. *A Self Portrait in Letters*. Ed. Linda Gray Sexton and Lois Ames. Boston: Houghton Mifflin, 1977. Print.

Snodgrass, W. D. *Heart's Needle*. New York: Alfred A. Knopf, 1959. Print.

———. "Mentors, Fomentors, and Tormentors." *A Community of Writers: Paul Engle and the Iowa Writers' Workshop*. Ed. Robert Dana. Iowa City: U of Iowa P, 1999: 119–46. Print.

Spivack, Kathleen. *With Robert Lowell and His Circle: Sylvia Plath, Anne Sexton, Elizabeth Bishop, Stanley Kunitz, and Others.* Boston: Northeastern UP, 2012. Print.

Travisano, Thomas. *Midcentury Quartet: Bishop, Lowell, Jarrell, Berryman, and the Making of a Postmodern Aesthetic.* Charlottesville: UP of Virginia, 1999. Print.

Wegs, Joyce M. "Poets in Bedlam: Sexton's Use of Bishop's 'Visits to St. Elizabeths' in 'Ringing the Bells.'" *Concerning Poetry* 15.1 (1982 Spring): 37–47. Print.

Worthen, W. B. "Disciplines of the Text: Sites of Performance." *The Performance Studies Reader.* Ed. Henry Bial. New York: Routledge, 2004: 10–25. Print.

# ...4

## Reading, Voice, and Performance

### "The Freak Show" Revisited

VICTORIA VAN HYNING

Anne Sexton came into poetic being at a time when poets were increasingly expected to deliver poetry readings and make studio and live recordings of their poetry.[1] Growing demand for oral performance radically changed the lives of poets from the second quarter of the twentieth century onwards: they now had to write for the stage, the sound booth, the airwaves, and the page.

Derek Furr has argued that the mid-twentieth century witnessed the rise of two distinct schools of poetry recording: a formal style cultivated at the Library of Congress (LOC) and a more performance-oriented style cultivated by Barbara Holdridge (née Cohen) and Marianne Roney, the founders of Caedmon. The Caedmon label began with a reading by Dylan Thomas on 22 February 1952 that "took advantage of effects associated with live, stage recordings" (Furr 41). A decade earlier, in 1943–44, Allen Tate, as Consultant in Poetry to the Library of Congress (forerunner of the post of Poet Laureate), had initiated an important program in which each laureate was expected to record a selection of their poems for the library archive and give a number of readings. Robert Lowell, Tate's successor, expanded the project by inviting other poets to record and give readings (Furr 28). Even the public-shy Elizabeth Bishop, who once asked Lowell, "If I get the Washington job [Laureateship]—I don't *have* necessarily to give a lot of 'readings,' do I?" was induced to make a LOC recording and read publicly during her Laureateship in 1949–50, despite deep misgivings (Bishop 181 and 199). As Bishop's experience demonstrates, the poet's voice and bodily presence were increasingly in demand from the 1940s onwards. It was not enough to write; one had to perform, and one had to sound like a poet reading at the LOC. According to Furr, "the Library of Congress project narrowed the range of vocal performance to reflect the preferences of mid-century formalism" (100).

Anne Sexton was mentored and influenced by proponents of the LOC and Caedmon schools of recording. While she learned from them, and indeed made a Caedmon recording herself, she also rebelled against them. She did so most notably by forming Her Kind, a rock band named after her eponymous poem, with which she performed her poems to music. Sexton formed the band after winning the Pulitzer in 1967. She was inspired by the new generation of rock and roll artists, such as Bob Dylan and Janis Joplin, whom she lauded as "the popular poets of the English-speaking world" (qtd. in *AS* 305) and admired for their ability to reach young audiences. According to a review in the *Boston Sunday Globe*, Sexton formed Her Kind in order "to relax from the rituals which surround our major contemporary poets . . . [and] enhance the poetic message with music" (qtd. in *AS* 305–06).

Sexton's various performance styles drew mixed responses from her fellow poets, including her friend, Maxine Kumin, who "hated" not only Her Kind but also Sexton's unaccompanied poetry readings. Kumin felt that Sexton was too dramatic and overblown as a public reader and that her florid style detracted from the "texture" and content of her work (*AS* 306). Her Kind exacerbated the excesses present in Sexton's usual live performance style. Others were more positive about Her Kind. Like many others, Paul Brooks was seduced by Sexton's live performance: "Last week at the De Cordova I realized why your readings have been such a wild success. As you well know, you are something of an enchantress" (qtd. in *AS* 305).

This essay examines Sexton's attitudes toward performance with a focus on live readings, as opposed to studio sessions or her more colorful musical sessions. I specifically attend to works from the bookends of her career including Sexton's second ever published poem, "The Reading" (*Christian Science Monitor* 1958); her article "The Freak Show" commissioned to stand alongside some of her poems in the *American Poetry Review* (May/June

1973); and Sexton's last public reading, delivered and recorded at Goucher College in Baltimore on 1 October 1974, three days before her suicide.

Live recordings constitute one of the richest elements of Sexton's oeuvre, and they are central to the material legacy that she consciously created in the hope of preserving her poems and her voice for posterity. Sexton arranged for her public performances to be recorded at almost every venue in which she performed, and she gifted the reel-to-reel tapes to each host institution for their future use. We have not paid enough attention to these recordings, and our window of opportunity in which to do so is rapidly closing as reel-to-reel technology becomes worse than obsolete: unsalvageable. We need to preserve the swiftly decaying media on which Sexton left her voice before these vanish altogether.

"The Reading"

Between 1957 and 1958, Sexton attended poetry readings by W. S. Merwin, Marianne Moore, Robert Graves, and Robert Frost in the company of her new friend and fellow poet, Maxine Kumin (*AS* 72). Sexton's poem "The Reading" manifests her fascination with public performance and her rejection of the rules that dictated its delivery within the academy.[2] The poem sardonically portrays a famous, unnamed poet, whose rhymes and charm have the power to hoodwink his audience into believing he has said something of substance. Sexton refers to the poet as being in his sixties, and it is likely she is referring to Graves, a rhyming poet in his sixties at the time who performed in Boston. Yet "The Reading" is not simply a critique of any one poet, it concerns broader themes of performance, poetic fame, and the role of the academic audience in creating and sustaining a poet's reputation.

"The Reading" does not appear in Sexton's *Complete Poems*, but a copy of the poem is reproduced in *Self-Portrait in Letters* (1977, 30).[3] I reproduce the text from *Self-Portrait* here in full, for ease of reference:

### The Reading

This poet could speak,
There was no doubt about it.
The top professor nodded
To the next professor and he
Agreed with the other teacher,

Who wasn't exactly a professor at all.
There were plenty of poets,
Delaying their briefcase
To touch these honored words.
They envied his reading
And the ones with books
Approved and smiled
At the lesser poets who
Moved unsurely, but knew,
Of course, what they heard
Was a notable thing.

This is the manner of charm:
After the clapping they bundled out,
Not testing their fingers
On his climate of rhymes.
Not thinking how sound crumbles,
That even honor can happen too long.
A poet of note had read,
Had read them his smiles
And spilled what was left
On the stage.
All of them nodded,
Tasting this fame
And forgot how the poems said nothing,
Remembering just—
We heard him,
That famous name. (30)

The following stanza is from an earlier draft of the "The Reading." This version of the poem consists of three stanzas that each begin with the refrain: "He spoke well, / there was no doubt about it." This draft offers a more strongly worded, and far less subtle, condemnation of the anonymous male poet and his audience, than Sexton's printed version of the poem. The second stanza reads:

He spoke well,
there was no doubt about it,

his word[s] tumbled over pony tails,
crew cuts and the blab [bald][4] heads that
sat as placid as nund [nude] statues.
Words swam to their hurried currents
and troubled some out.
Others were caught to his prose advice,
at least it[']s not all poetry,
they thought.
That poetry, at the least,
was very new, his recent work
and impressed
the impressionable.[5]

All surviving versions of "The Reading" direct criticism at the unnamed poet and his audience in roughly equal measure, but there is an important shift in Sexton's critique between this earlier draft and the printed version. Whereas the draft portrays the audience as "impressionable" and "placid," the published version splits the audience into two constituencies. The callow would-be poets are separated from the published poets, critics, and professors who, Sexton implies, ought to exercise their power to shape opinion. Sexton's speaker castigates the poets and professors for perpetuating the reputation of the male poet, despite his too-easy rhymes and his flimsy stage persona.

In the manuscript and printed versions of "The Reading," Sexton draws vital distinctions between speaking well, writing good poems, and delivering a compelling performance. The anonymous male poet's ability to speak, Sexton suggests, masks all of his other failings and weaknesses: his not very good poems "crumble" once they stop sounding; he is old; he has low energy and delivers a weak performance. Sexton famously likened her own experience of performing for an engaged audience to orgasm: "When there is a coupling of the audience and myself, when they are really with me, and the Muse is with me, I'm not coming alone" (Kevles 27). Although not overtly sexual, the lines within the third stanza of this draft in which the speaker observes the poet's "energy had crumbled" and, "A poet of note had read, / Had read them his smiles / And spilled what was left / On the stage," suggest impotence and incontinence, as well as a lack of visceral connection between audience and poet. What is left to be spilled? Surely not the metaphorical sexual fluid passed between audience and poet in Sexton's experience; surely not the blood that Sexton later felt she was letting in her own public performances. In "The Reading" and in describing her own relationship with a turned-on audience, Sexton places equal onus on poet and audience to achieve satisfaction.

It is significant that one of Sexton's earliest forays into print constituted a rejection of another poet's reading and writing style and a reproof of members of the academy who fail to interrogate whether a poet's fame is merited. Each draft of this poem reveals a poet-in-the-making trying to navigate the poetry world from an outsider's perspective. Its publication simultaneously marks Sexton's entry into that sphere and her rejection of the rules that govern poetry performance and the assessment of poets within it. "The Reading" foreshadows Sexton's development of a vivid reading style of her own and reveals, in some measure, what she hoped to avoid and what she hoped to achieve as a public reader of her own work. The remainder of Sexton's career as a poet and performer should be read with this poem in mind, not because it is a particularly good poem, but because it signals some of her earliest impressions of the poetry world, the reader-audience dynamic, and the nature of fame.

## Voice

In August 1958, shortly after "The Reading" was published, Sexton attended a weeklong seminar at Antioch led by W. D. Snodgrass, "then her favorite poet" (*SPL* 33). There, according to Diane Middlebrook, Sexton repeatedly asked her professors whether her poems: "have my voice, *my* voice?" (*AS* 81). This concern is a natural progression for the author of "The Reading" keen to make her mark as poet and performer. Poetic voice is twofold. First, it is the product of the arrangement of words, punctuation, and lineation on the page—and the way in which this directs a reader to read and hear a poem. Second, it consists of the way in which the poet voices her work aloud. Voice is central to performance, but they are not one and the same. Sexton understood this and thus tried to cultivate a powerful voice on the page and another, separate voice in performance, which developed her poems and helped to connect her with her readers and listeners.

The next stage of Sexton's education had a deep impact on the development of her voice. After attending Antioch, Sexton wrote to Lowell seeking to audit his poetry class at Boston University. She enclosed several of her poems for his consideration, and "The Reading" is likely to have been among them.[6]

In response to an anxious letter from Sexton asking if her poems were good enough to gain her a place in his class, Lowell wrote: "Of course your poems qualify. They move with ease and are filled with *experience*, like good prose. [ . . . ] have been reading them with a good deal of admiration and envy this morning after combing through pages of fragments of my own unfinished stuff" (qtd. in *AS* 91; emphasis added).

The rest of the story is known to readers. Sexton began by auditing Lowell's workshop, but by 1960 she was fully enrolled. Lowell became deeply ambivalent about the poetry of "experience"—the key ingredient he identified in the poems Sexton had sent him in 1958, and which made him feel "envious." As Christopher Grobe demonstrates, Lowell was uneasy about the fact that much poetry of "experience" seemed to be written for performance. Grobe illustrates how Lowell acknowledged a debt to the relatively simple Beat style, which he encountered while he was reading poems from *Life Studies*, over and over again, on a tour of the West Coast. The Beat style taught Lowell how to simplify his language in order to better suit public performance (Grobe 219). Yet Lowell was skeptical of any style that reduced substance and meaning.

In his acceptance speech at the National Book Award ceremony in 1960, Lowell summarized a crisis at the heart of contemporary American poetry performance that is fundamental both to our understanding of him and to our understanding of his relationship to Sexton as a student and fellow poet:

> Two poetries are now competing, a cooked and a raw. The cooked, marvelously expert, often seems laboriously concocted to be tasted and digested by the graduate seminar. The raw, huge blood-dripping gobbets of unseasoned experience are dished up for midnight listeners. There is a poetry that can only be studied, and a poetry that can only be declaimed, a poetry of pedantry, and a poetry of scandal.

He concluded: "When I finished *Life Studies*, I was left hanging on a question mark. I am still hanging there. I don't know whether it is a death-rope or a life-line" (1960). This question mark applies to Sexton as well as to Lowell: was the "confessional style" a "life-line" to the next generation of poetic expression or was it a rope with which to hang oneself—to end one's career as a poet of the academy in order to become a popular poet of the midnight masses? Was the "raw" a rope with which to bind oneself too closely to the confessing "I" of the poems?

"Confessionalism" coincided with increased demand for live performance and poetry recordings during the mid-twentieth century, as David Haven Blake, Jo Gill, Furr, Grobe, and others have demonstrated. Public performance laid peculiar burdens on "confessional poets," whose seemingly autobiographical work easily elided the persona of the poem with the speaker on the stage.[7] Even when poets themselves were keenly aware of the importance of dividing persona and poet, their audiences were not necessarily interested in making that distinction, and there was commercial gain to be had from avoiding the distinction (Blake 719). Part of the draw of confessional poetry is the ostensibly autobiographical nature of its content. The allure of the confessional performance is, by extension, the audience's belief that they will see the poet performing her true self.

In his reflection on her life, written after her suicide, Lowell suggests that for Sexton, the confessional style—the raw—was no life-line:

At a time when poetry readings were expected to be boring, no one ever fell asleep at Anne's. I see her as having the large, transparent, breakable, and increasingly ragged wings of a dragonfly—her poor, shy, driven life, the blind terror behind her bravado, her deadly increasing pace . . . her bravery while she lasted. (Lowell, "Anne Sexton" 71)

Read in this light, Sexton succeeded in creating a powerful performance style, but it cost her her life.

## "The Freak Show"

Sexton seems to anticipate Lowell's assertion in her article "The Freak Show," written in 1973. In it she proclaims "the death of Anne as a performer" at the hands of vociferous viewers ("Freak Show" 38). She asks her fellow poets why they read publically at all and commands audience members to ask themselves: "What is it I want of this person, this human being, who is going to reveal his deepest thoughts?" (38). The piece includes a few examples of readings at which Sexton felt particularly vulnerable and uncertain of audience members' reactions to her performance. Sexton describes one event in New Hampshire when she was reduced to tears by one of her own poems and forced offstage to find a tissue and compose herself. To her surprise, she says, the audience cheered. She speculates as to why: were they impressed to see her cry, feeling they were getting more for their money, or "Maybe they only meant, 'Anne, we're with you'" (38). Was this a moment of predatory voyeurism or were her auditors being supportive? She never resolves the question, and indeed, passes it on to the audience. According to Sexton, the reaction of one audience member is not a mystery. She lambasts her unnamed agent (from Redpath lecture bureau) for selling her spontaneous grief as a staple of her act. Sexton alleges that upon the first agent's suggestion, the whole bureau speaks "proudly of my presentation to their clients thusly: 'It's a great show! Really a pow! She cries every time right on stage!'" (38).

Although Sexton was attuned to the importance of poetic performance from the early stages of her career, as we see in "The Reading," she was ambivalent about public readings long before 1973. When asked by William Packard in an interview in 1970 how she felt about performance, Sexton responded, "I care very much about my audiences. They are very dear to me, but I hate giving readings" (47). In another oft-quoted interview Sexton proclaimed: "It takes three weeks out of your life[.] . . . Readings take so much out of you, because they are a reliving of the experience, that is, they are happening all over again" (Kevles 27).

Sexton alternately describes readings as useful to the poet and as damaging to them. On the one hand, she could aver that "The final test of a poem often comes during a public reading" ("Comment" 17), but, on the other hand, she could write, "I ask all you poets what in hell are we doing to ourselves—why are we making ourselves into freaks when we are really some sort of priest or prophet or hermit?" ("Freak Show" 38). In a letter to poet Erica Jong, after they met at one of Sexton's readings in June 1974, Sexton laments that Jong has seen her read because "that isn't the real me, the woman of the poems, the woman of the kitchen, the woman of the private (but published) hungers. Perhaps you knew that?" (SPL 413–14).

Sexton bemoans the commodification of the soul of the poet in "The Freak Show," and yet, as Jo Gill has convincingly argued, this article is yet another form of self-commodification and performance for Sexton: "Spectators pay money to see her, and she gives them a little part of herself in return" (Gill 129). Even after the publication of "The Freak Show," in which Sexton declares she will never give another public reading, she continued to perform and charge large sums for her time.

Sexton's final reading at Goucher College exemplifies this uneasy exchange. In a letter to Professor Brooke Peirce in the English Department, regarding the arrangements for her reading, Sexton writes, "I do hope you can have the check of $1500 ready for me that evening as I am terribly broke, or as one puts it more politely, in debt. I will try very hard to give you a good reading" (Sexton to Peirce, 10 Sept. 1974). When Peirce initially approached Sexton, he asked her to read for thirty minutes alongside other poets, but it was later agreed that she would speak alongside only one other artist, Goucher alumna and film star, Mildred Dunnock. Then, just days before the event, Dunnock withdrew due to filming commitments in London, and Sexton was asked if she could fill the hour and a half long slot alone. In a memorial article commemorating the reading and Sexton's life, Peirce recalls a phone call from Sexton in which she agreed to perform solo: "a throaty voice said, 'I understand you got trouble[.] . . . Give me the dough and I'll give you a hell of a show.'"

According to Peirce and Sexton, she did just that. In her post-performance letter to him, written the day before she killed herself, Sexton wrote:

> Dear Dr. Brooke Peirce,
> Thank you so much for *all* you did to make my reading as good as possible. I hope you feel it was as successful as I do and that I did justice to the occasion. I promise you I gave it my ALL.
> If you have any feelings about the reading (positive, of course) if you could write me a little blurby thing, it would help promote me at other colleges and would be a kindness to me.
> Enclosed please find the expenses for my travel.
> With all best wishes,
>     Anne Sexton (Sexton to Peirce, 3 Oct. 1974)

In the Goucher performance itself Sexton links her performance to payment when she jokes: "As you see I have to do something to this book. Break its spine it's called. It's just a paperback—don't get upset. They're only $2.95! Uh! All of them in print. Every one! Purchasable! A small ad here and there doesn't hurt." One could hardly ask for clearer evidence of Sexton's self-commodification.

"The Freak Show," Gill contends, "should be read as the culmination of a longstanding anxiety about the spectacular, theatrical, and finally exploitative nature of confession, and as an expression of Sexton's unease with the lascivious and predatory tendencies of the audience" (129). She describes Sexton as a victim of her own making and her victimhood as a centerpiece of her public persona, concluding:

> This, surely, is the point to be made about Sexton's article. . . . The "freak"/performer is complicit in, even solicits, her own exploitation. . . . Her complaint about confessional performance is simply a sequel, a further confessional performance inviting the exact same voyeuristic attention as the original. "Look at me," Sexton declares, look at me suffering as people look at me—a mise-en-abyme—which sees her locked in the endlessly reflecting mirrors of the confessional role. (135–36)

There is another important commodification aspect of "The Freak Show," which Gill does not mention, and which requires further examination: Sexton's solicitation of the record label Caedmon. Midway through lamenting the detrimental impact of readings on poets, Sexton asks,

> Couldn't Caedmon put out tapes? If there were one hundred people who really wanted just to hear how the words were spoken by me, I would be glad to do a record for Caedmon. . . . If there is anyone reading this who would like to hear how I read my poems, write Caedmon. Tell them they need a record by me. (38)

Although Sexton speculates that a Caedmon recording would not make much money, her solicitation of Caedmon was as much a commercial or commodifying impulse as a desire to retreat from the public eye. In theory, the tapes would give readers "interested in her voice" just that—her voice—not a performance, but the poems as Sexton sounded them out.

In June 1974, Sexton recorded twenty-four of her poems for Caedmon, selected from each of her published books, as well as the posthumously published "The Play" and "The Rowing Endeth," then in galley. After Sexton's death, Caedmon marketed the recording as important on the basis that it was made only months before her suicide, the implication being that this was Sexton's last word on Sexton: these were the poems she wanted us to hear.

Yet Sexton appears not to have been too familiar with the record label at the time of writing "The Freak Show," referring to it in her first drafts of the article as "Cadmion." This seemingly minor detail takes on new significance in light of Sexton's schedule of public readings during the last year of her life. I argue that her long-term interests lay in recordings of her live readings, rather than studio recordings. In light of these new findings, Furr's two-pronged paradigm of twentieth-century poetic soundscape (LOC and Caedmon) requires recalibration, at least insofar as Sexton is concerned.

Sexton ostensibly engaged Caedmon to make a studio recording that would offer up her disembodied voice in lieu of the "freak." However, if the Caedmon recording was intended as a substitute for live performance, it did not keep Sexton from the stage for long. Sexton performed at Harvard before a packed audience on 7 March 1974, three months before the Caedmon recording was made (but while the contract was under discussion), and seven months before her death. She began performing again, according to Middlebrook, because she felt she needed money after her divorce from Kayo and in order to promote her "posthumous book," *The Death Notebooks* (385). Between 7 March and 1 October 1974, Sexton delivered over a dozen public readings.

Middlebrook describes the Harvard reading in great detail, but it is worth adding a few additional observations to her account. It was rare for Sexton to have to explain the value of recordings to her host institutions and rarer still for her to intervene and manage her own publicity once she was an established poet. Yet, in a letter to Jeffrey Lant at Harvard, regarding her reading, it is evident that Sexton did need to spell out the importance of recordings: "It is nice, I think, for Harvard that I will be taped. (I have never been at any university where this did not happen and thought it a matter of course for it gives the university a wider use of what happens for an hour.)" (*SPL* 407). Moreover, according to Gray Sexton and Ames, Sexton "was disgusted with the publicity the Harvard group had arranged"—a small poster with the title of *Death Notebooks* misspelled and no advertisements on local radio or in the papers (*SPL* 406). Sexton, therefore, undertook the advertising herself and succeeded in attracting a large audience comprised of students, locals, poets, friends, family, and several of her psychoanalysts (*AS* 389–92). There are inherent in this episode, and Sexton's management of it, the complexities of her feelings toward performance: she was anxious about appearing in public, but determined to draw a large audience. She demanded large sums for her readings, but was keen for them to be recorded for future, free use.

In addition to Middlebrook's speculations about why Sexton performed in March 1974 (money, her new book), there are two additional explanations for Sexton's return. First, although readings were emotionally exhausting for Sexton, they were also a crucible for her poetry—"the final test of a poem." Given that Sexton was still writing new poems during the last two years of her life, and that she had usually arranged for her live readings to be recorded, we can conclude that she wanted to read publically, at least in part, in order to test new poems and make recorded versions of them available for future audiences.

There is ample evidence that Sexton used live performances to test new work throughout her career. J. D. McClatchy's disclaimer in the booklet accompanying *The Voice of the Poet* (an audio compilation stretching from 1959 to 1974) reflects this reality. He notes that some of the recorded poems differ from Sexton's published work. One of the most striking examples of Sexton reworking a poem between live performance and publication, in McClatchy's audio edition, is "All My Pretty Ones" (1961) recorded in Boston on 14 September 1959. In the third stanza, which describes a scrapbook and news clippings started by Sexton's father at her birth, the printed version contextualizes her coming into the world with these lines: "news where the *Hindenburg* went / down and recent years where you went flush / on war" (*CP* 50), while Sexton in performance reads "as Maine goes, so goes the Nation and other years where you go flush on war." The printed poem places Sexton's birth in an international context, whereas the recorded version ties her birth and her family's interests to Maine, albeit in such a way that emphasizes Maine's political import to the rest of the United States.

In addition to testing her poems in live performance, I contend that Sexton returned to the stage because live readings were a more compelling medium for the delivery of her poetry than studio recordings. The Caedmon recording is of very good quality, but for those interested in Sexton as a performer (including Sexton herself), it pales in comparison to her public readings, such as the 92nd Street Y recording (1964), which has been remastered for a teaching audio edition (1994), the Goucher reading, and many of the live recorded poems included by McClatchy in his audio edition (2000).

There are two key differences between Caedmon recordings in the twentieth century and live performances. Studio recordings almost always exclude anecdotal or explanatory material about the poems contained in the edition. They are, as Caedmon's logo boasts, "a third dimension for the printed page." In contrast, live poetry performances, then and now, almost always incorporate anecdotes and extra details about a poet and their work, indeed, Sexton remarks on the "prosey" anecdotes of the anonymous poet in a draft of "The Reading." The details revealed about specific poems may change from performance to performance. Witness "Her Kind." At the 92nd Street Y, Sexton introduces it as follows: "My first poem tells you what kind of woman I am, 'Her Kind.'" By the end of her life, Sexton does not even name the poem before she reads it: "I've always started my readings with this poem, and I won't stop now" (Goucher).

The second difference between the studio session and Sexton's live re-cordings is the quality and range of her voice. In all of the live recordings that I have heard, Sexton's voice is dramatic, undulating, musical. Of course, Sexton's voice changed over time. Early on in her career, she sounded a lot like Edna St. Vincent Millay, as Furr argues (83–113). Her performance at the 92nd Street Y exemplifies this. But by the end of her career, as the Goucher reading witnesses, Sexton's voice is harsher and her delivery is more sar-donic, self-assured, and commanding, and occasionally dismissive as when she prefaces "Ringing the Bells" thus: "I was formerly known as the poet of madness, *To Bedlam and Part Way Back,* etc. All that jazz, bum" (Goucher). While the Caedmon-Sexton could easily be mistaken for a slightly more exciting than usual American Laureate reading for the LOC (Furr and I dif-fer in our assessments of this recording) the Goucher-Sexton trills, gasps, smokes, sasses, swears, laughs, loses her composure, apologizes for her vul-garity (twice), and consistently *performs.*

Whatever she professes in "The Freak Show," a casual listener might guess that Sexton enjoyed live performances more than studio sessions. This is not to cast aspersions on the Caedmon recording: it is, as "The Freak Show" says it should be, a recording for people who want to know what Sexton sounds like when she reads her poems. However, if we want to know how Sexton performed her poetry, we must turn to the live recordings.

The Last Reading

Sexton's last public performance was given under the auspices of "The Creative Woman" series, a three-day long program of events delivered by women artists and professionals to mark the inauguration of Rhoda Dorsey, the first woman president of Goucher College. According to Professor Peirce, the performance was attended by more than one thousand people and it was audio recorded at Sexton's request. Sexton enquired whether a local television station might film the event, but this does not appear to have happened.

In the aftermath of Sexton's suicide, Peirce attempted to send the reels to Linda Gray Sexton. For a variety of reasons, the reels never reached her and remained at Goucher until 2005, when they were re-discovered by Jeffrey Dieter, a Goucher student who had been informed of the recording's existence by poet and Goucher professor, Elizabeth Spires. When Dieter attempted to listen to the reels all he heard was silence: they had decayed (Kiehl). Dieter worked with the college library and Kratz Center for Creative Writing to have the last reading professionally restored and digitized, and it is to Dieter, in particular, that we owe a debt of gratitude that the reading was preserved.

The eighty-five-minute-long recording features twenty poems spanning Sexton's career, held together by a rich connective tissue of personal anecdote and reflections on the poems themselves. She reads poems from all of her published books and adds "The Rowing," "The Play," and "The Rowing Endeth" from *The Awful Rowing Toward God* (1975), then still in galley. Sexton begins by outlining the shape that her reading will take, and, as if the performance were a book, she appends to it a dedication and an epigraph:

> I'm going to shift from book to book. Someone asked me today, "How many books have you written?" I said nine, but I'm not sure how many are printed, uhhh, I just haven't counted yet. I'd like to start in a strange way—two strange ways. I'd like to dedicate my reading to my very dear friend, Pauline Schwartz, a November Scorpio, as I am. And I would like to say, I would like to give you a quotation, first of all I would like to quote John F. Kennedy's unsaid words. The speech of course was given to the press in advance, in Dallas, 1963. He said:

"Unless the Lord keepeth the city, the watchman guardeth in vain. The watchman guardeth in vain." (Goucher)

This dedication recalls Sexton's induction as an honorary member of Phi Beta Kappa at Harvard on 11 June 1968. She read from "Eighteen Days Without You" and dedicated her reading to another Kennedy—Robert—assassinated on June 5, just a week before the ceremony (*AS* 302).

Sexton never explains her quotation from the Kennedy speech in her last reading, but it sets the tone for proceedings. Surely it is significant that Sexton, who took her own life three days later, and who had attempted to do so many times before that, should speak the unsaid words of a dead man, killed before his time. The reading includes poems in which Sexton celebrates her joyful meeting with God, as in "The Rowing Endeth," but this epigraph implies a darker side of Sexton's understanding of the relationship between the human and the divine. Neither the city nor the individual can be preserved without God's aid. What good are watchman, such as Schwartz, if God does not keep the poet, the city?

As Gill points out in a public event held to mark Sexton's last reading, the Kennedy quotation serves as an opening bookend for the reading while Sexton's final poem, "The Touch" links back to it (Van Hyning et al.). The poem concludes:

My hand is alive all over America.
Not even death will stop it,
death shedding her blood.
Nothing will stop it, for this is the kingdom
and the kingdom come. (*CP* 174)

After the dedication and opening epigraph, Sexton performs "Her Kind," and reflects: "I ought to give up her kind, but I feel like it's a lucky omen." Her opening poem is succeeded by "The Ambition Bird," which is followed by another poem that Sexton tended to read publicly, "The Truth the Dead Know." In her 92nd Street Y reading, Sexton introduced the poem as follows: "[It] was written about my father's funeral or about the day of my father's funeral. It was written to my husband as a protest against mourning, as a celebration of the ritual of love-making as opposed to the rites/rights of the dead."

In the Goucher recording, Sexton expands upon this explanation in several significant ways using a combination of humor and anecdote. (Italics indicate nonverbal actions. The ambiguity of rites/rights is preserved):

> Now for a while I'm going to have to be serious because uh, unfortunately I'm taken to it. They tell me this is my best poem. And when they tell me [gesture, followed by some audience laughter and scattered applause]. So what do I do? I say it's my best poem. But I'll tell you, there were 300 versions, and it's a short lyric. And I worked like hell. But I worked to get at the truth. That's what you work for: to get at the truth. And the truth is in the title. In it I refuse the rites/rights and celebration of the dead for the rites/rights and celebration of the body.

One of the ways in which Sexton challenged autobiographical readings of her work was to draw a distinction between poetic truth and factual truth. In an interview in 1965, Patricia Marx asked Sexton, "Do you find that you are more truthful in your poetry than you are to yourself?" She responded, "Yes, I think so. That's what I'm hunting for when I'm working away there in the poem. I'm hunting for the truth. It might be a kind of poetic truth, and not just a factual one, because behind everything that happens to you, every act, there is another truth, a secret life" (NES 74). This question and answer sequence implies that poetic truth is higher than factual truth, truer than fact. Sexton's comments at the Goucher reading extend this claim in a new direction: not only is poetic truth supreme, it is the reason we write.

"The Truth the Dead Know" is followed by "Ringing the Bells," which Sexton performs with humor, evoking her resistance to the group music therapy, and then her acquiescence to it with changes of tone, pace, and vocal pitch. She then asks her audience if the sound quality is okay; they applaud to reassure her it is, and Sexton moves on to "Some Foreign Letters," which she introduces as follows: "I'd like to read this long poem. I haven't . . . I haven't read it in nine years, ten years, I bet. I don't know how well I'll read it. It's been in many anthologies. It's about the person I love the most" (Goucher). Sexton's reading of this poem is nuanced, dramatic, and capable, despite her disclaimer. She only stumbles on "coat" and "cage" and misses out (or intentionally excludes) the line, "You were the old maid aunt who lived with us," without missing a beat. At the close of this long poem, Sexton clears her throat repeatedly and sounds a little flat in contrast with the energetic performance of the poem itself. She explains to the audience that she cannot read the next (unnamed) poem that she had intended to include: "I've got to skip [it] 'cause it's a little too much. I might have a cigarette and relax a little up here, because I loved that old lady—young girl—old lady—human being."

In Lowell's reflection on Sexton's life (mentioned above) he attempts to point readers away from the damaging, performative poems of Sexton's oeuvre and toward what he describes as one of her "finer and quieter" poems: "Some Foreign Letters." Lowell devotes an astonishing two-thirds of his reflection to quoting from it. He is not merely praising "Some Foreign Letters," so much as offering it as an antidote to Sexton's vivid public persona and her "raw" output. If this was indeed one of Sexton's "quieter" poems, it had the power to move her to the sort of performance and audience interaction that Lowell laments and that ostensibly drove her to announce her intention to give up readings in "The Freak Show."

Although Sexton states that she had not read "Some Foreign Letters" since around 1964 or 1965, in a commentary on the poem ("Comment"), she claims to read it frequently. Sexton's assertion that she has not read the poem publicly for a decade (whether true or not) suggests that the Goucher audience is special, that Sexton's emotional reaction is authentic, that her show of vulnerability stems from her love of Nana and her reliving of events in the moment of performance. The Goucher performance of "Some Foreign Letters" ineluctably joins the "I" of the poem with the "I" speaking onstage in a particularly visceral way. How can her audience resist the autobiographical reading? Should they? According to Sexton's teaching notes, they should, to some extent:

There is some persona going on in "Some Foreign Letters" because it is not all true. It is not all the confessional Anne Sexton speaking for her great aunt. Some of it isn't true and some of it is. I'd like you to guess which. But is it important which? That's a job to be left to eventual biographers, but then aren't you all biographers in a sense? ("Lecture Materials" 3, 3)[8]

Sexton's approach to this poem varies depending on the setting. For the sake of performance, this is an autobiographical poem—she uses anecdote to encourage the autobiographical reading. In her lectures, writings, and interviews about it, Sexton challenges her readers to discern autobiography from craft. Sexton's academic readers, unlike members of her live audiences, are asked to disentangle poetic truth from factual truth. Inversely, Sexton the performer obscures these distinctions, while Sexton the learned commentator tried to inject a bit of objectivity into the analysis of her work. Arguably, she never really succeeded in the latter because live performance was so much a part of her career and art.

Seeming autobiographical disclosure abounds in the last reading and takes many forms. In addition to her disturbance over "Some Foreign Letters," Sexton harnesses autobiographical detail to reveal the material confluence of her poetry and her domestic life, as when she regales the audience with stories about how her dog has chewed the manuscript of *Death Notebooks*: "This is actually *The Death Notebooks*[.] . . . It's here, but jeepers, here's the manuscript. See how my dog ate it? My dog loves manuscripts and books" (Goucher). Interestingly, no such dog-eaten manuscript is known to survive. Was this just an amusing fiction?

Anecdotes about past public readings are deployed in the Goucher reading in such a way as to suggest to that audience that they are more pleasant to read to than other audiences. Sexton describes the sexism she encountered at Harvard in 1974 concerning the outcome of her card game with God in "The Rowing Endeth." In this poem God wins because he has five aces, and Sexton wins because she has a royal straight flush, at which point they collapse, laughing, into one another's arms:

> When I read it at Harvard there was a lot of screaming and yelling going on about whether I was right about Poker. And if you have any advice, although it's now in galley, and I demand it go this way . . . I don't . . . you know how they say, men say, "Women don't know anything about Poker, they're terrible you know." They like the five, you know that, whatever they call it. Just the five dealt out. I don't like that, I like, uh . . . seven card stud is my favorite, with uh, uh deuces and jacks wild or something like that. Then I'm having a good time! Penny ante, why not? Ok this is the end of the book. It's a very serious book, but it ends on this moment—of glory—I think.

This disclosure also serves to curtail feedback of the kind she received at Harvard. Public performances could not only help Sexton with the writing and rewriting process, but also with controlling the interpretation of her poems. The readings are to some extent an extension of Sexton's classroom—"Anne on Anne," live.

In addition to using personal disclosure to shape the reception of her work, Sexton also uses autobiographical disclosure to amuse, as when she describes her invention of a new word for "The Little Peasant":

> I have to read this unfamiliar story because there's a word in it I like to say. [*audience laughter*] You see, after all, I've got to get my kicks too, don't I? At any rate, the word, uh, came through on the galley sheets, which you get. They're long sheets, from the copywriter, as the book is going through its process of getting printed, and the copywriter said, "Author, Au: What is 'dingo-sweet'?" I wrote, "Dear Copywriter, 'dingo-sweet' is an image for sexual intercourse." I don't add, "And I made it up." I mean, she probably looked through every damn book there is, you know, and she couldn't find any "dingo-sweet." I came out of sex and said it. 'Scuse my vulgarity. I wish no insult to anyone. But we've got to be a little comic in these times. These are bad enough times without a little laughter.

Sexton reads "The Little Peasant" with exaggerated humor, rendering each "dingo-sweet" a fusion of sensual purr and rumbling growl. This version of the poem is markedly more dramatic than the Caedmon recording and might give us a clearer picture of how Sexton wanted the poem to be read and heard.

Finally, Sexton used public readings, including the Goucher event, to articulate her understanding of poetic truth on the most fundamental level of her poetry: she discusses her use of punctuation and the ways in which poems should, ideally, be read. She deployed punctuation consciously to elicit particular physical responses in her reader. Sexton does not highlight these facts in her printed works, but she comments on them in her public performances. At the 92nd Street Y, Sexton explains that "I Remember," "is a love poem, all to be said as if in one breath. It's written in one sentence, and can't be said in one breath at all, but it's written that way." She says much the same of "Ringing the Bells" during her Goucher reading: "it might interest you to know that it's all written in one long form as though it could be said in one breath, and then there are three more words. You know, period, three line [*sic*] sentence. But of course, this is impossible. Can't do it that way. But you can read it that way." Sexton's use of punctuation that is physically impossible to voice mirrors her distinction between poetic truth and factual truth. In an ideal world, Sexton would be able to read these poems aloud in a single breath. The fact is that she cannot—few humans can. That does not change the truth of their intended form.

While Sexton did not always tax her live audiences with the job of discerning fact from fiction, she did ask them to pay attention to poetic form and punctuation. Raw though Sexton's live performances were, they also reveal her concern for the details of her art. Sexton's public performances ask us to do two things: internalize her voice and then return to the pages of her books. By fusing our experiences of performance and reading, we ultimately hear Sexton within an inner soundscape. What better way for the poet to outlive herself?

Unlike many of her predecessors, Sexton developed her poetics and her reading style in tandem from the outset of her career: she wrote with the expectation that she would read publically, and performance was central to her art. She was a performance innovator who exploited the power of public appearance to a greater degree than many of her predecessors and peers.

Maybe Sexton really did intend to walk away from the "freak show" by way of making studio recordings. We will probably never know to what extent the article was a gimmick, and to what extent it was a real statement of Sexton's intention to withdraw. In any event, live performance featured heavily in the last months of her life. Recorded readings suggest that Sexton could not cut the cord of which Lowell spoke—the lifeline/death-rope—which bound Anne Sexton, the woman, so closely to the "I" of her poems.

### Notes

1. I am grateful for Linda Gray Sexton's and Goucher College's permission to quote from "The Last Reading" and Linda Gray Sexton's permission to reproduce "The Reading" in this essay.

2. See Kamran Javadizadeh's "Anne Sexton's Institutional Voice" in this collection for further analysis of Sexton's self-fashioning within institutional settings.

3. Sexton probably gave this poem to her mother, along with nearly forty pages of work from her first year of writing, on Christmas Day, 1957 (*SPL* 30–33).

4. Linda Gray Sexton has pointed out that this is probably a typo for "bald" and that her mother would not have used the colloquialism "blab" at that stage in her life. If the intended word is "bald" this evokes the dual audience we encounter in the unpublished draft: the younger auditors are signified by pony tails and crew cuts, while the bald heads signify the old guard whom Sexton castigates.

5. Anne Sexton, "The Reading," Sexton Papers, box 10, folder 9.

6. A manuscript copy bears the note, "L. Likes," and it is probable that "L" stands for Lowell. Anne Sexton, Sexton Papers, box 41, folder 1.

7. See Grobe's chapter in this collection, which explores the varied responses or "reading poems" written for Sexton by fans who attended her readings.

8. Gill brought this passage to my attention (91).

## Works Cited

Bishop, Elizabeth. *One Art: Letters*. Ed. Robert Giroux. New York: Farrar, Straus and Giroux, 1995. Print.

Blake, David Haven. "Public Dreams: Berryman, Celebrity, and the Culture of Confession." *American Literary History* 13.4 (Winter 2001): 716–36. Print.

Furr, Derek. *Recorded Poetry and Poetic Reception from Edna Millay to the Circle of Robert Lowell*. New York: Palgrave Macmillan, 2010. Print.

Gill, Jo. *Anne Sexton's Confessional Poetics*. Gainesville, FL: UP of Florida, 2007. Print.

Grobe, Christopher. "The Breath of the Poem: Confessional Print/Performance Circa 1959." *PMLA* 127.2 (2012): 215–30. Print.

Kevles, Barbara. "The Art of Poetry: Anne Sexton." *Anne Sexton: The Artist and Her Critics*. Ed. J. D. McClatchy. Bloomington: Indiana UP, 1978. Print.

Kiehl, Sexton. "Hearing Again the Life-altering, Haunting Words of Poet Sexton." *Baltimore Sun*. 31 March 2006: 1C. Print and web. 28 Sept. 2009.

Lowell, Robert. "Anne Sexton." *Anne Sexton: The Artist and Her Critics*. Ed. J. D. McClatchy. Bloomington: Indiana UP, 1978. 71–73. Print.

———. "National Book Awards Ceremony Acceptance Speeches." 1960. Web. 17 July 2013. <http://www.nationalbook.org/nbaacceptspeech_rlowell.html#/>.

Marx, Patricia. "Interview with Anne Sexton (1965)." *No Evil Star: Selected Essays, Interviews, and Prose*. Ed. Steven Colburn. Ann Arbor: U of Michigan P, 1985. 70–82. Print.

McClatchy, J. D., ed. *Anne Sexton: The Artist and Her Critics*. Bloomington: Indiana UP, 1978. Print.

Middlebrook, Diane Wood. *Anne Sexton: A Biography*. Boston: Houghton Mifflin, 1991. Print.

Packard, William. "Craft Interview with Anne Sexton." *Anne Sexton: The Artist and Her Critics*. Ed. J. D. McClatchy. Bloomington: Indiana UP, 1978. 43–68. Print.

Peirce, Brooke. "Anne Sexton at Goucher." N.d. Sexton file. Baltimore, MD: Goucher College Special Collections.

Sexton, Anne. *Anne Sexton Reads Selections of Her Poetry*. New York: Caedmon, 1974. Audiotape.

———. *Anne Sexton: A Self-Portrait in Letters*. Ed. Linda Gray Sexton and Lois Ames. Boston: Houghton Mifflin, 1977. Print.

———. "Comment on 'Some Foreign Letters.'" *No Evil Star: Selected Essays, Interviews, and Prose*. Ed. Steven Colburn. Ann Arbor: U of Michigan P, 1985. 14–17. Print.

———. "The Freak Show." *American Poetry Review* 2.3 (May/June 1973): 38, 40. Print.

———. "The Freak Show." Sexton Papers, box 16, folder 1.

———. "The Last Reading." Goucher College, Baltimore. Rec. 1 Oct. 1974. Reel-to-reel tape. Remastered 2005. CD. Web. 10 Nov. 2015. <https://www.wolfson.ox.ac.uk/clusters/life-writing/podcasts>.

———. "Lecture Materials for Colgate University Course." Sexton Papers, box 26, folder 1.

———. Letter to Brooke Peirce. 10 Sept. 1974. Sexton file. Goucher College Special Collections, Baltimore, MD.

———. Letter to Brooke Peirce. 3 Oct. 1974. Sexton file. Goucher College Special Collections, Baltimore, MD.

———. New York Poetry Center 92nd Street Y Reading. Audio-Forum. Reel-to-reel. 1964. Remastered by Sussex Tapes: Pre-Recorded Educational Discussions and titled *The Poetry of Anne Sexton*. London, AS41. 1994. Audiotape.

———. "The Reading." Sexton Papers, box 10, folder 9 and box 41, folder 1.

———. *The Voice of the Poet*. Ed. J. D. McClatchy. New York: Random House, 2000. Audiotape and print.

———. "Worksheets for 'Elizabeth Gone.'" *Anne Sexton: The Artist and Her Critics*. Ed. J. D. McClatchy. Bloomington: Indiana UP, 1978. 51–68. Print.

Van Hyning, Victoria, with Jo Gill, Erica McAlpine, and Leo Mercer. "Re-reading with Anne Sexton." 9 June 2015. Web. 10 Nov. 2015. <https://www.wolfson.ox.ac.uk/clusters/life-writing/podcasts>.

# ...5

## From the Podium to the Second Row

### The Vanishing Feel of an Anne Sexton Reading

CHRISTOPHER GROBE

...we go to hear you sing our songs for us.

Letter from Theresa Reis Kennedy to Anne Sexton, 7 August 1973

When a cosmopolitan performer tours, the periphery meets the center. But something subtler happens when that performer works in a culturally peripheral art form—and represents, to boot, a marginalized identity. Then the margins meet and, if all goes well, they invent their own centrality. Tim Miller, a self-dubbed "wandering queer performer," has often enjoyed such moments of *communitas* on tour. As he once explained, with his signature blend of sarcasm and sincerity: "I know this is what George W.'s daddy was really talking about with that 'thousand points of light' nonsense a few years back" (91, 94–95).

By all accounts, Anne Sexton's poetry readings were exactly such galvanizing events—for people suffering from mental illness, for women racked by "the problem that has no name," and for dissenters from Cold War American culture more generally. The mere fact of these readings was alone a powerful thing: that, at midcentury, before second-wave feminists made spectacles like this a bit more common, a woman stood behind a microphone in Cazenovia, NY, and Fayetteville, AR, and Muncie, IN, and she spoke the truth of her experience (Fig. 5.1). But can we truly understand

FIGURE 5.1. Map of Anne Sexton's readings.

today how she startled and enthralled her audiences back then—in Phila-
delphia and Fargo, from Houston on up to Maine?

With a question like this, our house style as critics won't cut it. There's
little here to close-read, and critical distance won't help when our topic is
modes of immersion. What we need, then, is new language—new words
for the current that flowed through a Sexton poem—that shiver or shock—
when she performed. Reflecting in a similar mood on the limits of music
criticism, Roland Barthes once suggested that, "rather than change [our]
language . . . it would be better to change the . . . object" ("Grain" 180). In
a way, that is what I also propose to do. Barthes's new object was not mu-
sic, not performance, not audience response, but what he called "the grain
of the voice." This "grain" didn't *really* belong to the voice. It wasn't *there*
in the singer's cords, nor was it hidden in the vinyl that spun on Barthes's
turntable. Instead, it was "the space" of an "encounter between a language
and a voice," between "music and language," between a listener and all of
these (181). Affective intensities, tacit relations—between tones, beyond
words—these were Barthes's new objects of criticism, and now they are
mine. The only question is: what evidence remains of them?

◆  ◆  ◆

from watching you . . . [I] learned . . . about giving myself to the poem-
audience[.] . . .

Letter from C. K. Williams to Anne Sexton, 28 October 1971

sometimes it's good, great, zany, electricity, all that

Letter from Anne Sexton to Donald Hall, 26 July 1973

Fifteen months before Sexton's death, in July 1974, the Sunday *Boston Globe*
ran this rave review:

> Her voice in its maturity has lost none of its feeling, its zing and zap.
> It reaches out and demands your innermost response.
> Now the large pink scarf in her hand is held beside her cheek as if
> for comfort, as if for safety. The scarf going up often to her moist brow
> or suddenly flying outward toward us to bring us closer, closer[.] . . .
> She keeps evoking the audience directly with the pink scarf, teasing
> us with it and with the words "Come on Man! Come on Man!" and
> leaves the stage calling "Right on man!"

Now, be honest: how far did you get in that passage before you realized it
wasn't about Sexton? Did "zing and zap" sound quite right? Would Sexton
really wear pink? And, *Right on*? You must have doubted by then.

Then again, who could blame you for believing it was Sexton—maybe
even right up to the end? It does feel like her, doesn't it: the way she "de-
mands your innermost response," *an axe for the frozen sea*? Sure, the words
are all wrong—*Come on, man! Right on, man!*—but the vibe is pure Anne
Sexton. And so is that scarf—not its style, but its effect. One second it
makes her seem haunted, hunted; the next, she flings it back into your face.
*Take that! Come here . . .*

Alright, it's time to come clean: this passage actually comes from a review
of Ella Fitzgerald—but a review, I should add, written by none other than
Anne Sexton ("Poetry of Ella"). As far as I can tell, this was Sexton's only
stab at writing performance criticism, but it shows what a knack she might
have had for the genre. Not only does she manage to conjure an elusive
feeling—Ella's presence in performance—but she manages to hang all of
that on the tip of a scarf, a punctum in pink.[1] As it clings to Ella's face and
slices through the air, this scarf measures the space between Ella and Anne.
It twists in each current of Ella's charisma; it tacks back and forth with each

gust of desire. In short, it *is* Ella's relationship with her audience in solid state.

To me, it is no surprise that Sexton could write this way about performance—that she could see another performer's work so clearly. She was, after all, not only a famed performer of her poems but also a bit of a performance hound on the side. During the formative years of her poetic career she immersed herself in the theater. From 1961, when she completed her first draft of a play, until 1964–65 when she served as author-in-residence at the Charles Playhouse in Boston, she "bought at least fifty plays in paperback" (many of them avant-garde titles), she "subscribed to *The Tulane Drama Review*" (then, a leading theater journal; soon thereafter, ground zero for performance studies), and she "started seeing plays everywhere and anywhere" she could ("Reactions of an Author" 3). If those years taught Sexton how to read drama and appreciate performance, her residency at the Playhouse brought her into the workaday theater itself. Peeking in on a season of rehearsals and using the company's actors to workshop new scenes, Sexton witnessed firsthand how performers work—how they slowly transform a writer's words into the stuff of repeatable action—how a scarf or a skull might be as crucial to that process as a lyric or a line of prose. *One day, maybe Monday . . . a fellow of infinite jest . . . will come . . .*

◆　◆　◆

it was not entertainment (as so many "performances" tend to be) but an experience—a poet living his poems (pardon! *her* poems!) to the edge of our common humanity.
Letter from Perle Epstein and Shelley Neiderbach to Anne Sexton, 26 November 1964

was shaken once again by your power with words and, for the first time, with your power as an actress. You live your poems when you read them in a way I have never seen.
Letter from Bob Abzug to Anne Sexton, 7 November 1973

Why *don't* we have accounts of Sexton's readings as good as her review of Ella's concert?[2] For one thing, though Sexton was famed for her readings, they were rarely understood *as performance* (in the way that, say, Allen Ginsberg's were). Fans and friends may have praised her as "a splendid actress," but they were usually careful to assure her that this "acting" was extraneous to her work as poet—let alone her identity.[3] "You in your role of lovely and exciting actress-persona were the perfect complement to Miss Sexton, the poet," wrote one fan, cutting "Miss Sexton" neatly in two.[4] Suppose they *had* praised her performance as something integral to her poems; unless they phrased it just right, Sexton would only have shuddered in response. "I have a certain guilt about the ham in me," Sexton confessed to the woman who called her "a splendid actress"—though it might help to know that the woman in question was one of her former therapists.[5] Even when such compliments weren't coming from Freudians, though, Sexton occasionally treated them as accusations of fakery. "I don't think I'm a fraud onstage," she protested in one letter to a fan, "but the theatricality does creep in, not to entertain but to emphasize."[6] Amid the fog of such anti-theatrical terror, who could see—who would waste any time to describe—her performance?

Back then, though, as Sexton would surely have known, the loudest preachers of such "anti-theatricalism" were, in fact, the theater-makers themselves. With ample encouragement from *TDR*—the theater journal that, remember, Sexton was reading—they were practicing the Method, staging environmental theater, orchestrating happenings, and making performance art. No more imitation; we want action; we want *life!*—no more fakery; we want something *real* onstage! (This must have sounded awfully agreeable to Sexton: her copy of *Stanislavsky on the Art of the Stage* is emphatically dog-eared where it tells of Stanislavsky's hatred for "arts of imitation" and his advocacy for the "art of direct experience" [32].) And though her friends and fans didn't quite have the language to say it, they placed Sexton's readings in this tradition. She gave audiences, they said, an "experience" at a reading, unlike "so many 'performances'" did. She was an "actress," sure, but one who "live[d her] poems"—a Method actor of the self. Sexton—who was troubled, not jazzed by the thought that her poems were fictions; her readings, masquerades—must have thrilled at such sensitive praise. After all, she spoke often of "the strain of being what [she] wrote" at poetry readings, and all she wanted from her audience (as she confessed to a therapist) was to know that she had succeeded: "I wish sometime you'd come see me read and figure out if that's me," she once begged Dr. Orne.[7] (Her red-faced reaction to Dr. Brunner—Orne's mother—should make a little more sense in this context: Sexton wanted a therapist's okay, but "splendid actress" was precisely the wrong compliment.)

Sexton's readings *deserve* to be remembered as performance, at least in this more-than-theatrical sense, and (assured of this caveat) Sexton herself would have argued the point. "For me poems are verbal happenings," she once said—meaning, I guess, that they are events in themselves, even on the page (*NES* 114). Poetry readings, in turn, were "a reliving of the experience, that is, they are happening all over again" (*NES* 109). So, if what's "happening" in performance is what's "happening" in the poem—and if it's hard to tell the difference between these and what's happening in real life—well, this, for Sexton, was a mark of her performative success. "I . . . become the private poet who wrote the poem," she once said, describing her favorite moment at a reading (*NES* 17). And "the private poet who wrote" was, in turn, always teetering on the brink of real life, real emotion. "Emotion recollected in tranquility is nonsense," she once scrawled, "I write in a frenzy of recreated experience" ("Untitled Talk"). Combine this frenzied vision of writing with the idea that, in performance, she becomes the "poet who wrote the poem," and Sexton's readings must have seemed doubly saturated with "experience" in all its vitality—its volatility.

◆　◆　◆

we can only hear Anne Sexton read
in poor remembrance of having heard, once.

Anonymous, "Upon Hearing Anne Sexton," Cambridge, MA, Fall 1968

I have never given a reading or a lecture that was not taped.

Letter from Anne Sexton to Stephens College, 29 June 1964

Sexton is hardly unique in garnering less attention for her readings than they patently deserved, and that's where the story I'm telling about Sexton is much more than a biography of one poet. Despite the significance of readings to poetry's public life, the academy remained—until the last two decades—almost entirely indifferent to them. This may sound surprising, given how essential colleges were to the postwar demand for readings, but just because they hosted these events does not mean they understood them as performances—nor does it mean that they valued what documentation of them was kept. For proof, look no further than the dustiest corner of your own university's archive: there you will likely find dozens of reel-to-reel tapes simply rotting on the shelf. (Someone, it seems, has forgotten to throw them out.)[8] These recordings were made with the best of intentions—that the reading might remain available into an unknown future—but now they are reaching the end of their playable life, and (*let's not kid ourselves*) most of them have rarely, if ever, been played. Institutions seem to have collected these tapes the way readers once collected locks of hair: to say, *Poet was here.*

Meanwhile, the comforting whirr of the recorder seems to have licensed our "poor remembrance" of what we saw. For decades, we attended readings without attending *to* them. Want proof? Just ascend from the acetate crypt of the archive to your library's main stacks. There, you will struggle to find rich, contemporary accounts of poetry readings published in print. Thin descriptions abound around the edges of memoir and biography. And there are plenty of polemical essays about how readings *ought* to be.[9] But until the last two decades, when poetry scholars took a shine to (the idea of) poetry performance, thick descriptions of readings remained pretty thin on the ground. This is because most folks thought of them (still do) as mere "poetry listenings."[10] If an audio recording was made, then—well, what's left to say?

To this day, much writing on poetry readings is caught in this cul-de-sac. You see it in the titles of many books and essays, where "listening," "sound," and (audio) "recordings" are key terms, to the exclusion of other senses and archives. There are a few decent reasons for this narrow focus—*we work with what we have*—but there's also a fair amount of disciplinary inertia. Too often, we seem to scramble for familiar ground, mistaking performance for a more familiar object: *a body-as-text,* we are told, *gives rise to a phonotext.* Or else we take as our object of study a rediscovered archive (for example, recorded sound)—forgetting, meanwhile, that it is *the thing recorded,* not the recording, that ostensibly interests us. There is more to performance, after all, than a text turned audiotext, and we need more evidence of this surplus. If we simply replace "close reading" of texts with "close listening" to recordings, we'll expand our archive (a bit) without broadening much at all the horizons of our thought.

◆  ◆  ◆

performance remains, but remains differently.
Rebecca Schneider, "Performance Remains"

traces, glimmers, residues, and specks of things.
José Muñoz, "Ephemera as Evidence"

It is not just a matter of finding different archives; we need to approach the same ones differently. Live performance, after all, is an ephemeral thing: the moment it enters our world, it is already beginning to vanish. But it can never succeed in disappearing altogether. Instead it carries, like starlight, its past into our present. Performance historians are connoisseurs of such radiant decay. They know that the faintest light leaves a mark, given a long exposure—that even an absence of remains, the hollow fossil of an invertebrate, will nonetheless keep its shape.

When I enter the archive as a performance scholar, I know I'll never lay hands on a performance—but, all the same, my hands are somehow never empty. Theorists used to argue that performance is ephemeral and, thus, that it eludes the archive. I say: it is ephemeral and, thus, it fills the archive with ephemera. You need only expand your sense of what *counts* as evidence to find it everywhere. Ephemera, writes performance theorist José Muñoz, are a kind of "anti-evidence," a "kind of evidence of what has transpired but certainly not the thing itself" (10). Theater and performance scholars are so accustomed to this thinness, this obliquity in our archive, that we take such anti-evidence in stride. As theater historian Tracy Davis once put it, we find what traces we can, then shade these strokes into "*rondeur*—an illusion of convexity" (205). Performance history, I mean to say, is an art of creative evocation—and so the one thing we can *never* do is take our object of study for granted.

When scholars of poetry performance turn first to printed poems and then second to audio recordings (especially studio recordings), I worry that we are settling for a familiar feeling: the sensation of beholding "the thing itself." Deny yourself that feeling, and new horizons will open up to you. Even the printed page and the reel-to-reel tape have more to offer a scholar who views them as "traces, glimmers, residues" of a fuller event.

◆  ◆  ◆

I sort his odd books and wonder his once alive words. (*CP* 20)

a photostat of your will. (*CP* 42)

This is the yellow scrapbook [ … ]
These are the snapshots [ … ]
I hold a five-year diary [ … ] (*CP* 50–51)

I have read each page of my mother's voyage.
I have read each page of her mother's voyage. (*CP* 134)

I read your Paris letters [ … ] (*CP* 135)
I try [ … ]
to reach into your page and breathe it back[.] … (*CP* 9)

If we are looking for new evidence of poetry performed, I can hardly think of a better place to start than with Anne Sexton: not only because of her successful performance career but also because of her unusual faith in the archive. She had a feel for old paper; in her poems, she is always rifling through the remains of her family history. It was her passion to hoard such scraps and "breathe [them] back." This passion would guide not only her choice of subject matter but also her attitude toward finished poems. When Sweet Briar College, for instance, asked Sexton to discuss her poetry with their students, she didn't prepare a lecture or suggest a Q-and-A; instead, she stood there and read verbatim from the worksheets and drafts of one poem (then another), complete with cross-outs, false starts, loose ends, and a line-by-line narration of what she was up to.[11] No wonder that Sexton was so relentless a historian of herself, so indiscriminate an archivist. She saw the past as something restorable from its paper trail, and so she kept in triplicate what other poets might have trashed. Her papers, as a result, exceed the limits of prejudice: including the one against poetry readings.

There is so much in Sexton's papers to spark a performance historian's imagination. Many books and typescripts of her poems are annotated for performance; she carefully preserved and arranged hundreds of the letters and contracts in which she conducted the business of her career on the circuit et cetera. But because poetry readings were, at the time, such *unserious* objects of attention, I always knew I'd find the best material in the least reputable wing of Sexton's papers: her fan mail, a dozen fat folders quarantined from the rest of her correspondence. Poring through this mail, I found plenty of what I expected: breathless accounts of her readings, sensitive descriptions of her manner, detailed reports on audience response. But I also found a new genre of document I never imagined might exist: poems by Sexton's fans about the experience of seeing her read. (I came to call them "reading poems"; a selection of them will follow this essay.) How all of them hit upon the same idea we will never know, but, unaware of each other, these writers gravitated toward the same habits, feelings, and forms. In the process, they captured something hard to see and harder still to preserve: the precise quality of Sexton's presence, the social and emotional charge these readings held, and the way this charge electrified the minimal affordances of the reading.

◆  ◆  ◆

I'm sorry I couldn't hold my breath through your reading—even that was too much noise.

Letter from Tinsley Crowder to Anne Sexton, 21 December 1959

I do not want to break the silence of living your poems . . . [that] you imparted in your reading.

Letter from Martha Kearns to Anne Sexton, 18 April 1966

Take the simplest event in any poetry performance—one so hard to make sense of when you are listening alone in the archive—an audience's silence. It can terrify even a career performer, but Sexton bravely embraced this terror, larding her lines with one pause after another.[12] These often erupt in the middle of a phrase, without regard to syntactic or typographical breaks. This was a calculated effect. You can hear as much by listening to several recordings of the same poem: Sexton's cadence, however odd, remains consistent from reading to reading, year to year. She also left some proof of the precision with which she measured each of these silences. When, in 1968, she was invited to read at Harvard for a Phi Beta Kappa ceremony, she decided to perform a few sections of a very new poem, "Eighteen Days Without You." Since the poem was unfamiliar, and since the stakes were so high, she took the unusual precaution of marking her pauses with a series of typed and handwritten slashes (Fig. 5.2). Notice how they come in twos, threes, and fours—sometimes more—scoring the void that her voice refuses to fill. Notice how you can find them just about everywhere, but how they seem to have filtered to the bottom, filling the last stanza with their weight. And then, as a conductor might do at the close of a symphony, she plans a three-phased, lingering silence after the final line. Letting the overtones die, she holds the audience in limbo—before releasing them gently: "thank you."

But why focus entirely on her delivery? These silences also belonged to her audience. A performer's silence, after all, is always an invitation—to suspense, to embarrassment, to sympathy, to boredom, to fear. (Recordings cannot tell you exactly which.) That is where fan mail and reading poems prove their worth: they tell us not only how a few individuals experienced

```
Look lout!  Say yes!
Draw me like a child.  I shall need
merely two round eyes and a small kiss.
Two earings would be nice.  Then proceed,
to the shoulder.  You may pause at this.

Catch me.  I'm your disease-----
Please go slow all along the torso////
drawing beads and mouths and trees
and o's///  a little graffiti and a small hello
for I grab, I nibble, I lift, I please.

Draw me good,  Draw me warm.
Bring me your raw-boned wrist and your
strange, Mr. Bind, strange stubborn horn.
Darling, bring with this an hour of undulations,////for
this is the music for which I was born.

Lock in!  Be alert, my acrobat/////
and I will be soft wood// and you the nail////
and we will make fiery ovens for Jack Sprat
and you will hurl yourself into my tiny jail////
and we will take a supper together///and that///
will be that./////////////
                   //////////
                   ///////////

        ----silence----

                    thank you
```

FIGURE 5.2. Anne Sexton, "Eighteen Days Without You" (Sexton Papers, box 6, folder 6).

and interpreted these silences but also how they thought Sexton *meant* these pauses to be felt. And since they based these judgments on cues and contexts no longer available to us, their conclusions are themselves a residue of Sexton's bearing in performance. Says one fan, even breathing "was too much noise" amid the tension of a Sexton silence; we dare not "break" it, frets another, showing the reverence and fear for Sexton that her pauses somehow inspired. These were, after all, moments of extreme vulnerability for Sexton (and for her audience). As such, they were a signature feature of her confessional style—more than anything she said.

Sexton's fans, to judge from their letters and poems, shivered in sympathy with her silent exposure. Some of the reading poems give direct evidence of this—for example, "Pausing . . . / She glances at us / With haunted eyes" (anon., "Poet"). But even poems that do not directly address the topic are full of the feeling these pauses impart. Every detail in these poems that does not describe Sexton's voice has something to tell us about her silence. When one poet speaks, for instance, of Sexton's "yearning to be sure / Of cadences, thought, sadnesses, man" and then proceeds to describe her "thunderstruck" eyes, we are getting, I would argue, an interpretation of Sexton's pauses (Plunkett). In this view, they are live ordeals—emotional struggles meant to be shared—not *with* audience, but *by* them. Indeed, in the very act of sending Sexton a poem—which most of them did *instead of* (or in apology for) having approached her—these authors return to this silence once more. There is always "Something more to say" in these poems—because it is "easier to write than to speak while others can / hear" (Plunkett; Roach). Silence, it seems, is their secret covenant—and poetry, their "speech." Having refused to "break" Sexton's silence, they finally "speak" in these poems; or maybe they *perform* their silence, filling out line by line what Sexton had excised—slash by slash—from her performance.

◆  ◆  ◆

If I can stand up [behind a podium], then I can own the audience. . . . It gives you more distance between the audience and yourself, and I need that because I speak so intimately. Anne Sexton, therapy tapes, 29 April 1961

The microphone's ability to capture subtleties of vocal timbre and inflection faithfully opened up the possibility of new forms of performance marked by a quiet intensity and subtle shadings of inflection, suggestive of intimacy and emotional density.

Jacob Smith, *Vocal Tracks: Performance and Sound Media*

Equally inaudible on tape is the simple yet affecting materiality of a Sexton reading. Reading poems speak of her "angular" physicality, her "conspicuous hands," the dramatic "thrusting" of her gestures, but I'm intrigued by the intensity with which they attend to the minimal props of the poetry reading: podium, manuscript, microphone, water glass, cigarette, et cetera. (anon., "Poet"; Clardy; Loewenstein). They obsess over these items, treating them the way Sexton did Ella's scarf: as the performer's tools for forging a relationship with her audience, and, thus, as an anchor for audience members' drifting desires. Take the reading poem called "Full Fathom," whose very title suggests the sea change Sexton wrought on each element of the reading (Friend). As she breathed those rustling poems back to life, each other object onstage also turned into something rich and strange. The cigarette smoke pouring from Sexton's mouth is the first and boldest image of this liveliness: "Thin vapors unbend. / Like a glassblower / she tongues / a filter cigarette; / under full copyright, / grey sorrows quiver / and ascend." (One evocative newspaper account corroborates the detail: "She would drag deeply," it attests, "and then start talking again, letting the smoke roll out of her mouth and over the microphone.")[13]

But the detail is less important than what it is made to mean: Sexton the poet makes beautiful vases (well-wrought urns?) that Sexton the performer heats into elasticity, then breathes into diffusion. ("She breathes her words, they are alive. She is so alive!" one fan reports her friend exclaiming.)[14] Each prop is transformed in this way and, together, they give ground to a peculiar array of feelings and affects: Sexton's uncanny blend of "terror" and "calm" onstage, the patented "sorrows" of the poems, and finally the strange joy that her audience came to feel. The poet never mentions this joy, but it is there on the page—in each burst of creativity, with each twist of a metaphor.

Among these various affects, Sexton confessed most often to the terror, but she did not invite or receive much comfort from her audiences. Quite the opposite: most of the best reading poems are a bit tetchy—dismissive of those who mistook her, of course, but also wary of Sexton themselves— in other words, ambivalent to the core. Notice, for instance, the blend of intimacy and strangeness in the opening lines—in the first word, even— of "Spectacle: a reading": "Lady, you're not a safe poet," it begins, either chiding or in awe of Sexton—who can say (Clardy)? And in the next line this poet makes the same double-move, either patronizing Sexton by saying mere poetry isn't worth it, or else praising her for her courage: "You risk too much for words." By the end of the poem, she writes earnestly of Sexton "daring" her audience to "bear / the sight and hear the words / you risk yourself to form," but not until she has put Sexton through ten lines' worth of (plausibly deniable) irony. This is a common pose among fans and reading-poem authors: loving yet prickly; intimate, and yet ever so slightly aloof (out of fear? out of respect? out of candid confusion?). Sometimes it is all of these at once.

Another reading poem literalizes this blend of intimacy and distance as a measurable, physical space. Titled "To Anne Sexton: From the second row," this poem turns its author's seating choice into a source of pride—into a claim that he knows how her poems (and her readings) are *really* meant to be received (Wing). He and his ilk in the second row are like moths attracted to her flame—but held back by cobwebs. They gather near her like boys around a campfire, huddling close, but also knowing how far to hang back. Their eyes water from the smoke—that is, they cry; they see *her* cry— an embarrassing reaction their slight distance permits. If the poem does not spell all of this out, the enclosing letter does: it reveals the sort of person who had actually dared to claim a first-row seat at this particular reading. He was a boor—in point of fact, an "English prof"—who faulted Sexton for her lack of "aesthetic distance" and who "felt that [her] presentation, however effective, detracted from the 'art' of [her] poetry" (Wing). In his poem, the student turns this critique around on his "prof." *Doesn't he know? Those who never expect art to keep its distance know to keep a bit of their own. They sit in the second row.*

◆ ◆ ◆

Reading your poems can kill us but hearing your voice is something else again.
Letter to Anne Sexton from Carter Bottjer, early summer 1967

what we look for is . . . ways in which the poet is like the rest of us—so that the poetry can be admitted as something that belongs naturally and normally in our lives.
Letter to Anne Sexton from Ottilie Ketchum, mid-August 1973

This repeated gambit—an offer of intimacy *just* held back by a posture of restraint—mimics the ambivalence Sexton's own performances were said to project. One reading poem refers to Sexton's "screaming poems," but it is clear she did anything but scream them (Legler). As Derek Furr has pointed out, critics who hated Sexton's work tended to hear her poems as *loud*, even there on the page; they were "sobbing" or "shrill," but her voice at a reading was none of these things (106). "What struck me most about your reading," wrote one fan, "was the softness of it—some of your hardest phrases stepped onto a soft carpet. . . . I think if you didn't do this, if your voice was sharp or something, no one would be able to bear your poetry— everyone would start screaming."[15] This palpable contrast—hard words and soft carpets, poems that screamed and a poet who whispered into a microphone—was the source of Sexton's greatest power, especially for the most desperate among her audience. If Peter Middleton is right that readings can show us "what it means for a life to say these words," then Sexton's readings seem designed to surprise us by showing how *livable* these words might be (34). Her audiences wanted

> to see how you carried
> your words, your images,
> your ways of dying
>     and being born—(Gibson)

And that is what Sexton *did* show them. Though she shook under the burden, she always proved she could carry the load. *Maybe you can, too.*

## The Anne Sexton Reading Poems: Fan Poetry as Performance Criticism

The documents I collect below are the fruits of my opportunism in the archive. I hope they provide some fodder for your imagination. They are idiosyncratic. I would not expect to find their like in another poet's archive, but perhaps they can help us reconsider what counts as evidence of poetry performance. I call them "reading poems." Fans wrote them in remembrance of her readings and then sent the poems in letters to her. The preceding essay outlines a few ways of approaching them; there are surely many more.

One tactic I particularly recommend is to watch how these poets play the role of "audience." Many of them play it like a game of cat's cradle: taking images from Sexton's poems, they give them a twist, and then hand them back to her. In this connection, it is useful to remember two facts. First, the only texts spoken at every Sexton reading were the poem "Her Kind" and, later, this line from a Kafka letter (first published by Sexton as an epigraph to *All My Pretty Ones* [1962]): "the books we need are the kind that act upon us like a misfortune, that make us suffer like the death of someone we love more than ourselves, that make us feel as though we were on the verge of suicide, or lost in a forest remote from all human habitation—a book should serve as the ax for the frozen sea within us" (*CP* 48). Second, the other texts most often performed (and most cited in these poems) seem to have been: "For John, Who Begs Me Not to Enquire Further," "The Double Image," "The Black Art," "Flee on Your Donkey," and "Little Girl, My String

Bean, My Lovely Woman." If you return to these poems—even better, to her whole oeuvre—before you proceed to the reading poems, you will understand their engagement with Sexton on a whole new level.

Finally, some curatorial notes: I selected these poems from the many that I found in the archive. Even these I have cut internally to meet space constraints. I have labeled each poem with the name of its author, as well as the location and date of the reading the poem describes. Where available and relevant, I have also included (in italics) language from the letters that accompanied the poems. I begin with a single, brief poem that provides, in my opinion, the best overview of Sexton's performances. After that, they are arranged as most poem cycles are: along vague, symphonic lines. They do, however, follow a narrative—not the historical chronology of their writing, but the order of the poetry reading. So, we begin with poems of anticipation, then turn to poems of performance. The structured aftermath of the Q-and-A and autograph line follows, and then the audience returns to the comforts and terrors of their lives. As fate would have it, the second and penultimate poems were written by authors who attended the exact same reading—as neat a symbol as you please for the way these isolated voices might add up to a larger audience.

I. Spectacle

Andrea Fleck Clardy•Weston, MA•May 1967

*I would be most grateful if you would let me know if you have any reservations about my sending it out. [ . . . ] The poem accomplished its primary function when you read it.*

**Spectacle: a reading**

*for Anne Sexton*

Lady, you're not a safe poet;
you risk too much for words.
For those whose only relation to you
is in being also human,
you pose, defiant, finally dressed
in only gaudy eyes,

conspicuous hands and, quite
miraculously, your dignity.
Leaning hard on crutches of pain,
you crack away at the shells
of your life, willfully daring
the righteous ladies, the acres of nuns,
the kids to really bear
the sight and hear the words
you risk yourself to form.

## II. Anticipation

Stephen Wing•Williamsburg, VA•April 1966

*Your version of "aesthetic distance" became the topic of some debate. One English prof. who sat in the front row felt that your presentation, however effective, detracted from the "art" of your poetry. Fooey. What we need is communication first, then art. I admit, though, that you and your comments smashed "the frozen sea within us" as well as your poems, and that reading your books lacks a powerful dimension you gave the material.*

**To Anne Sexton from the Second Row**
We cautious moths
Caught in cerebral cobwebs; all
But the very last
Filled every row but the first,
Lest we be burned,
Lest we betray
Our hungry ears,
Listened to your sad fire
Sputter, snap, sing.
Eyes watering
Watched you talk, live, cry;
Heard
You laugh.

III. Performance

Barbara Friend•Hamilton, New York•1973

*This poem came close to being published recently, and I suddenly realized I had second thoughts—not about the poem, though it is far from perfect, but about how it might strike you.*

*It is written partly from impressions of your reading at Colgate, and in some versions is dedicated to you. It is intended to be more about the people watching the reading (or any reading with its mixture of myth, drama, strip-tease) than about you or any poet.*

**Full Fathom**

The figurehead turns
in terror
to her prow.
She throbs
above the canted podium.
Her eyes are as calm
as vodka.

Thin vapours unbend.
Like a glassblower
she tongues
a filter cigarette;
under full copyright,
grey sorrows quiver
and ascend.

Her soul is transparent,
has become the water
in her hand.
She is as real
as any bleached page
of the Parthenon.

Thicker than caviar
the red eyes wait.
They have packed the Institute

to see her famous smile—
last Friday's curdled
prom gardenia;
to hear the flawed voice
ebb and flow
on its crystal radio;
and, of course,
to observe the poems:

how, against Nature,
they continue to rise
and make love.
like circus balloons
    escaping,
    like Roman candles
    dying,
    like Noah's dove.

Eugenia Plunkett•Lincoln, MA•Winter 1967

*here is another [poem]—one which I wrote after hearing and seeing you
read at de Cordova Museum [ . . . ]. I hope it gives you as much pleasure in
the reading as it gave me in the writing. It is odd that so few poets talk about
the actual, almost physical satisfaction that getting something right on paper
can afford the poet or would-be poet.*

## To Anne Sexton, After Her Poetry Reading

With your "glass ball" for a head, your
Painful "stars" inside it, Anne,
Your uncertain yearning to be sure
Of cadences, thought, sadnesses, man,
Your thunderstruck and green-white eyes,
Anne-on-a-donkey, your surprise—
You seem to gesture those broken stars away.
And however insular we are,
Star, thought, man . . . yet, bonne Anne,
I feel there is something to be said,
Something more to say. [ . . . ]

Author Unknown•Location Unknown•October 1969

**Poet**

She stands, reading
In a spotlight
Quiet voiced,
Angular, lonely.

Pausing, her tongue
Ranges her lips.
She glances at us
With haunted eyes.

And tears bits of her heart
Upon the podium
For us to swallow
And transplant slowly
Into lifeblood.

IV. Aftermath

Tina Van Sickle•Baltimore, MD•February 1974

**Evening of Baltimore, Md. Poetry Reading**

The eyes, pale with a blue distance,
gazed,
not looking,
not receiving,
but accommodating to the
necessary aftermath of the movable reading.

Tired, waiting with
a repose, seeking the dream that
has faded out of focus from the
vibrant red and performance, you
sat and answered pedestrian questions
from naïve and interested students.

Baltimore and breadcrumbs take on
new meaning.

Muriel Cole•Hanover, NH•January 1968

**To Anne Sexton**

Your Stanwyck aloofness and furcoat height
speaks to me
all the way down to your low-heeled warmth.

You listen intently:
then speak with clarity
as you dismiss the question.

I love you for your complex simpleness
and the honesty you radiate.

Janice Gibson•Boston, MA•November 1973

*Labeled by Sexton: "given by hand at [Boston] Globe reading"*

   i came here
because i *was* curious
to see how you carried
your words, your images,
your ways of dying
   and being born—
   my curiosity was respecting—
i appreciated your reading.
i don't want your autograph—
   you brought tears to my eyes.

V. Return

Andrea Freud Loewenstein•Lincoln, MA•January 1967

*It was wonderful for me to see you, because you are my favorite poet, and it added so much to hear you read your poems. [ . . . ] I think Poetry Reading is a pretty bad poem, but maybe you'd like to see it anyway; it's a kind of thanks.*

## Poetry Reading

Coming back
Into the mess of my room
Strange woman
I disentangle myself from you
I sat, hemmed in between my mother and a girl I know
While you read your poetry, and spoke dramatically
of a nervous breakdown—thrusting your arm out
I wished I were somewhere where I didn't have to think so much
about what my face was doing
My mother's face was stuck in a smile of frozen teeth
She doesn't like to remember
Coldly I noted: you are beautiful
wondered which one was your husband
how I will describe you to someone, form the words
But then you read about yourself, your frozen mother
and just for a moment I'm not aware
Of me

Judith Kerman•Rochester, NY•November 1965

*You may remember a tall girl with a braid who got rather upset at the University of Rochester reading last Friday evening [ ... ]. I wrote the enclosed poem later Friday night, in a bit of a rush but working more intensively than I usually am able to. [ ... ] I hope you will like it, and that it explains what I was so teary about.*

## To Anne Sexton
## Her Poem for Her Daughter

Mother
I wish my mother had
written a poem like that for me
I know why I cried when you were reading
because the things you told, unasked
were the things I was afraid to ask (because I love my mother)
until they had eaten my heart for a year or so
until the pain of hiding questions

doubts about my body, ignorance
of things I somehow should have known
was worse than shame, and I would blurt
a casual, single-sided detail
of a question
that left the doubts unsaid
unanswered

Thomas Eustis Roach•Williamsburg, VA•April 1966

*Communication between two people is so difficult that I sometimes despair of it altogether. But your reading [ … ] made me feel communicated with. And I wanted, in turn, to talk to you. Temporarily the best I can do in that respect is what I have enclosed, a very unfinished poem of my own. I don't have time to let it lie still and then revise it, nor do I have the strength to type it, because as soon as I get officially withdrawn from college (tomorrow), I'm going home to have another nervous breakdown, which only Dexedrine is keeping me from having right here.*

**To Anne Sexton**

in the orderly and endless procession
a black-haired head visible above the rest
reading and drinking water and smoking
speaking of poison
speaking of death
not looking back to see the blond boy following her [ … ]

easier to write than to speak while others can
    hear what we need to say alone
easier to send what should be said [ … ]

oh god what happened to the time when
screaming branches could be silenced with
only one drink or one pill
if the mood could be silenced I would kill it—

if there will be a day when the procession
    halts long enough for the black-haired
    woman and me to meet

even if only to make a procession of martinis
to duplicate the march we're in
perhaps then there will be a longer day
a single long fine day
when the procession moves along
starting up again while we are talking
and will move along without us

Philip Legler[16]•Sweet Briar, VA•April 1966

**Privileges**

Now one day here, my first
Floor room near the entrance
On Franklin, yesterday showing
The visible scars
And an intern checking all those curable
Childhood diseases,
From my open window I watch
Your Sunday lunatics [ … ]

Oh crazy Annie, baby,
Two days ago
(Knowing before your visit
I was heading this way,
Trapped, to be sent like a basket case
Or a dirty word
In a book some library's shelved
Out of circulation)—
I heard your screaming poems
Slash, tearing at the Van Gogh ear.
Now I shall bring you mine—
This room, these walls.

Poems are lies, you said,
That tell the truth.
Truth in this home's the lie
I diet on:
Poet, you've made me eat your words. [ … ]

Look straight into this light,
The intern said
Then poked my fish's body, bloated
He wondered why.
I sit and watch TV;
A nurse brings in
My special pills and meal
Again. You talk about abundance?
Oh Annie baby. I'm eating
Your leftover trays.


## Notes

1. I borrow this term from Barthes's *Camera Lucida*, where it describes the one detail that overwhelms an image, at least according to a particular viewer (27 and passim).

2. The only one of much substance is John Mood's essay "A Bird Full of Bones," but it is a rather limited resource—too simply a document of one man's lust for Anne Sexton. As he wrote in a letter to Sexton, enclosing a draft of the essay, "it is obviously a *love letter* to you—& I very much want your response to that."

3. Letter, Brunner to Sexton, 8 Mar. 1974, Sexton Papers, box 18, folder 4.

4. Letter, Todd to Sexton, 29 Nov. 1973, Sexton Papers, box 29, folder 6.

5. Letter, Sexton to Brunner, 1 Apr. 1974, Sexton Papers, box 18, folder 4.

6. Letter, Sexton to Haden, 5 July 1973, Sexton Papers, box 36, folder 4.

7. Letter, Sexton to Legler, 11 Sept. 1966, Sexton Papers, box 22, folder 2. See also Sexton Therapy Tapes, Sexton interview by Martin Orne, 14 Feb. 1961, reel 5, *APAS*.

8. The exceptions are rare enough to prove the rule. Harvard's Woodberry Poetry Room has done well to digitize and preserve their fine recordings. Lately the University of Cincinnati has begun dusting off and digitizing their own collection. But hundreds of institutions hold troves nearly this rich but lack the will or the money to preserve them. PennSound/Ubuweb, the most comprehensive online archive of poetry recordings, is a wonderful model for future projects but does not seem poised to solve the larger problem. They have basically treated their archive as an exercise in canon-formation, focusing mainly on L=A=N=G=U=A=G=E poets and adjacent members of the avant-garde. They have also privileged variety over versioning, rarely including more than one recording of a single poem.

9. When I speak of "polemical essays," I'm thinking of essays by Denise Levertov in *Light Up the Cave*, Donald Hall in *American Scholar*, David Wojahn in the *New England Review*, etc. The era of poetry scholars' growing interest in the readings roughly dates to the 1997 release of *Sound States* (ed. Morris) and the 1998 release *Close Listening* (ed. Bernstein).

10. The phrase is Denise Levertov's from her essay "An Approach to Public Poetry Listenings."

11. This discussion was taped and can be found at the Harry Ransom Center for Humanities Research under the title "R0084 'at Sweet Briar' ([1966])."

12. I am not the first one to notice this: commenting on the sparse wave-form of a recording of Sexton reading "Her Kind," Derek Furr has declared, "Silence was essential to Sexton's dramatic effect" (103). He means *her* silences of course, but they also belong to the audience.

13. A clipping of this article was enclosed in a letter from the reading's organizer. Letter, Todd to Sexton, 5 Dec. 1973, Sexton Papers, box 29, folder 6.

14. Letter, Hunken to Sexton, n.d. [1974], Sexton Papers, box 34, folder 5.

15. Letter, Goetz to Sexton, 28 June 1967, Sexton Papers, box 20, folder 2.

16. A substantially different version of this poem appeared in Legler's 1972 book *The Intruder*.

## Works Cited

Abzug, Bob. Letter to Anne Sexton. 7 Nov. 1973. Sexton Papers, box 17, folder 2.

Anonymous. "Poet." 22 Oct. 1969. Sexton Papers, box 33, folder 7.

Anonymous. "Upon Hearing Anne Sexton Read." N.d. [Fall 1968]. Sexton Papers, box 33, folder 5.

Barthes, Roland. *Camera Lucida: Reflections on Photography*. New York: Hill and Wang, 1980. Print.

———. "The Grain of the Voice." *Image-Music-Text*. New York: Hill and Wang, 1978. 179–89. Print.

Bottjer, Carter. Letter to Anne Sexton. N.d. [1967]. Sexton Papers, box 33, folder 4.

Clardy, Andrea. "Spectacle: a reading / for Anne Sexton" and letter to Anne Sexton. 16 Oct. 1968. Sexton Papers, box 33, folder 4.

Cole, Muriel. "To Anne Sexton." 16 Oct. 1968. Sexton Papers, box 33, folder 5.

Crowder, Tinsley. Letter to Anne Sexton. 21 Dec. 1959. Sexton Papers, box 19, folder 2.

Davis, Tracy. "The Context Problem." *Theatre Survey* 45.2 (2004): 203–9. Print.

Epstein, Perle, and Shelley Neiderbach. Letter to Anne Sexton. 26 Nov. 1964. Sexton Papers, box 33, folder 3.

Friend, Barbara. "Full Fathom" and letter to Anne Sexton. 27 Feb. 1974. Sexton Papers, box 34, folder 5.

Furr, Derek. *Recorded Poetry and Poetic Reception from Edna Millay to the Circle of Robert Lowell.* New York: Palgrave Macmillan, 2010. Print.

Gibson, Janice. [Untitled poem]. N.d. [1973]. Sexton Papers, box 34, folder 4.

Kearns, Martha. Letter to Anne Sexton. 18 Apr. 1966. Sexton Papers, box 33, folder 3.

Kennedy, Theresa Reis. Letter to Anne Sexton. 7 Aug. 1973. Sexton Papers, box 34, folder 4.

Kerman, Judith. "To Anne Sexton / Her Poem for Her Daughter" and letter to Anne Sexton. N.d. [1965]. Sexton Papers, box 33, folder 3.

Ketchum, Ottilie. Letter to Anne Sexton. N.d. [1973]. Sexton Papers, box 34, folder 4.

Legler, Philip. "Privileges." 25 Apr. 1966. Sexton Papers, box 22, folder 2.

Levertov, Denise. "An Approach to Public Poetry Listenings." *Virginia Quarterly Review* 41(1965): 422–33.

Loewenstein, Andrea Freud. "Poetry Reading" and letter to Anne Sexton. 15 May 1967. Sexton Papers, box 36, folder 4.

Middleton, Peter. *Distant Reading: Performance, Readership, and Consumption in Contemporary Poetry.* Tuscaloosa: U of Alabama P, 2005. Print.

Miller, Tim. "The Battle of Chattanooga." *Cast Out: Queer Lives in Theater.* Ed. Robin Bernstein. Ann Arbor: U of Michigan P, 2006. 91–102. Print.

Mood, John. Letter to Anne Sexton. 17 July 1969. Sexton Papers, box 23, folder 2.

Muñoz, José Esteban. "Ephemera as Evidence: Introductory Notes to Queer Acts." *Women and Performance* 8.2 (1996): 5–16. Print.

Plunkett, Eugenia. "To Anne Sexton, After Her Poetry Reading" and letter to Anne Sexton. 1 Feb. 1967. Sexton Papers, box 33, folder 4.

Roach, Thomas Eustis. "To Anne Sexton" and letter to Anne Sexton. 24 Apr.1966. Sexton Papers, box 33, folder 3.

Schneider, Rebecca. "Performance Remains." *Performance Research* 6.2 (2001): 100–108. Print.

Sexton, Anne. "Reactions of an Author in Residence in a Little Town Called Boston." *The Charles Playbook.* Vol. 5 (1964–65). Boston: Charles Playhouse, 1965. Print. Sexton Papers, box 16, folder 1.

———. "The Poetry of Ella." *Boston Globe.* 28 July 1974. 46, 51. Print.

———. "Untitled Talk on Poetry." Sexton Papers, box 16, folder 4.

———. Interview by Martin Orne. 29 Apr. 1961. Sexton Therapy Tapes, Reel 18. *APAS*

———. Interview by Martin Orne. 14 Feb. 1961. Sexton Therapy Tapes, Reel 5. *APAS.*

———. Letter to Donald Hall. 26 July 1973. Sexton Papers, box 20, folder 4.

———. Letter to Stephens College. 29 June 1964. Sexton Papers, box 28, folder 1.

Smith, Jacob. *Vocal Tracks: Performance and Sound Media.* Berkeley: U of California P, 2008. Print.

Stanislavsky, Konstantin. *Stanislavsky on the Art of the Stage.* Ed. David Magarshack. New York: Hill and Wang, 1961. Library of Anne Sexton, Harry Ransom Center for Humanities Research.

Todd, Robert. (Worcester State College). Letter to Sexton. 29 Nov. 1973. Sexton Papers, box 29, folder 6.

———. Letter to Anne Sexton. 5 Dec, 1973. Sexton Papers, box 29, folder 6.

Van Sickle, Tina. "Evening of Baltimore, Md. Poetry Reading." 1 Feb. 1974. Sexton Papers, box 34, folder 5.

Williams, C. K. Letter to Anne Sexton. 28 Oct. 1971. Sexton Papers, box 29, folder 5.

Wing, Stephen. "To Anne Sexton: From the second row" and letter to Anne Sexton. 1 Aug. 1966. Sexton Papers, box 33, folder 3.

# ··· 6

## "Two Sweet Ladies"

### Anne Sexton and Sylvia Plath's Friendship and Mutual Influence

DAVID TRINIDAD

I should say at the outset that I am, have been—on and off—since the 1970s, a Sexton- and Plath-oholic. When I first encountered Anne Sexton she was on the cusp of being, thanks largely to the women's movement, co-opted by academia. Sylvia Plath was already being taught in literature classes at my college; *Ariel* had been published in this country in 1966 and, due to the shock value of Plath's suicide and the role that suicide plays in her poems, she was very popular. Both writers' preoccupation with death, of course, connected them in my mind, as did the fact that they had been friends. For me there was an irresistible glamour about their friendship. It has always felt like I was honoring—in my devotion to and my obsession with their lives and their work—the bond between them. Something intimate and yet Olympian, if you will, touched by creative genius. Over time, however, I began to question the depth of their friendship. There are a number of holes in the story, mysteries of a sort. And although it is an accepted fact that Sexton and Plath influenced each other's work, there has been very little scholarship, to my knowledge, in this area. It is these holes, these blind spots, that I would like to explore.

For many years the accepted (and pretty much sole) record of Sexton and Path's friendship has been Sexton's brief memoir "The Bar Fly Ought to

Sing." In the fall of 1966, *TriQuarterly* magazine published a "womanly issue" that featured a special section called "The Art of Sylvia Plath"—one of the earliest, if not the first, tributes to Plath. A year earlier, *TriQuarterly*'s editor Charles Newman had contacted Sexton about "a feature section devoted to Sylvia Plath," originally intended for spring 1966, to coincide, no doubt, with the June publication of *Ariel*. Sexton's response to Newman is basically a rough draft of her memoir. At first she tells him she has "no contribution to make," but then proceeds to describe her friendship with Plath. At the end she offers to expand her letter into a "small sketch." And adds: "I am ashamed of America—when I think of Sylvia's last poems. I read at many universities and yet no one mentions her work. Are they all fools?" (*SPL* 272, 274). This is an interesting glimpse of Plath's neglect, at least during the three years between her suicide in 1963 and the American publication of *Ariel* in 1966, in light of the immense attention she was about to receive.

Sexton fleshed her memories into "The Bar Fly Ought to Sing" and included two poems: "Sylvia's Death," an elegy she wrote on 17 February 1963, just six days after Plath's suicide, and "Wanting to Die," which she wrote one year later. "I knew her [Plath] for a while in Boston," says Sexton, and tells how they both grew up in Wellesley, Massachusetts, though didn't meet until they were both adults, both poets (*NES* 6). Plath and George Starbuck learned, she says, "that I was auditing a class at Boston University given by Robert Lowell" and "kind of followed me in, joined me there" (6). Lowell was then a leading American poet; Sexton depicts him as a merciless judge of student poetry, but a personally kind father figure. She describes how after class she, Starbuck, and Plath would

> pile into the front seat of my old Ford and . . . drive quickly through the traffic to, or near, the Ritz. I would always park illegally in a LOADING ONLY ZONE, telling them gaily, "It's okay, because we are only going to get loaded!" Off we'd go, each on George's arm, into the Ritz and drink three or four or two martinis. George even has a line about this in his first book of poems, *Bone Thoughts*. He wrote, "I weave with two sweet ladies out of The Ritz." Sylvia and I, such sleep mongers, such death mongers, were those two sweet ladies. (*NES* 7)

In the "plush, deep dark red" Ritz-Carlton bar, the three would eat "free potato chips" and drink "lots of martinis," and Sexton and Plath would discuss, "like moths to an electric light bulb," their passionate flirtation with death (7). Later they made their way to the nearby Waldorf Cafeteria, where dinner could be purchased for a mere seventy cents. After Plath moved back to England, Sexton tells us, they "exchanged a few letters. . . . I have them now, of course. . . . Sylvia wrote of one child, keeping bees, another child, my poems—happy, gossip-letters, and then, with silence between us, she died" (10). Sexton also tells us, regarding Plath's talent: "Something told me to bet on her but I never asked it why" (9). Although in her original letter to Newman she states: "I never guessed that she had it all in her" (*SPL* 274).

It takes a little detective work, culling facts from various letters, journals, memoirs, and biographies, to get the timeline down and to fill out the details. In another, earlier "small sketch" of Robert Lowell as a teacher, Sexton says she studied with him "during the fall of 1958 and the winter of 1959"; she doesn't specify these dates in "The Bar Fly Ought to Sing" (*NES* 3). In September 1958, Sexton, who had yet to publish her first book, applied to Lowell's graduate writing seminar at Boston University. She did so at the suggestion of W. D. Snodgrass (himself a former student of Lowell's), whom she had met earlier that year at the Antioch Writers' Conference. A week later she received a letter from Lowell accepting her into the class. Lowell praised the poems she had submitted to him: "They move with ease and are filled with experience, like good prose. . . . You stick to truth and the simple expression of very difficult feelings, and this is the line in poetry that I am most interested in" (Lowell 326).

The editorial notes in *Anne Sexton: A Self-Portrait in Letters* inform us that "The class met on Tuesdays from two to four in a small room. Although smoking was forbidden, Anne lit up furtively, defiant as in her high school days, using her shoe as an ashtray" (38). According to Sexton's Lowell sketch, the class "consisted of some twenty students—seventeen graduates, two other housewives (who were graduate somethings), and a boy who snuck over from M.I.T. I was the only one in that room who hadn't read *Lord Weary's Castle*" (*NES* 3). By 6 October, Sexton is writing to Snodgrass: "I am learning more than you could imagine from Lowell" (*SPL* 40). In the same letter she says "Lowell just called," as if they're suddenly chums, and passes on some professional gossip (39). But such chumminess is short lived: on 26 November, after a brief stay in a mental institution, Sexton writes Snodgrass:

Went to Lowell's class yesterday. I guess I forgive him for not liking me
(if he didn't like me as I thot [*sic*]) because he has such a soft danger-
ous voice. He seemed more friendly yesterday. He is a good man; I
forgive him for his sicknesses whatever they are. I think I will have to
god him again; gods are so necessary and splendid and distant. (43)

Still, in November, again according to Sexton's Lowell sketch, she gives him
a manuscript of her poems, "to see if he thought 'it was a book'" (*NES* 4).

Another letter to Snodgrass, written on 11 January 1959, confirms that
Lowell is still looking over Sexton's manuscript. This same letter gives us
a pretty good idea of what it was like to have Anne Sexton as a workshop
peer:

The class is good. I am learning leaps and boundaries. Tho I am very
bitchy acting in class. I don't know why but I am very defensive around
Lowell (I think I am afraid of him) . . . so I act like a bitch with these
sarcastic remarks[.] . . . The class just sits there like little doggies wag-
gling their heads at his every statement. For instance, he will be dis-
secting some great poem and will say "Why is this line so good. What
makes it good?" and there is total silence. Everyone afraid to speak.
And finally, because I can stand it no longer, I speak up saying, "I don't
think it's so good at all. You would never allow us sloppy language like
that." . . . and so forth. But I don't do this for effect. But because the
line *isn't* good. What do you do—sit there and agree and nod and say
nothing . . . ? . . . As you say, I do act aggressive. (*SPL* 48–49)

On 1 February she writes Snodgrass:

Lowell is really helping me. . . . he likes the looks of my 'book,'
with some critical reservations, and has shown it to Stanley
Kunitz . . . who . . . agree[s] with his enthusiasm . . . He is going to
show it to somebody Ford at Knopf this week to see if he would be
interested. And Houghton Mifflin wants to see it. . . . in total he likes
my work a lot." (51–52)

Enough to also share it with Randall Jarrell, among others. Lowell coaches
her on which poems to delete from the manuscript and encourages her
to replace them with new ones. Though Sexton puts the word "book" in
quotes, indicating she's not sure it is yet a book, she is already calling it "To

Bedlam and Part Way Back," a title that would stick. A few days later, 5 February, Sexton writes poet Carolyn Kizer that Lowell is "pushing me to send out fat groups [of poems] to the big places," that is, the most visible literary magazines (56).

In the midst of all this exciting tutelage, February 1959, Sylvia Plath began auditing Lowell's poetry class. Plath, living in Boston with husband Ted Hughes and still very much in his shadow, had recently finished a year of teaching at Smith College. To her friend Lynne Lawner, Plath wrote, "I have been auditing a poetry course [Lowell] gives at BU with some bright young visiting poets, George Starbuck, who is an editor at Houghton Mifflin, & has published everywhere, and Anne Sexton, another mental hospital graduate, who Lowell thinks is marvelous" (45). From the 25 February entry in her journal: "Lowell's class yesterday a great disappointment: I said a few mealymouthed things, a few BU students yattered nothings I wouldn't let my Smith freshmen say without challenge. Lowell good in his mildly feminine ineffectual fashion. Felt a regression. The main thing is hearing the other student's poems & his reaction to mine" (UJ 471).

Unhappy at first with the workshop, Plath perked up when Lowell started comparing her work to Sexton's. Lowell suspected, perhaps intuitively, and ultimately correctly, that they might benefit from each other's differences. Plath's journal, 20 March: "Criticism of 4 of my poems in Lowell's class: criticism of rhetoric. He sets me up with Ann [missing the "e"] Sexton, an honor, I suppose. Well, about time. She has very good things, and they get better, though there is a lot of loose stuff" (475). That looseness—in person as well as on paper—was a potential antidote to Plath's compulsive togetherness.

Kathleen Spivack, then nineteen and a student in the class, remembers Plath as "curt and businesslike," as "reserved and totally controlled as well as unapproachable to the younger writers" (29). She was "composed, neat, held in, in a tightly buttoned print blouse and neat cardigan. She spoke quietly, with utmost control" (27). In contrast, Sexton

was often late, and wore splashy, flowing dresses and flashy jewelry. Her hoarse voice breathed extravagant enthusiasm and life. Her hands shook when she read her poems aloud. She smoked endlessly. Anne's poems were ragged; they flew off the page. She was an instinctual poet rather than, as Sylvia, a trained one. (27)

In class, Sexton named William Carlos Williams as a favorite poet; Plath, Wallace Stevens. Their own poems, at this time, reflect their preferences: Sexton's are personal, colloquial, direct; whereas Plath's are intellectual, mythological, and formally complex. These stylistic differences were clear to Plath. From her journal, 23 April: "She ["Ann Sexton," the "Ann" again without its "e"] has none of my clenches and an ease of phrase, and an honesty" (477). Sexton poems Plath read or saw workshopped include "The Double Image" (Sexton's painfully open and seamlessly crafted sequence about her mother's death from cancer and her separation, due to breakdown, from her infant daughter; both answer and homage to "Heart's Needle," a Snodgrass sequence Sexton deeply admired), "Kind Sir: These Woods," and "A Story for Rose on the Midnight Flight to Boston." (Mimeographed copies of these three poems, with Plath's penciled scribblings, are in Plath's papers at Smith College.) To Lawner, Plath wrote this about Sexton: "I like one of her long poems, about a very female subject: grandmother, mother, daughter, hag trilogy ["The Double Image"], and some of her shorter ones. She has the marvelous enviable casualness of the person who is suddenly writing and never thought or dreamed of herself as a born writer: no inhibitions" (45). Plath was writing such poems as the stilted "Electra on Azalea Path" and the gimmicky "Metaphors," two poems that would fail to make their way into the American edition of her first book, *The Colossus* (1962).

It seems the gay afternoons at the Ritz-Carlton, the mutual infatuation between Sexton and Plath, would have occurred during the months of March and April 1959. In April, to Snodgrass, Sexton wrote:

> Ted Hughes and his wife (Sylvia Plath) are in Boston this year (he is an english poet) and they are going to Yaddo for 2 months next fall. She wants to know what it's like if you can drink and etc. She is going to Lowell's class along with George Starbuck . . . and we three leave the class and go to the Ritz and drink martinis. Very fun. My book is at H.M. now. (*SPL* 73–74)

"*Not* martinis," insisted Starbuck when he was interviewed by Sexton biographer Diane Wood Middlebrook some thirty years later: "Anne drank stingers at the time—awful stuff—I don't remember what Sylvia drank" (*AS* 107). Middlebrook would have us believe nothing at all; she makes the following assertion about Plath's drinking habits in *Her Husband* (her study of the Hughes/Plath marriage): "Sexton says they drank martinis at the

Ritz—this would have been very unusual behavior for Plath" (125). Could Sexton have misremembered, or projected? And could she have exaggerated about the frequency of the trio's outings to the Ritz? About Sexton and Plath's death talks, Starbuck concurs (although the tone of their conversations seems lighter than Sexton implies): "They had these hilarious conversations comparing their suicides and talking about their psychiatrists." Then he adds: "It was just a few times that I was privileged to eavesdrop on them" (*AS* 107). Starbuck was a junior editor at Houghton Mifflin and, according to Middlebrook, would "now and then . . . [take] off from work . . . to drop in on . . . [Lowell's] seminar" (106). So it doesn't appear he was a regular presence in the class or at the Ritz. From the vantage point of age and more modest accomplishments, Starbuck said this about Plath: "Her journals indicate that she was wary of me, which is odd. Everybody at that age thinks the other people are the lions" (107).

Indeed, judging from her journal entries, the honeymoon ended, for Plath, almost as soon as it had begun. On 23 April she acknowledges that Sexton and Starbuck are having an affair—a fact Sexton would discreetly omit from "The Bar Fly Ought to Sing" (*UJ* 478) Sexton is obviously referring to Starbuck in this quote from a letter to Snodgrass, also written in April: "There is a rather nice poet in Boston who is in love with me. I guess I'd better give up and sleep with him" (*SPL* 75). Maybe Plath felt like the odd poet out, witnessing the beginning of her friends' affair, but she was no prude. A 3 May journal passage makes it clear that it was a different kind of jealousy—not sexual, but career-related—that was getting under Plath's skin: "Retyped pages, a messy job, on the volume of poems I should be turning in to Houghton Mifflin this week. But AS is there ahead of me, with her lover GS writing New Yorker odes to her and both of them together: felt our triple martini afternoons at the Ritz breaking up." (Plath, it would appear, *was* capable of putting back three martinis.) She goes on: "That memorable afternoon at G's monastic and miserly room on Pinckney 'You shouldn't have left us': where is responsibility to lie? I left, yet felt like a brown winged moth around a rather meagre candle flame, drawn. That is over" (*UJ* 480).

This sounds pretty final, but Starbuck and Sexton have really gotten under Plath's skin. On 18 May she dreams "George Starbuck had a book of poems published by Houghton Mifflin, a spectacular book, full of fat substantial poems I hadn't seen, called 'Music Man'" (483). Then two days later, on 20 May:

All I need now is to hear that GS or MK [Maxine Kumin] has won the Yale [Younger Poets Prize] and get a rejection of my children's book. AS has her book accepted at HM and this afternoon will be drinking champagne. Also an essay accepted by . . . [the *Christian Science Monitor*], the copy-cat. But who's to criticize a more successful copy-cat. Not to mention a poetry reading at McLean. And GS at supper last night smug as a cream-fed cat, very pleased indeed, for AS is in a sense his answer to me. And now my essay, on Withins, will come back from . . . [the *Christian Science Monitor*], and my green-eyed fury prevent me from working. (483–84)

On 6 June Plath learns that her manuscript (an early incarnation of *The Colossus*, then titled "The Bull of Bendylaw") has lost the Yale "'by a whisper'"; it came in second. Angrily, she calls the judge, Dudley Fitts, "a fool." She rails about her lack of support: "I have no champions. They will find a lack of this, or that, or something or other. How few of my superiors do I respect the opinions of anyhow. Lowell a case in point. How few, if any, will see what I am working at, overcoming" (492). The last straw comes a few days later, 12 June, when Starbuck calls Plath and announces, smugly, that *he* is the poet who has beaten her out for the Yale: "'O, didn't I tell you.'" Perhaps Plath had good reason to be wary of Starbuck, after all. Unable to sleep, she stays up until three in the morning "feeling again the top of my head would come off, it was so full, so full of knowledge" (494). Knowledge, she goes on to explain, of corrupt, political string-pulling in Poetryland—of the private boys' club variety. In a letter to a college friend, Plath calls Starbuck a "louse" and dismisses his work as light verse (Alexander 233). (Ironically, Plath makes an appearance, you'll recall, in a poem in Starbuck's winning manuscript, *Bone Thoughts*, as one of "two sweet ladies" of the Ritz.)

Sexton and Starbuck high on the acceptance of their first books—and Plath fuming, the success of her friends triggering feelings of jealousy and frustration, perceived failure. This in June 1959, two months after Lowell's *Life Studies*, the book that will crown him king of Confessional poetry, is published. On 1 April Sexton had written to Carolyn Kizer about Lowell's new volume: "Tho I haven't seen . . . [it], I hear it is full of personal poetry and think that he is either copying me or that I'm copying him (tho I haven't seen his new stuff) or that we are both copying [Snodgrass]" (*SPL* 71). This is a fair appraisal, in my opinion. More could be said about all this influence—the freedom of subject matter that these poets sparked in each other. But for now I will leave Starbuck's sweet ladies to their summer plans: Sexton to a fishing trip to Maine with her husband Kayo, followed by the Bread Loaf Writers' Conference in late August (with her lover/editor George); Plath to a car camping trip across North America with Hughes, during which she realizes she is pregnant, followed by a stay at Yaddo in the fall. While at Yaddo, on 6 October, Plath will jot the following bitter entry in her journal: "George Starbuck's immortal love poem ["Technologies"] to Anne Sexton in the NY [*New Yorker*] this week. A reminder" (*UJ* 515).

◆ ◆ ◆

Something that has always puzzled me is the absence, in all that has been published by and about both poets, of the correspondence between Sexton and Plath. Sexton, we are told, kept carbon copies of all of her letters; this is why *Anne Sexton: A Self-Portrait in Letters* is so comprehensive. Missing from the volume, however, are Sexton's letters to Plath. Plath's letters to Sexton ("I have them now, of course," says Sexton in "The Bar Fly Ought to Sing") are in the Anne Sexton Papers at the University of Texas at Austin (*NES* 10). There are two letters from Plath to Sexton, but no carbon copies of Sexton's letters to Plath. Two letters in the three and a half years between Lowell's workshop and Plath's suicide? At Smith College and Indiana University, the two schools that house Plath's papers, there are no letters from Anne Sexton to Sylvia Plath.

Plath wrote the first letter to Sexton on Sunday, 5 February 1961, in response to a card Sexton had sent her. Plath received the card while a letter she'd started to Sexton was still lodged in her typewriter. After professing admiration for *To Bedlam and Part Way Back* (1960), Plath announces she has given birth to a daughter, says her own poems have been well-received in England, and boasts of hobnobbing (on Hughes's arm, we can imagine) with London's literati: Stephen Spender, Louis MacNeice, W. H. Auden, Thom Gunn, and just a few days before, American Theodore Roethke. She expresses her wish for news about Sexton's poems and for literary gossip, especially about their mentor Robert Lowell, and recounts a dinner party she and Ted attended at the house of T. S. and Valerie Eliot. She also thanks Sexton for her reactions to *The Colossus*, which had been published in England the previous October and which Plath presumably sent to Sexton.

In the summer of 1962, Sexton sent Plath an advance copy of her second book, *All My Pretty Ones* (1962). Plath apparently received the book on 17 August, the date she inscribed, along with her name, on the half-title page (the book is in the Plath collection at Smith), and read it over the next few days. She responded on 21 August with a generous letter (this is Plath's second letter to Sexton, only Middlebrook calls it a "thank-you note"): "I was absolutely stunned and delighted with the new book. It is superbly masterful, womanly in the greatest sense, and so blessedly *un-literary*" (*AS* 174). (In Plath's actual letter, "*unliterary*" is not hyphenated.) Paul Alexander, author of the Plath biography *Rough Magic*, reminds us that Plath wrote the letter from Court Green, Plath and Hughes's home in Devon, at a time when her marriage to Ted Hughes was breaking up; Hughes was spending much of his time away from Plath, in London with his lover Assia Wevill. Alexander comments on the contents of the letter: "Plath predicted—she was blessed with clairvoyance, she said—that *All My Pretty Ones* would earn Sexton a Pulitzer Prize and a National Book Award." *All My Pretty Ones* would indeed be nominated for the National Book Award, and Sexton's next book, *Live or Die* (1966), would win the Pulitzer in 1967. "Then," Alexander continues,

> Plath asked Sexton a most revealing question. How did it feel, she wanted to know, to be a female Poet Laureate? With *The Colossus* a failure in England and America, Plath posed the question out of at least some unacknowledged jealousy. Next, Sylvia told Sexton about Nicholas and Frieda, about tending bees and planting potatoes, and about trudging into the BBC to record broadcasts. However, she did not so much as allude to Ted, or her marriage. (288–89)

Within a week, Plath would write her mother that she intended to pursue a legal separation from Hughes.

Among the poems Plath lists as favorites are "The Black Art," "Letter Written on a Ferry While Crossing Long Island Sound," "Flight," "Old," "For God While Sleeping," and "Lament." She wonders who the lover mentioned in several of the poems might be and again presses Sexton for literary gossip, saying she would love to tack one of Sexton's news-filled letters on the wall above her desk. She ends by complimenting her on "The Sun"—one of Sexton's post–*All My Pretty Ones* poems, which she'd read in the *New Yorker* three months before—and bestowing a blessing: Sexton has everything she needs for success; more power to her. Unlike Plath's acrid journal entries, the timbre of her letters to Sexton is warm, admiring, and affectionate.

So these are Plath's "happy, gossip-letters." But where are Sexton's? Did they even survive? In her second letter, Plath asks Sexton to write one of her "newsy letters," as if she had already received such a missive. Did Sexton not make carbon copies of her letters to Plath? We know that Sexton sent Plath a card in 1961 (and she certainly wouldn't have made a carbon copy of a postcard or, God forbid, a Hallmark) and, a year and a half later, a letter? a note? another card? to accompany *All My Pretty Ones*. They were friends, but poet friends, each ambitious and self-absorbed, one of them, at least for the moment, more successful than the other. Sexton was able to have a nurturing and intimate relationship with Maxine Kumin, who lived nearby and was a lesser poet, therefore nonthreatening; Sexton was always the star. Similarly, Plath, when she knew Sexton, posed no threat. Sexton admitted in "The Bar Fly Ought to Sing" that she didn't notice in Plath her determination to succeed, to be a "great writer." "I was too determined to bet on myself," Sexton recalled, "to actually notice where . . . [Plath] was headed in her work" (*NES* 9). After her breakup with Hughes, Plath would begin to develop close friendships with other women, including the poet Ruth Fainlight. I suppose one could say that Plath and Sexton knew each other as well as they could know each other, given the time, given the circumstances, given their personalities. In 1967, Sexton would write to Ted Hughes, the person who knew Plath better than anyone, that, regarding research being done on Plath, she "had little to add. That poem of mine ["Sylvia's Death"] makes everyone think I knew her well, when I only knew her death well" (*SPL* 308).

◆  ◆  ◆

Regardless how well the poets actually knew each other, one thing is certain: they both had had breakdowns and had courted death (*"our* boy," Sexton says possessively in "Sylvia's Death"), and this shared experience drew them to one another, an attraction—moths to the bulb—impossible to resist. Another thing is certain: Plath knew and liked Sexton's poetry. I think it is important to point out that Plath read *All My Pretty Ones* just weeks before beginning to write her *Ariel* poems. Plath wrote no poems between 13 August 1962 (a week before she wrote her letter to Sexton) and the end of September, when she, in essence, kicked Hughes out of Court Green. Alone, she desperately threw herself into her work. On 30 September she wrote "A Birthday Present," the first of her amazing month-long outpouring—twenty-six poems, many of them her most famous, in almost as many days. Of Plath's poems, Sexton declared she didn't "need to sniff them for distant relatives of some sort" (*NES* 11). I, on the other hand, seem to have that need, or perhaps knowing Sexton and Plath's work as well as I do, cannot help but notice resonances. Here are a few:

Sexton:
. . . the brown mole
. . . . . . . . . . . . . . .
[on] my right cheek: a spot of danger
where a bewitched worm ate its way through . . . [my] soul
in search of beauty. (*CP* 66)

Plath:
Soon, soon the flesh
The grave cave ate will be
At home on me
. . . . . . . . . . . . . . .
They had to call and call
And pick the worms off me like sticky pearls. (*Collected Poems* 244, 245)

Sexton:
Oh God,
although I am very sad,
could you please
let these four nuns
loosen from their leather boots
and their wooden chairs
to rise out
over this greasy deck,
out over this iron rail,
nodding their pink heads to one side,
. . . . . . . . . . . . . . .
My dark girls sing for this.

They are going up.
See them rise
on black wings, drinking
the sky, without smiles
or hands
or shoes.
They call back to us
from the gauzy edge of paradise,
*good news, good news.* (CP 82–83, 84)

Plath:
I think I am going up,
I think I may rise—
The beads of hot metal fly, and I, love, I

Am a pure acetylene
Virgin
Attended by roses,

By kisses, by cherubim,
By whatever these pink things mean.
Not you, nor him

Not him, nor him
(My selves dissolving, old whore petticoats)——
To Paradise. (*Collected Poems* 232)

Sexton:
The snow has quietness in it (CP 89)

Plath:
The snow has no voice. (*Collected Poems* 263)

All harmless, probably unconscious echoes. Did the image of the sun as a "hot eye" in Sexton's "To a Friend Whose Work Has Come to Triumph" prompt the "red eye" at the end of "Ariel"? (CP 53; *Collected Poems* 240). Did the mention of "daddy" in the last line of the same poem give Plath her famous title? And did the reference to Lazarus in Sexton's "The Hangman" inspire the title of "Lady Lazarus"?

A more overt example is the way Plath appropriated rhythms, rhymes, and phrases from "My Friend, My Friend," an obscure Sexton poem, for "Daddy." "My Friend, My Friend" was first published in *The Antioch Review* in the summer of 1959 and remained uncollected until 2000, when Diane Middlebrook included it in Sexton's *Selected Poems* (it was not included in Sexton's *Complete Poems* in 1981). The poem, Middlebrook conjectures, "was almost certainly critiqued in [Lowell's] class" (*AS* 105). Plath undoubtedly knew it—and knew it well. In 1987, Heather Cam published a brief essay in *American Literature* called "'Daddy': Sylvia Plath's Debt to Anne Sexton." In it she compares the two poems and delineates their similarities. The first stanza of each poem will give you the general idea:

> Sexton:
> Who will forgive me for the things I do?
> With no special legend or God to refer to,
> With my calm white pedigree, my yankee kin,
> I think it would be better to be a Jew.
> (*Selected Poems* 5)

> Plath:
> You do not do, you do not do
> Any more, black shoe
> In which I have lived like a foot
> For thirty years, poor and white,
> Barely daring to breathe or Achoo.
> (*Collected Poems* 222)

Cam shows how Plath twice alters Sexton's "I think it would be better to be a Jew" line: 1) "I think I may well be a Jew" and 2) "I may be a bit of a Jew"; how Plath borrows the end-rhymes "do," "you," and "Jew," but adds inventive rhymes of her own: "shoe," "Achoo," "blue," "du," "true," "through," "who," and "glue"; and calls special attention to Plath's "gobbledygoo" versus Sexton's "bugaboo." One similarity Cam fails to "sniff" is the reference to white skin in the opening stanza of each poem: Sexton's "calm white pedigree" (repeated later in the poem as "my calm white skin") and Plath's metaphor of herself as a "poor and white" foot.

That Plath pilfered so heavily from one of Sexton's poems, albeit a minor one, is a bit of a revelation. Sexton believed Plath hid her real influences. But Plath always wore her influences on her sleeve. Throughout her work, one can detect traces of her idols (W. H. Auden, Dylan Thomas, Theodore Roethke) as well as her friends and contemporaries (Anne Sexton, Robert Lowell, W. S. Merwin). And, of course, quite prominently, Ted Hughes. In 1961, when Knopf was considering the British edition of *The Colossus* for publication in America, editor Judith Jones asked that Plath cut poems that struck her as "deliberately stolen from Roethke," so much so that she "would almost fear the charge of plagiarism" (Alexander 254). Plath obliged, deleting most of the derivative "Poem for a Birthday" sequence. In "The Bar Fly Ought to Sing," Sexton "remember[s] writing to Sylvia in England after *The Colossus* came out and saying something like: 'if you're not careful, Sylvia, you will out-Roethke Roethke,' and she replied that I had guessed accurately and that he had been a strong influence on her work" (*NES* 10). In her poem "Sylvia's Death," Sexton refers to Plath as a "funny duchess"—a nod, for sure, to "Duchess of Nothing," a line from one of the excised Roethke-influenced pieces in "Poem for a Birthday" (*CP* 128).

On 30 October 1962, just a few days after writing "Ariel" and "Purdah" and putting the finishing touches on "Lady Lazarus," Plath recorded for the British Council in London fifteen of the twenty-six poems she'd written that month. Afterwards, Peter Orr conducted an interview. When asked if there were any themes that attracted her as a poet, Plath had this to say:

> I've been very excited by what I feel is the new breakthrough that came with, say, Robert Lowell's *Life Studies*, this intense breakthrough into very serious, very personal, emotional experience which I feel has been partly taboo. Robert Lowell's poems about his experiences in a mental hospital, for example, interest me very much. These peculiar, private, and taboo subjects, I feel, have been explored in recent American poetry. I think particularly of the poetess Anne Sexton, who writes also about her experiences as a mother, as a mother who's had a nervous breakdown, as an extremely emotional and feeling young woman, and her poems are wonderfully craftsman-like poems and yet they have a kind of emotional and psychological depth which I think is something perhaps quite new, quite exciting. ("1962 Interview")

It was Plath who was now high on her own achievement (she knew that she had done it—written poems that would "make . . . [her] name"), and she could afford to set jealousy aside and be generous, acknowledge the impact Lowell and Sexton had had on her (*Letters Home* 468). They had given her

permission to explore, in her work, "peculiar, private, and taboo subjects."
With the exception of "Lady Lazarus" ("The second time I meant / To last
it out and not come back at all") and "Daddy" ("At twenty I tried to die /
And get back, back, back to you"), the *Ariel* poems do not deal, directly,
with Plath's experiences in a mental hospital, or with nervous breakdown
per se (*Collected Poems* 245, 224). She had already covered that ground in
*The Bell Jar* (1963), which she'd written the previous year. Plus Lowell and
Sexton had been there before her—he in *Life Studies*, she in her Bedlam
poems. Instead, Plath locates us, dead center, in the extreme emotions and
feelings of a young woman who, if not in the throes of a nervous breakdown,
is experiencing intense psychological distress.

The restored edition of *Ariel*, which honors Plath's original selection, dra-
matizes the source of that distress: outraged by Hughes's "desertion . . . and
doubleness," she angrily liberates herself from the relationships that have re-
strained her—husband, dead father, mother—reinventing herself literarily,
in poem after poem, as a man-eating phoenix, as a transcendent whore/
Madonna, as an avenging ("More terrible than she ever was") queen bee
(*Collected Poems* 210, 215). Plath's *Ariel* sequence is not a dead end; on the
contrary, the story it tells leads, ultimately, to emancipation and hope.
Nonetheless, poems such as "Tulips," "Cut," "Poppies in October," and "The
Moon and the Yew Tree" are vivid simulations of a mind that is "not right,"
to quote Robert Lowell. And poems like "Ariel" and "Lady Lazarus," which
triumphantly proclaim Plath's death wish, owe much to Sexton. In her first
two books, Sexton often confesses her desire to die, most purely in "The
Starry Night":

> Oh starry starry night! This is how
> I want to die:
>
> into that rushing beast of the night,
> sucked up by that great dragon, to split
> from my life with no flag,
> no belly,
> no cry. (*CP* 54)

Plath's poem "Ariel" is, in a sense, a response to Sexton's "The Starry Night."
Both are celebrations of the suicidal impulse—that impulse the poets ex-
citedly shared over martinis at the Ritz. Whereas Sexton describes Vincent

van Gogh's famous painting and projects her death wish onto the scene, Plath is an active participant in the action: riding her horse at sunrise, she imagines dissolving, physically, and "flies / Suicidal at one with the drive / Into the red // Eye, the cauldron of morning" (*Collected Poems* 240). Sexton's moon rebukes, "push[es] children, like a god, from its eye"; Plath's rider ("God's lioness") sails like an arrow straight into the sun's red eye (*CP* 54; *Collected Poems* 239). You can feel (and surprisingly relate to) the immediacy of Plath's dissolution—her letting go, her own astonishment, and then her glee; Sexton's death, though wished for, is kept from her—it is a desire locked in the painting. And because "Ariel" takes place at daybreak, Plath's suicidal vanishing act seems like a beginning, a renewal, compared to the negation of Sexton's silent "split." Plath's tone is proud and empowered, the effect heroic. She clearly surpasses Sexton here: utilizes her own (rather than someone else's) imagery; fully realizes the emotional experience for herself and the reader; risks and accomplishes more.

◆ ◆ ◆

In the Orr interview, Plath mentions Sexton's poems about motherhood. She could only have known two: "The Double Image" (the heartfelt sequence addressed to Sexton's daughter Joy, which had been workshopped in Lowell's class and published in *To Bedlam and Part Way Back*) and "The Fortress" (a tender poem about taking a nap with her daughter Linda, which Plath would have read first in the *New Yorker*, then in *All My Pretty Ones*). It is easy to imagine how these might have inspired Plath to write such poems as "Magi" (a feminist statement about her newborn daughter, which Plath intended to be included in *Ariel*, but which Hughes cut), "Parliament Hill Fields" (a poem about her miscarriage—which occurred, incidentally, on 6 February 1961, the day after Plath wrote Sexton praising *To Bedlam and Part Way Back*; she wrote the poem just five days after she miscarried), and "Morning Song" (addressed to her daughter and written a week after "Parliament Hill Fields"; it would be the opening poem in *Ariel*). Once Plath and Hughes's marriage dissolved, motherhood—or finding herself a single mother—became one of Plath's great themes. She wrote "For a Fatherless Son" before Hughes officially moved out of Court Green. Then, in the midst of the *Ariel* poems, she wrote "By Candlelight," "Nick and the Candlestick," and "The Night Dances"—also addressed to her nine-month-old son.

Both Plath (in "Nick and the Candlestick") and Sexton (in "The Fortress") express concern for the safety of their children, given the dangers that exist in the outside world. "Darling," says Sexton, "life is not in my hands; / life with its terrible changes / will take you"; take her, Sexton then envisions, via bomb or cancer (*CP* 67). "Love, love," says Plath, "I have hung our cave with roses, / With soft rugs—/ The last of Victoriana." She knows delicate antiquities will not "ward off the world's ills"; still she implores, "Let the stars / Plummet to their dark address, / Let the mercuric / Atoms that cripple drip / Into the terrible well" (*Collected Poems* 241, 294, 241–42). Sexton's poem captures a calm, loving moment: mother and daughter napping under a pink quilt, trees and birds in the window. Plath wakes in the dark and by candlelight tends to her son; instead of a sweet nursery scene, we're taken underground, into a cave where "Black bat airs / Wrap [her], raggy shawls, / Cold homicides," where a fish mobile becomes "A vice of knives, / A piranha / Religion, drinking // Its first communion out of my live toes," where "The pain / You wake to is not yours" (240–41). Different poets, different situations.

The first two poems in *All My Pretty Ones* ("The Truth the Dead Know" and the title poem) are both elegies to Sexton's father. Her father is also characterized, in "The House," as a lecherous alcoholic. One can almost miss (I did for many years) the importance of this moment in Sexton. Her father's face is "bloated and pink / with black market scotch"; "His mouth is as wide as his kiss." The climax of the poem, a suicidal declaration ("*Father, father, I wish I were dead*"), is directly related to "the bender that she kissed last night" (*CP* 72, 74). Diane Middlebrook is uncertain whether such incestuous depictions were true—were they based on Sexton's memories or her fantasies? True or not, a similar kiss is described at the end of the last poem in *Transformations*, "Briar Rose (Sleeping Beauty)." The whole book, which turns Grimm fairy tales on their head, leads to this final dark admission:

It's not the prince at all,
but my father
drunkenly bent over my bed,
circling the abyss like a shark,
my father thick upon me
like some sleeping jellyfish. (294)

Later, in *The Book of Folly*, Sexton is more graphic. While dancing with her father at her cousin's wedding, her father has an erection: "The serpent, that mocker, woke up and pressed against me." When they kiss, his tongue "like a red worm ... crawled right in." But Sexton never expresses anger at her father; rather, she seems resigned to "swallow[ing] down his whiskey breath" and concludes her "Death of the Fathers" sequence with a kind of metaphorical affection: "Father, / we are two birds on fire" (324, 328, 332). Of course Plath did not read *Transformations* or *The Book of Folly*. But she did read "The House" and she did read the elegy "All My Pretty Ones," in which Sexton claims that she forgives her father, though she doesn't tell us what she forgives him for. She calls him "my drunkard" and refers to his "alcoholic tendency." The poem ends, oddly enough, with Sexton bending down her "strange face" to kiss the image of her father (51). In interview she admitted "it's ... a kind of sexual thing there" (*NES* 49). She also said that she had not actually forgiven her father; she'd only written that she had.

Anger is, in a way, the ingredient that is missing from Sexton's early poems; she would learn, from *Ariel*, how to more openly channel such emotion into her work. And anger is, in a way, the thing that is unique to Plath, her contribution to the poetic dialogue she was engaged in, the way she extends, adds to what Lowell and Sexton had confessed before her. For Plath, forgiveness is not an issue: she is fighting back with the only weapon she has; she wants to wound. Father, mother, husband, husband's lover, husband's uncle, older female poet, eavesdropping neighbor—Plath fires furious poems at them all. It is an exhilarating spate of poems, one that, from Plath's point of view, seems justified. Naturally Hughes received the brunt of her fury: at least half of the poems in her version of *Ariel* are directly or indirectly aimed at him. Though now in book form, it is impossible to read Plath's *Ariel* the way she intended it to be read, impossible to experience it as it would have been experienced then, in the sixties and seventies, as an incipient feminist text. In this way, I think her version will always remain lost to us.

I like to believe that, had she lived and published *Ariel*, Plath would have been as influential a figure as Adrienne Rich, only wittier, and less stringent. When Plath edited a selection of American poetry for *Critical Quarterly* in 1961, she included Sexton, Starbuck, Merwin, Rich, and Snodgrass, but also included Barbara Guest, Denise Levertov, and Robert Creeley. In her introduction she says that she wanted to include Gregory Corso as well, but could not obtain permission. This shows how open she was to different kinds of writing—to poets associated with the Beat movement, with the New York and Black Mountain schools. Based on this, I also like to believe that she would have been receptive to and inspired by much of the poetry that emerged in the decades after her death.

♦ ♦ ♦

Sexton's work opened doors for Plath; after her suicide, Plath's work did the same for Sexton—up to a point. Plath died when Sexton was well into—about halfway—her third book, *Live or Die*. The poems in *Live or Die* are dated and arranged chronologically, so we see, thanks to the poem "Sylvia's Death," exactly where that death falls. *Live or Die* is the first book in what I would call Sexton's middle period—where she begins to let go of the formal strategies that dominated her first two books, and to write looser, longer poems. A number of poems prior to "Sylvia's Death" retain the rhyme schemes and visual order (tidy, identical stanzas) that Sexton was fond of, but a number of them—like "Flee on Your Donkey," "Those Times . . . [,]" and "To Lose the Earth"—are composed in this freer, more expansive style.

After "Sylvia's Death," Sexton abandons rhyme (with one exception) and writes the rest of the poems in *Live or Die* in her new mode. These poems span the next three years—from February 1963 to February 1966. In this period, dashes and exclamation marks (abundant in Plath's *Ariel* poems) abound in Sexton as well. Skimming through the second half of *Live or Die*, you can see these punctuation marks increase; it is as if we can witness Sexton becoming more and more familiar with Plath's last poems—and responding to them in her own. Many of Plath's poems appeared in magazines in the years following her death ("Fever 103°," "Purdah," and "Eavesdropper," for instance, were published in the August 1963 issue of *Poetry* magazine); Sexton would have read them as they came out, and there would have been discussion of them in Sexton's poetry circle.

"Cripples and Other Stories," the one rhymed poem in the second half of *Live or Die*, written in October 1965, is sing-songy, self-mocking, and deliberately lewd—a far cry from Sexton's previous impeccability when using form. (In fact Sexton will never, from this point forward, be able to return to rhyme schemes with her earlier seriousness.) She lets us know, at the beginning of "Cripples and Other Stories," that she is using "silly rhymes"; this enables the reader to get into the spirit of the piece:

> God damn it, father-doctor.
> I'm really thirty-six.
> I see dead rats in the toilet.
> I'm one of the lunatics.
>
> Disgusted, mother put me
> on the potty. She was good at this.
> My father was fat on scotch.
> It leaked from every orifice. (CP 160–61)

Toward the end of the poem, Sexton gives us the following stanza:

> My cheeks blossomed with maggots.
> I picked at them like pearls.
> I covered them with pancake.
> I wound my hair in curls. (162)

An obvious rip-off of "Lady Lazarus": "They had to call and call / And pick the worms off me like sticky pearls." But because she is making fun of herself (and her fixation with Plath), Sexton gets away with it.

"Live," the final poem in *Live or Die*, ends with one of Sexton's first Nazi references and points toward a tendency Sexton will later abuse:

> . . . in spite of cruelty
> and the stuffed railroad cars for the ovens,
> I am not what I expected. Not an Eichmann.
> The poison just didn't take. (170)

Here Sexton is mimicking the Nazi imagery that Plath employed and which so shocked (and surely continues to shock) first readers of *Ariel*. The representation of Plath's father, in "Daddy," as a "Panzer-man," and of Hughes as a "man in black with a Meinkampf look," and of Plath as a concentration camp victim in that poem as well as in "Lady Lazarus," are a few of the most famous examples.

What Sexton most admired about the *Ariel* poems, she tells us in "The Bar Fly Ought to Sing," is Plath's "openness to metaphor, the way

[she] . . . jump[s] straight into [her] . . . own image and then believ[es] it"
(*NES* 10–11). In *Live or Die* and in her next two books, *Love Poems* (1969)
and *Transformations* (1971), which round out her middle period, Sexton
practiced, and benefited from, this technique. She is able to throw herself
right into a poem, into an image, often to thrilling effect, although more
theatrically than Plath. Sexton, at this stage in her public life, is becoming an
exhibitionist; she is too exaggerated and flamboyant, too aware of an audi-
ence she thinks sees her as "the living Plath"—a comment she once made
to John Malcolm Brinnin. "I was influenced [by Plath] and I don't mind
saying it," Sexton confessed (93). Although envious of Plath's tremendous
posthumous success (Sexton narcissistically felt Plath had robbed her of *her*
suicide), Sexton's own fame grew because of her association with Plath.

Tulips and blood (Plathian images) suddenly make their way into Sex-
ton's poems. "Life rushed to my fingers like a blood clot," she writes in
"The Touch" (*CP* 174). Then in "The Kiss": "My mouth blooms like a cut"
(174). One thinks, naturally, of Plath's poem "Cut," of her lines "A mouth
just bloodied. / Little bloody skirts!," of her "Black sweet blood mouth-
fuls" (*Collected Poems* 203, 239). In "The Breast" Sexton even "ris[es] out of
the ashes" à la Lady Lazarus (*CP* 176). *Ariel* is peppered with tripled words
and phrases: "wars, wars, wars"; "my fear, my fear, my fear"; "that kill, that
kill, that kill." Sexton (remember that Plath called her a "copy-cat" in her
journal) adopts similar repetitions: "his job, his job"; "my head, my head";
"the child in me is dying, dying"; "an offering, an offering"—these just in
the first few *Love Poems*. She not only steals from Plath, she starts to steal
from herself. "No one's alone," she says in "Eighteen Days Without You,"
cannibalizing one of her best-known poems, "The Truth the Dead Know"
(214).

Then there is the Nazi trope. Nazi images appear here and there in *Love
Poems*: "Oh my Nazi, / with your S.S. sky-blue eye," for example (too close
for comfort to Plath's "Aryan eye, bright blue") or "you dragged me off
by your Nazi hook" (187; *Collected Poems* 223; *CP* 207). At first a Sexton-
oholic like myself could forgive her such thefts, and such lapses in taste; she
was, after all, Anne Sexton, and she did have a special, firsthand connec-
tion to Plath. But this Nazi business soon gets out of hand; in Sexton's later
books, the trope appears with increasing frequency. There's "Herr Doktor!"
(spelled with a "k" as in Plath), "that Nazi Mama with her beer and sauer-
kraut," the Nazi in "After Auschwitz" who sautés a baby for breakfast in a

frying pan (302, 351, 432). These are just a few random examples. It becomes embarrassing, to say the least, a kind of *Cabaret* burlesque that, along with other flaws in her deteriorating craft, serves to undermine her entire art.

Most dismal of all is the posthumously published *45 Mercy Street* (1976), which Sexton had yet to finish at the time of her death. I read it with great interest when it was published in 1976; in retrospect, however, I wish it had been suppressed. The section of divorce poems is littered with dreadful Nazi-isms. Sexton, separated from her husband, seems to be play-acting at being Plath: "Mr. Firecracker, / Mr. Panzer-man"; "a gas chamber for the infectious Jew in me"; "I see the killer in him / and he turns on an oven, / an oven, an oven, an oven / and on a pie plate he sticks / in my Yellow Star" (510, 518, 526). I could go on, but it seems pointless, and given my love of Sexton's work, too painful. This is, undeniably, the downside of influence. Sexton's desire to out-Plath Plath undid her in the end. In an attempt to produce her own *Ariel* "at white heat," Sexton wrote *The Awful Rowing Toward God* (1975)—thirty-nine poems—in a mere fifteen days. It is the last book in her third period (which also includes *The Book of Folly* [1972] and *The Death Notebooks* [1974]), characterized by her ribald tone and her slowly unraveling style. Sexton's efforts in this period are not without merit; as Jeffery Conway says, there are still some Lucky Charms there. But who can write a book of poetry in two weeks? The day she corrected the galleys of *The Awful Rowing Toward God*, Sexton committed suicide.

◆ ◆ ◆

When I saw the 2003 movie *Sylvia*, I was disappointed that the filmmakers failed to include a scene of Plath, Sexton, and Starbuck drinking martinis at the Ritz bar. So vividly, thanks to Sexton's "The Bar Fly Ought to Sing," has that scene lived in my imagination. I thought Gwyneth Paltrow made a fairly decent Plath, though the script was awful, and Daniel Craig, who played Ted Hughes, was physically too small for the role. (Sexton once jokingly called Hughes "Ted Huge.") But who could have played Sexton? For a while I thought Mercedes Ruehl could do her justice—but maybe it was just her big brunette hair. Sexton said she and her Ritz cohorts always wished the waiters would mistake them for celebrities, "some strange Hollywood types" (*NES* 7). Plath and Sexton did indeed become celebrities—in the poetry world and beyond. Due, in large part, to the mystique of their brief, intense friendship.

## Works Cited

Alexander, Paul. *Rough Magic: A Biography of Sylvia Plath*. New York: Da Capo Press, 1999. Print.

Cam, Heather. "'Daddy': Sylvia Plath's Debt to Anne Sexton." *American Literature* 59.3 (Oct. 1987): 429–32. Print.

Lowell, Robert. *The Letters of Robert Lowell*. Ed. Saskia Hamilton. 2005 New York: Farrar, Straus and Giroux, 2007. Print.

Middlebrook, Diane Wood. *Anne Sexton: A Biography*. Boston: Houghton Mifflin, 1991. Print.

———. *Her Husband: Hughes and Plath—A Marriage*. New York: Viking, 2003. Print.

Plath, Sylvia. *The Collected Poems*. Ed. Ted Hughes. New York: Harper and Row, 1981. Print.

———. "A 1962 Sylvia Plath Interview with Peter Orr." Cary Nelson. *Modern American Poetry*. U of Illinois at Urbana-Champaign. Web. 10 Nov. 2015. <http://www.english.illinois.edu/maps/poets/m_r/plath/orrinterview.htm>.

———. *Letters Home: Correspondence 1950–1963*. Ed. Aurelia S. Plath. New York: Harper Perennial, 1992. Print.

———. "Nine Letters to Lynne Lawner." *Antaeus* 28 (Winter 1978): 31–51. Print.

Sexton, Anne. *Anne Sexton: A Self-Portrait in Letters*. Ed. Linda Gray Sexton and Lois Ames. Boston: Houghton Mifflin, 1977. Print.

———. *The Complete Poems*. Boston: Houghton Mifflin, 1981. Print.

———. *Selected Poems of Anne Sexton*. Ed. Diane Wood Middlebrook. New York: Mariner Books, 2000. Print.

Spivack, Kathleen. "Poets and Friends." *Anne Sexton: Telling the Tale*. Ed. Steven E. Colburn. Ann Arbor: U of Michigan P, 1988. Print.

## ... 7

## Are We Fake?

Images of Anne Sexton, Twentieth-Century Woman/Poet

KATHLEEN OSSIP

### It is as a poet that she must be remembered

" ... to direct our attention away from the woman and back toward her art. She may hold interest as a cultural phenomenon or 'figure' ... [but] Sexton's importance is and will remain as a poet ..." wrote J. D. McClatchy in his preface to *Anne Sexton: The Artist and Her Critics* (1978), a collection of interviews, reviews, and retrospectives on Sexton.

Thirty years later, I think: Well, yes and no; well, mostly no; no.

The wooden platitude after the death of a flamboyant artist—it's her art that matters, not her biography—is understandable in the context of the time. By 1978, confessional poetry had burnt itself out pretty appallingly.

The survivors with personal connections to the freshly dead poets must have found it unbearable to think that these showy deaths themselves had any cultural value—and McClatchy was a friend of Sexton.

Furthermore, "good" academics and "serious" critics were still living under the constraints imposed by the New Criticism, still dutifully escaping from personality (even if the Confessional poets and, eventually, the mainstream culture had moved far away from such priggishness).

Thirty years later, we can repeat the platitude but we can't believe it. Anne Sexton's biography doesn't merely "matter" as much as her writing; the two can't be separated.

In fact, her life story—what we know of it, what we read of it in her letters, biographies, memoirs, interviews, remember and misremember of it, project onto it—forms an important part of her work, her gift to her readers. The entirety of this gift is precious; lose any of it, and you diminish it all.

Some puritanical readers and critics choose to think that she doesn't "deserve" to get "credit" for an achievement that has nothing to do with hard work at the typewriter and desk. But what matters is our pleasure and enlightenment (end result) not the number of hours put into planning and intention.

If aesthetic intent and achievement were all that mattered in assessing the cultural value of a work, then a brilliant one-off by a poet we know nothing about would be more "important" (more integrated into the minds and hearts of present and future readers) than a "bad" Sexton poem like "The Furies."

Any true lover of poetry knows this simply isn't so. The wrapped package of Sexton's poems, both sparkling and rotten, her life story, her letters, and her comments on her poems, as well as captivating glimpses via photos and video, form her work: her myth. We can't know the poems except as part of that oeuvre. Why should we?

This is a Romantic view of poetry: heightened emotions expressed by an extra-sensitive soul, complete with equivalency of poet and speaker. I come to it through no prejudices, affiliations, theories or axes to grind, only by observing my response to Sexton's work.

In which emotion and aesthetic appreciation are so intertwined that there ought to be a single name for the experience, a fascination with the person and the writing where both are enhanced by the other. Call it love.

Anne Sexton was a poet. Anne Sexton was a woman with a lived life. There ought to be a way to state these two facts the way we experience them when we read her poetry, concurrently, with each fact illuminating and rhyming with the other, one sentence on top of the other with both (or neither?) legible, as audio (the poems) and video (the life) combined.

## We're fake

Thanks to YouTube, we can get a glimpse of Anne Sexton circa 1966, when a public television documentary team filmed her at her home in Weston, Massachusetts.[1]

In the first section of the video, Sexton reads her poem "Menstruation at Forty" in a smoky voice. (This was the poem that *Harper's* critic Louis Simpson called "the straw that broke this camel's back" [qtd. in Pollitt 1].)

She seems thoroughly engaged, closing her eyes at times, at other times throwing coy or dramatic glances at the camera. You can tell how deeply she feels the rhythms of her lines and the assonance of her words, and she hasn't yet perfected (or imperfected) the hamminess that caused her friend Maxine Kumin to dislike her later public readings.

You can see her almost intentionally creating a new, more emotive, personal way of reading, in reaction to the declamatory style used by (male) poets of the generation ahead of hers: listen to Robert Lowell reading "Skunk Hour," for example.[2]

A dog barks. She worries to the director, "Should I let that damn dog in?" But while she's reading, you're a witness to her creating what she called "word magic."

Her husband Kayo hates how she reads poems, she tells the director— "like a minister." You wonder if this isn't an emblem of him resenting her enthusiasm about anything other than himself and their family life. (Now Lowell sounds like a minister.)

She adds, exuberantly, "But you give it kind of a royal touch when you read a poem, I think. I think *everyone* does." She seems genuine, confiding, sincere.

Then Kayo, home from work, hesitates at the door of her office and she becomes someone else:

> [wheedling] Darling, come here, come here, come here, honey [whining] don't be shy about this stupid television camera, [demanding] come here, for me, will you come here, and tell me about it? [as with a balky child] Oh, come on . . . [Kayo says he doesn't know where the camera is] [with anger-clenched jaw] Then say "Where the hell is it?" [sweetly but with venom that would be released if the camera crew weren't there] Honey, don't be camera-shy!

The irritation, even suppressed anger, comes through: he's ruining the impression she wants to make, perhaps of the successful dominant male she (and the rest of American culture) thought they should want.

In the next scene, Sexton appears with Linda, her thirteen-year-old daughter, and undergoes a remarkable series of moods and affectations, playing to the camera. At first, she appears to be counseling her daughter about a problem with a teacher at school:

> ANNE: Now she knows you better (Linda: yeah) [motherly concern and wisdom] Honey but you can't wait for people to know you, you've got to know that some teachers still have problems.... (Linda: I know but I didn't realize, you know . . . Cuz everybody else, you know . . . ) [fond irritation] No, I *don't* know. (Linda: She did it to another girl. . . . ) [fierce maternal protection] Well, she's not going to do it to you again, is she? [They both laugh.]

Another conversation between them is like a catalog of exaggerated feminine attitudes from a 1940s movie. They're discussing a business trip Kayo is taking:

> Linda: [sweetly plaintive, à la young Judy Garland] When is Daddy going to be away?
> Anne: [matter of fact, efficient mom à la Joan Crawford] Daddy's going away next week.
> Linda: [sweetly plaintive] What time and when?
> Anne: [there, there, darling] Monday to Friday.
> Linda: [teenage tragic] Monday to Friday!

There's a quick cut. I wonder what happened in the interval. A guess: Linda expresses anxiety about surviving the week without her father's caretaking—we know from her biography that Kayo usually cooked dinner, for example.

But there's no mention, no hint in the video of Anne's inadequacies as parent and caretaker—she presents herself as a reassuring compassionate maternal laughing loving figure. In fact, though, Linda's worries seem to have ratcheted up Sexton's own anxiety about her on-camera image, as shown in the next scene.

They're at the front door, about to go inside, nuzzling each other:

Anne: We'll make it! . . . [hugs] Are we fake, are we fake?
Linda: [laughing dutifully, a little nervously] Yeah.
Anne: [exuberant, for the cameras and director] Tell them we're fake!
Turn around (to face the camera) and tell them we're fake!
Linda: [nervous, dutiful] We're fake!
Anne: We don't love each other at all, right? We hate each other! We
despise each other! We just can't bear each other! How's the loving
between us?
Linda: Oh my . . . you're funny . . . [all the time laughing self-con-
sciously, she goes in]
Anne: [lingering on camera] It's so easy to be natural . . . when you've
got this. . . . I mean, that's for real! [with the actressy enthusiasm of a
USO girl selling war bonds]

It makes you cringe, like watching your mom sing a pop song in front of
your friends.

It's also hard to watch Anne draping her body over Linda's, in light of
Linda's later memoir, which reported her mother's occasional trips to her
daughter's bed, to cuddle and masturbate.

But watching this scene, my heart breaks for them both.

It was almost impossible to be a woman during that time and not be
fucked up, or faked up, not to spend most of your time being inauthentic.

The gaze and judgment of others was all-important. Nothing encouraged
an inner life, "this inward look that society scorns."

The camera's whirring must have felt like gaze and judgment times 1000.

I remember my mother's nicey-nice voice with an edge, used when "out-
siders" were around, if she felt anything that I or my siblings or my father did
reflected badly on her. I remember my mother prodding me forward with
relatives, with teachers, as if the cure for shyness was to be made ashamed
of one's shyness. At the time, I felt terror about displeasing her and about
her rejection; later, anger; now, sadness, because I realize the terror was hers
too.

## Women of That Generation

My mother's name is Ann. She was born in 1938, ten years after Sexton.

When I look at photos of Sexton in her 30s and 40s, she resembles my mother at the same age: both women are beautiful, with dark hair, fair skin, striking angular features, and tall slim sexy figures.

Like Sexton, my mother didn't go to college; she married young, had babies, and set out on an unexamined path as a housewife and mother.

The parallels should end there. My mother survived her traditional life (which she felt as privilege, not oppression) and in her 70s lives today with my father, her only husband, and enjoys an active and unambitious suburban life in upstate New York.

But different as they were, they were both inescapably *women of that generation*. Subject to the legacy of decades/centuries of devaluing. Subject to a desperation for the approval of others and an emptiness where the inner life should be.

As a bookish girl with mother issues, I'm a natural to feel connected to a writer who looked like my mother. If it's largely based on transference, Anne would understand that.

As someone with an ambivalent relationship with the past, I'm a natural to be obsessed with Anne Sexton, who represents spectacularly so many of the obsessions of the twentieth century.

As someone with an ambivalent relationship with her mother, I was a natural to want to spend time in a "safe" (because written and imaginary, not lived and physical) relationship with Anne Sexton.

I see my young mother not only via memory but also via snapshots, actual photos that exist in actual photo albums in her house. Through them, I tell myself, I understand her and how she affected me.

But the thing about snapshots is that they're posed—they're a presentation of the self as we want others to see us. Sometimes we imagine we can see a war between the neat presentation and the seething interior, but we can't be sure to what extent the subject of the gaze allowed that duality to appear.

I see Anne Sexton through a series of snapshots too, images that appear in her biographies and in my imagination. Except I see her moving through the scenery of her life, the roulette ball tumbling around the wheel, and then—the living image stops, like a freeze frame at the end of a cheesy 1970s movie.

The stills turn out to be emblems of poetdom and womanhood, all jumbled together, of feminine and artistic life in the upper middle-class United States in the third quarter of the twentieth century. These emblems feed my ideas about womanhood and poetdom.

In seeing a real woman, a real artist, through archetypal (stereotypical) images, I'm complicit with the culture that can't see women whole, as complex individuals, but instead fetishizes partial aspects of the feminine, like the various avatars and guises of the Virgin Mary I grew up with: Mater Dolorosa, Queen of Heaven, Our Lady of Lourdes/Fatima/Guadeloupe.

The facets of Mary the Catholic saint shed light on the anxieties of the faithful: birth, grief, death, afterlife.

The facets of Anne Sexton shed light on the anxieties of the twentieth-century United States: class, sex, success, addiction, suicidal depression. None of the images "true," "complete," but in absorbing those images, I absorb Anne, my mother, how they were diminished, how to steer clear.

## Pretty Anne

Like many bookish girls, I read *Little Women* over and over when I was a kid.

Unusual for a bookworm, I never wanted to be Jo, the budding novelist. Instead I fantasized about being Meg, the pretty sister and the one whose desires were cozy with society's expectations of a young woman in her time and place.

Whether or not I could live up to it, that was my ideal; I now understand it was my ideal because it was my mother's ideal. She had bartered her youthful good looks for the best kind of deal she could get: marriage, at age 20, to a man who would provide for her and for their children.

A pretty surface was very important. I had long golden curls, which my parents agreed I should never cut. On the other hand, they didn't encourage an inner life.

Among women poets of her generation, Anne Sexton was the pretty one.

Her good looks were important to her, and she worked them. I think, insecure as she was, she never quite believed in them, but she never quite disbelieved them either.

The circles in which she worked them set a low bar for glamour: Sexton's great friend Maxine Kumin described the effect of Pretty Anne in the first workshop they took together, "the ex-fashion model . . . totally chic" (*NES* 159), "all intimidating sophistication in the chalk-and-wet-overshoes atmosphere of the Boston Center for Adult Education" (qtd. in *AS* 50). (To return the compliment, Sexton labeled Kumin "the most frump of the frumps") (*NES* 159).

That glamour certainly helped her appeal to male mentors like Robert Lowell, W. D. Snodgrass, and many others.

Muriel Rukeyser reports hearing another woman poet say, after Sexton's reading at the Guggenheim Museum, "It's really the distinction between those woman poets who are attractive and those who really aren't, like poor _____, isn't it?"

In a review of *The Book of Folly*, Rukeyser responds, "Well, of course it isn't, but that adheres to the name in its own time, and beyond" (McClatchy 159).

For women in Sexton's own time, it was very much about that distinction, from birth onwards. Good looks conveyed an allure, and that allure bestowed confidence, and that confidence shows as authority in her work, even when she's confessing utter self-abasement.

In that way, the allure lives on beyond its own time.

Sexton enjoyed and profited from her looks; I'm sure she also found ways to turn them into a reason to self-loathe and to loathe others: Would they love me if I weren't pretty?

### Housewife Anne

My mother was a housewife. So was Anne Sexton. Letters show that Sexton at first tried to take this job quite seriously.

But it didn't hold her attention (other-directed tasks never did), and motherhood, which was supposed to hold her attention even more urgently, sent her to her first breakdown.

The problem with being a housewife is that nobody sees you. For my mother, this wasn't so debilitating: she didn't know how to expect more than the audience of her family. For Sexton, being seen was of primary importance; she seems to have been unable to really believe she existed without someone telling her she was a princess.

Not that she was a valuable human being: a princess.

Her understanding of what a princess was seems to have started out, true to her era, as the pretty, cosseted, provided-for daughter, then wife, of a man. (Unpredictably, it later morphed into the crown of being the prettiest, most glamorous, and most successful woman poet around.)

Pretty women who got married in the 1950s had this special problem: before marriage, their prettiness made them successes, but after marriage it mattered not at all—they were household slaves no matter what they looked like.

They turned reflexively to motherhood—the pregnant body made them into a different kind of object of envy with a similar audience reaction; then, after the birth(s), though their drudgery multiplied, they at least had a captive audience in their kids, as well as a target for their rage at being no longer valued.

Linda Sexton's memoirs are evidence that Anne Sexton used her children in both these ways, as did my mother, whose dry Irish wit (in the form of quips that made her children crack up) and Irish temper (in the form of stinging slaps) were the poles of my childhood emotional life.

As a teenager, I often thought that if my mother "worked," had a "career," she would have been more fulfilled, less angry. Looking at the example of Sexton, I'm not sure that's true.

American women of her generation were damaged in a very fundamental way, and the resulting rage didn't fade even after professional fulfillment and recognition—it could never be enough to heal the "shadow [that] mark[ed] my bone" which Sexton wrote about in "The Double Image."

In the poem, the shadow is a bequest from the mother. Anne Sexton turned around and passed it on to her own daughter. People with no power to express their rage at their diminishment will choose the even more powerless as scapegoats. For women, this often meant their daughters, powerless because of both age and gender. So the rage and damage was perpetuated.

Anne Sexton enjoyed her housewife-poet life. In some ways, both realms provided Sexton a place where her lack of impulse control didn't cost her as much as if, say, she had been forced to make her living as a single-gal *Mad Men*-style secretary.

There were aspects of her life that any writer might envy—freedom from having to earn a living, from childcare; material comfort; the almost unlimited patience of family and friends who nursemaided her.

Whether she would have been freer or would have written better under other circumstances . . . ?

## Stupid Anne

My mother wasn't smart, or so family legend had it when I was growing up.

She failed geometry in high school; this fact became a potent symbol for inferiority. My father, an accountant, made much of it, in a "don't bother your pretty head about that" kind of way, but also a "what can you expect from a woman" kind of way.

I got As = I was smart. So was I a (real) woman? This was a puzzle that took quite a bit of pain to solve. But it was the kind of puzzle that doesn't get solved; instead it gets lost or forgotten.

Anne's academic record was unremarkable. There seems never to have been a question of her going to college. Lack of education was a good bet for a girl looking for a husband; a man had to be superior in all ways to his wife.

I knew that my mother prized her non-smartness because she felt it fit her proper feminine role in her relationship with my father. The interior logic seemed to go "If I'm weak, I'll be taken care of. If I'm taken care of, then I'm precious."

Anne and Kayo Sexton enjoyed this logic too. Anne Wilder, Sexton's companion (and lover), reported that, during a 1965 reading tour, Sexton would call her husband every night before going to sleep: "'This is your princess . . .'—like a china doll on a music box" (AS 238).

It makes me wince with understanding: that stance was the only one that could make her feel like a good little girl, and that was all she'd ever been encouraged to be: she counted on it.

Later on, when she was working and traveling in circles that prized education, her lack of it, which the educated are quick to attribute to lack of intelligence, worried her. As late as 1970, she told a friend, "I know so little, just barely enough to write" (qtd. in AS 341).

If she had had more education, her writing would likely have taken different directions; at least she'd have had other options. As it was, she had nothing to dig in but the ground of her own nervous system.

## Classy Anne

Anne Sexton was successful because she came from the upper middle class; she almost innately knew how to milk and grow her initial success because she had absorbed the lessons of her upper middle-class family of prosperous businessmen and socialites.

As with looks, family money, summer homes, and leisure time give a person a baseline feeling of superiority, no matter how inferior, even suicidally depressed, they feel on other counts.

Undoubtedly, Sexton's patrician bearing, good clothes, and innate sense of entitlement attracted the male editors and mentors who "discovered" her (her word, used prolifically) in the early years of her career. Literary circles, then and now, hanker after class, the Ivy League variety and the moneyed variety, with a tug of envy and striving.

Elizabeth Bishop's famous gripe about Sexton, in a letter to Robert Lowell—"That Anne Sexton I think still has a bit too much romanticism and what I think of as the 'our beautiful old silver' school of female writing which is really boasting about how 'nice' *we* were. . . . They have to make quite sure that the reader is not going to misplace them socially, first—and that nervousness interferes constantly with what they think they'd like to say"—sounds like envy to me (*One Art* 386–87).

It was an era of class anxiety, class worship, and class envy. My mother expressed them all when she made it clear, through little frowns and eye-rolls, that she considered her Irish-American family, headed by her father the lawyer, superior to my father's Italian-American family, headed by his father the candy-store owner.

Anne had some of the same snobbishness: she scorned her move, as a married woman, to "the asshole of Newton, [Massachusetts]," away from classier Wellesley, where she had grown up. Later, when she and Kayo were financially able to move to a "better" neighborhood, they did.

Women of that generation were hyperaware of class distinctions, which were many and subtle. As Sexton moved from her haut-bourgeois background to literary and academic sets, she began to worry about being perceived as Classless Anne: in a letter to Snodgrass after meeting Frederick Morgan, the editor of *The Hudson Review*, for the first time, she wrote, "I might have axed myself—but I don't think I did" (*SPL* 50).

(Morgan reported that he liked her very much although she "didn't have a great deal of culture") (*AS* 95–96).

In some ways, Anne was well-equipped to deal with attitudes like Morgan's: she had her looks, financial security, and the example of her sales executive father's "glad-handing" to bolster her. It's easy to imagine, for example, a working-class man of equal talent but equally limited education having a very different experience with editors and other tastemakers.

Remembering the manic, controlling performance for the documentary cameras, though, you understand the ever-present alcohol and tranquilizers she relied on to make the public part of her literary career possible.

## Dead Anne

"A woman *is* her mother. / That's the main thing" (*CP* 77). Becoming a woman is a fraught task, turning from our mothers as we try to remake ourselves in and against their images.

If I now draw parallels between Sexton the woman and my mother, Sexton the poet was at one point in my life an alter-ego.

Like many young women, I began my relationship with Anne because I was drawn to her as a suicidal poet.

I wasn't suicidal, though I was afraid I might become so, and I was a latecomer. I didn't find my way to Anne until the last years of her century. I had my own little quarter-life crisis, a less flamboyant version of her breakdown and breakthrough.

I couldn't afford flamboyance. A working-class upbringing at least provides you with the survival-hope, rather than a death wish, praying to live rather than wanting to die, because your survival depends on your own sanity and effort.

After college, I was working in publishing, successfully but unhappily, with a mean boss and stress-making expectations. I got through the days with a mask of friendliness and civility, and cried every night because my life was so different from what I felt it should be.

I didn't know at the time that I could be "a writer"; that was a luxury a wage-slave couldn't dream of and an authority that a sobbing mess on the bathroom floor couldn't grasp. This was as near to a breakdown as I could come and still keep earning my paycheck.

I also didn't see how I could ever be a mother. Would I be a mother like my mother? Was I willing to inflict all that pain on another human being? On myself?

What was I sobbing about? Gender, class, depression, art.

On the weekends, I would walk to the Donnell Library on 53rd Street and read every poetry book I could find, something I had never done before in my life and felt to be outside of my control, a calling or compulsion. Anne Sexton was one of the poets I discovered at that time, a delayed adolescence.

Anne Sexton described the moment when she first realized she was a poet, watching an educational television program on sonnets: "I thought, well I could do that" (qtd. in *AS* 42).

Devouring my library poetry books, I also eventually came to the "I could do that too" moment, after my husband picked me up off the bathroom floor and found me a psychotherapist.

Anne Sexton's poetry attracted me because she had a lifelong taste for suicide and because she ended as a successful suicide. I dislike this fact but it's undeniable. With Sylvia Plath, her deathly sister, she was the model of the woman poet in the chapel perilous, who saw the light of truth too blinding to survive.

As a mother now myself, the mother of a daughter, I don't know how to justify my love for suicidal poetry, or anyone's love for it.

Seeing and expressing the truth kills you? Women poets are more interesting and more successful when they're dead, particularly if they kill themselves? When you're angry at reality, the most notable response is to kill yourself? The "real self" is always the darkest and most self-destructive part of you? "The woman is perfected"?

I remember in my non-suicidal but very profound misery encountering Sexton's poetry for the first time. There was an exhilaration in recognizing that something beautiful and significant and moving could come out of misery. There was a relief in knowing that someone of value (a poet, a label I never dreamed of applying to myself) had been equally miserable, equally unable to find a place of grace for herself in her conception of the world.

I didn't need to carry this through to its logical conclusion (suicide's a good idea); the extreme expression, in the poems, of feelings I felt akin to was enough—pure catharsis, pure pity and terror, then expurgation.

There was also, I think, an atavistic thrill to Poe's old saw: "The death then of a beautiful woman is unquestionably the most poetical topic in the world . . ."

Extremes are sexy, especially when embodied by a good-looking woman of childbearing years. Sexton never got old. The intersection of fertility (sex) and death is primitive and enthralling.

Unlike Plath, who had a corpse-obsession, Sexton's body is always vibrantly alive in her poems, so her death wish seems more like a wish for drama, for more life. Her actual death is presented with the accoutrements of the good life (cool car, suburban garage, fur coat) as opposed to Plath's sealed-tomb kitchen and morgue-slab oven rack.

The dual reasons given in her biography for the final successful act—unbearable loneliness after exhausting the support of many friends and family members plus fear that she was "losing her gift"—suggest that she didn't want to escape life, but she couldn't face a diminished life, a death-in-life.

## It is as a poet that she must be remembered

When I read real-time reviews of Sexton's books, I want to call an immediate and permanent halt on the reviewing of poetry books until the poet is dead for fifty years.

Poetry that is truly new and ongoing would seem to call on its readers to appreciate what they can't fully understand—and this challenge seems beyond most critics and reviewers, whose job description says "pin it down."

The review of *45 Mercy Street* by Patricia Meyer Spacks, for example, from the *New York Times Book Review*, consists of one staggeringly irrelevant and misguided judgment after another.

"The second book too (*All My Pretty Ones*, 1962) has its telling moments, particularly when the poet functions as observer ('Woman with Girdle,' 'Housewife') rather than self-devouring subject of the work."

(Anne Sexton was the subject of her most compelling poems.)

"In a sense, Anne Sexton can be seen as a victim of an era in which it has become easy to dramatize self-indulgence, stylish to invent unexpected imagery regardless of its relevance, fashionable to be a woman and as a woman display one's misery."

(Anne Sexton created the fashion and style Spacks is referring to, and it wasn't easy personally or professionally. If she was a "victim of her era," that victimhood manifested more in her life than in her work.)

Fakeness is part of Anne Sexton's poetic myth. The story goes: Beautiful, brilliant young woman is forced by repressive society into stifling domestic situation; she goes mad and is released into her real self, to speak the truth about her life.

So, partly fake by her own doing, she was also faked by reviewers during her life and faked by her readers and mythifiers to this day.

I suppose the myth means well, but it's a pretty dumb story. It is, though, a partial story that serves some readers at some point in their lives, and that's the way it worked for me. When I needed to hitch a wagon to that myth, I did; and when it was time to separate from it, I did.

What is Sexton's "lasting value," as the critics like to ask?

I've attained the critical mass of mortality: many people I love have died, and I've come to the consciousness of natural, inevitable death. I know almost all the time that I'm going to die; I'm all the more conscious of the sweetness of life (and less conscious of its pain). I no longer feel the allure of Sexton's death wish.

There's nothing good about ill-timed death; that poetry glamorizes it disturbs me. I think, "Didn't she know she was going to die anyway?"

One of the things that still attracts me to Anne's work is not her ending, but her beginning: she can be seen as the only 20th-century "major" poet who began writing poetry naively, purely.

Her early work was perhaps the last intersection of poetry and the mainstream culture in the United States—as opposed to her contemporaries and those who came after, who set out to become poets through doors marked "Bohemian" or "Academic" or "Intelligentsia," propelled by (along with love of poetry) careerist or social motivations.

That story of her watching the sonnet show, the aha moment—joy of poetry, the gift sparked, pure: an escape from fakeness. At first.

This purity shows in her work, especially in *To Bedlam and Part Way Back* (1960) and *All My Pretty Ones* (1962). Among the poems I love, still and seemingly for always, are "Music Swims Back to Me," "The Double Image," "The Division of Parts," "The Truth the Dead Know," "With Mercy for the Greedy," and "The Fortress."

*Live or Die* (1966) has moments of great authenticity ("Wanting to Die," "A Little Uncomplicated Hymn"), but it also has that programmatic feel-good ending: "I say *Live, Live* because of the sun, / the dream, the excitable gift" (CP 170).

In *Love Poems* (1969) the flavor of careerism is present, but her devotion to craft was still strong enough to produce some lovely work. By

*Transformations* (1971), she was a brand and had to produce, inspiration or not, craft or not: that shows in the formulaic poems.

In later poems (in my opinion, most of those from *The Book of Folly* on, although I do remain a sucker for any rhymed poem she ever wrote), addiction, aging, and loneliness had pushed her into another kind of desperation. Some of the poems again seem genuine rather than willed, but the sheen, the craft, are gone; she was either psychotic or feigning psychosis as the only thing left that could buy her attention, probably a combination of both.

Sexton's poems from her first two books have the clarity and timelessness and essential femininity of ninth- and tenth-century Japanese courtesans' poetry,[3] and finally, it's these Japanese poets that seem like Anne's closest peers, not Plath, not the other Confessional poets, not Sexton's feminist/memoiristic descendants.

Sexton's poems and the poems of these Japanese women poets are affecting for the same reason: they're spoken by women from cultures where their only social roles were to be and to feel. We see this, rightly, as oppression.

But being and feeling are two of poetry's grand subjects. In Sexton's case, a set of circumstances forced or allowed her to focus her energy, her powers of observation, her innate emotional intuition (which seems to have had the power to leap directly from sensation to metaphor) on remaking her life in words.

These circumstances didn't leave her much of a cushion between herself and her demons, didn't allow her to develop into emotional maturity—but did allow her to feel and to be without the distraction of humdrum tasks like being an effective parent, partner, or adult.

When she began, at her best, she was writing to figure out her life against long odds, not merely expose it, and that task seemed vital. Her life depended on it. This is my favorite kind of poetry.

The ability to pay a certain type of intense, concentrated attention to one's own life, and the ability to articulate, thrillingly, what one finds—without blurring, universalizing, or deferring to received concepts and narratives—is a rare and genuine gift.

Anne Sexton doesn't mean as much to me as she used to, but then my mother doesn't loom as large as she once did either. I love Sexton because of the associative chimes that happen between her poems, the emotional history of the century I was born in, and the work I do now: "my kitchen, your kitchen, / my face, your face" (*CP* 35).

## Notes

1. "Anne Sexton at Home 1 (VOSE)," web. 5 Nov. 2015, <http://www.youtube.com/watch?v=L4VlcVfgFJk&feature=related>.

2. Robert Lowell, "Skunk Hour," web. 5 Nov. 2015, <https://www.poets.org/poetsorg/poem/skunk-hour>.

3. See, for example, *The Ink Dark Moon: Love Poems by Onono Komachi and Izumi Shikibu.*

## Works Cited

Bishop, Elizabeth. *One Art: Letters.* Ed. Robert Giroux. New York: Farrar, Straus and Giroux, 1994. Print.

Gray Sexton, Linda. *Searching for Mercy Street: My Journey Back to My Mother, Anne Sexton.* Berkeley, CA: Counterpoint, 1994. Print.

Kalstone, David. *Becoming a Poet: Elizabeth Bishop with Marianne Moore and Robert Lowell.* New York: Farrar, Straus and Giroux, 1989. Print.

Komachi, Onono, and Izumi Shikibu. *The Ink Dark Moon: Love Poems by Onono Komachi and Izumi Shikibu, Women of the Ancient Court of Japan.* Trans. Jane Hirshfield with Mariko Aratani. Vintage Classics. New York: Vintage, 1990. Print.

McClatchy, J. D. Preface. *Anne Sexton: The Artist and Her Critics.* Ed. J. D. McClatchy. Bloomington: Indiana UP, 1978. Print.

Middlebrook, Diane Wood. *Anne Sexton: A Biography.* Boston: Houghton Mifflin, 1991. Print.

Plath, Sylvia. *The Collected Poems.* New York: Harper and Row, 1981. Print.

Poe, Edgar Allan. "The Philosophy of Criticism." *Great Short Works of Edgar Allan Poe: Poems, Tales, Criticism.* Ed. Gary Richard Thompson. New York: Harper Perennial, 2004. Print.

Pollitt, Katha. "The Death Is Not the Life." *New York Times.* 18 Aug. 1991. Web. Accessed 5 May 2016 <http://www.nytimes.com/1991/08/18/books/the-death-is-not-the-life.html>.

Rukeyser, Muriel. "On The Book of Folly." *Anne Sexton: The Artist and Her Critics.* Ed. J. D. McClatchy. Bloomington: Indiana UP, 1978. Print.

Sexton, Anne. *The Complete Poems.* Boston: Houghton Mifflin, 1981. Print.

Spacks, Patricia Meyer. "On *45 Mercy Street*." *Anne Sexton: The Artist and Her Critics.* Ed. J. D. McClatchy. Bloomington: Indiana UP, 1978. Print.

## The Poet Has Collapsed

### Coming to Terms with Anne Sexton's Late Poetics and Public Persona

JEFFERY CONWAY

> Is there some way to ride to old age and to fame and acceptance
> And pride in oneself and the knowledge society approves one
> Without getting lousier and lousier and depleted of talent?
>
> Kenneth Koch, "The Art of Poetry"

Anne Sexton was a brilliant poet. She was also a big mess. And thank God, for where there is no messiness, there is, ultimately, no interest. Great poets like Sexton allow themselves to let it all hang out—by wearing a striking Pucci-esque halter dress to a reading, by confessing secrets, and by letting whatever springs forth from her mind to land, unfiltered, right on the page (*splat*). There is no denying that many of Sexton's early poems, in *To Bedlam and Part Way Back* (1960) and *All My Pretty Ones* (1962), are works of sheer genius. Chiseled, intense, hand-wrought, exact—these are a few words that come instantly to mind.

Her poetic zenith, it has always seemed to me, is *Live or Die*, published in 1966. The poems are less constrained than earlier ones; there is an energy, an openness about them that draws me in. The poems are personal: they deal with the poet's familial relationships, her drug addiction, her pernicious Thanatos. Sexton's later poems are also intriguing, albeit for somewhat different reasons. *Après*-Pulitzer, her work begins a long slow slide toward mediocrity and a rather campy awfulness. Yet, amidst that rubble, there are some lucky charms to be found—moments of brilliance—that not only evoke the earlier poems but also declare, in a new way, Sexton's unique nakedness.

Interestingly, as the poems in Sexton's oeuvre deteriorate over time, they also announce "Late Sexton" as the true possessed witch younger Sexton wrote about in "Her Kind"—though perhaps the demons multiply, or "change wigs." There is, too, the poet's irresistible persona: genius, mother, housewife (with dark flip hairdo, long Salem cig protruding from what *must* have been hyper-orange lips, smoky voice, swirly-print shift) enjoying fame and success, and at the same time, a fragile woman struggling with addiction and suicidal tendencies. Sexton was bigger than life, and we love her for it. It is that largesse, though, that overshadows her later work, weakens it, and in the end leaves it overblown in a way that both repels *and* thrills.

My own introduction to Sexton was in a college poetry seminar. The professor handed out anonymous poems, poems she had typed, leaving out line breaks. They looked like blocks of prose. My task was to "re-write" one of the poems by putting it back into lines. I knew that I was working with a poem from the canon, but I did not know the author. Regardless, I was drawn to the imagery and language of the poem, and I felt a deep connection to the lines as I arranged them. The professor revealed the poem ("Your Face on the Dog's Neck"), and I compared my line breaks with the poet's. As an exercise, it was a good way to observe choices, to notice patterns, intent, et cetera. The real news for me was the discovery of Anne Sexton. Shortly after that class, I purchased *Live or Die* and read it over and over for weeks.

As poetry students are wont to do, I just had to read *all* of my new hero's work: I purchased *The Complete Poems* at a chain bookstore. In the years that followed, I re-read and studied the single collections included in the book. As best I can recollect, my first impression of the poems in later Sexton books (*The Book of Folly* [1972], *The Death Notebooks* [1974], *The Awful Rowing Toward God* [1975], and *45 Mercy Street* [a book in process at the time of her death but one which Sexton did not see to press; it was published in 1976]) was that they were definitely different from her earlier poems: surreal; looser; and just a bit, well, kooky in places.

That was in the late eighties. My first memories of discussing late Sexton poems as being "bad" are from the early nineties. I remember one particular occasion when I attended an "Anne Sexton birthday party." A group of friends got together on November 9th to celebrate and read Sexton poems aloud, share favorites. We also read some of the "bad" later poems, looking at each other from time to time, dumbfounded: *What was she thinking?* Around this same period, Diane Wood Middlebrook's biography of Anne Sexton was released. I remember overhearing a conversation between two guys at a gym in Provincetown, Massachusetts. They were cackling over the revelation in the book that Sexton had used money from a Radcliffe Scholars honorarium to pay for an in-ground backyard swimming pool. This fact (that someone "literary" would spend poetry grant money on a pool) added to the notion that Sexton was bigger than life, a little outrageous. In short, she was kind of a diva.

Once, I almost came to blows with an inflamed cater waiter I was working a party with; we sparred over the merits of late Sexton. He: *That's when she's most brilliant and raw.* Me: *Come on, "I flee. I flee. I block my ears and eat salami"? It's so* bad *it's* good—*I'll give you that much!* By then, I was listening constantly to the audiotape of Sexton reading her poems, which had become available in 1993. I was able to memorize whole poems, perfectly imitating her smoky voice and inflections as I relished her stagey reading style.

I was addicted to the concept of "Bad Anne." On Thanksgiving in 1999, snug in a little cottage in Upstate New York, my friend David Trinidad and I stayed awake late into the night (we were collaborating on "Chain Chain Chain," a one-hundred-stanza renga), chortling gleefully as we sent upside-down Bad Anne lines via email to Lynn Crosbie, the third collaborator: "Hep ap e7 'po6 we I 'sooq hueW 'sooq hueW" ("Many boos. Many boos. I am god, la de dah") and "S3I7 77V .ON .ON" ("No. No. All lies") ("Chain Chain Chain" 187). In a subsequent collaboration, *Phoebe 2002: An Essay in Verse*, Trinidad and I transformed the set of the Sarah Siddons Society in the film *All About Eve* into a *Laugh-In* joke wall. A portrait on the wall behind the character of Eve Harrington swings open:

... a cloud of cigarette smoke plumes

into the room. Anne Sexton, wearing one of her signature halter dresses (swirling black-and-white pattern), one leg wrapped around the other,

obviously stoned, slurs: "This next poem is called "The Little Peasant."
Krr. Krr." (*Phoebe* 2002 460)

A few years ago, in my tiny West Village studio, I sat atop my bed with my
boyfriend (a technologically adroit English PhD) and "mixed" several fa-
vorite Bad Anne lines (sampled from Sexton recordings) with house mu-
sic and disco beats in a GarageBand-type program on his MacBook. Some
highlights: "Miss Sexton went looking for the gods"; "Dybbuk! Dybbuk!";
"Why do I live in this house, who's responsible, eh?" (fading echo effect:
*eh?, eh?, eh?, eh?*). Late Sexton—Bad Anne—has been a steady fascination
for two decades.

I should reiterate that my personal overarching sentiment for Sexton is
one of profound admiration. My assessment of her body of work is that she
is one of the most important, talented poets of modern times. Perhaps it
seems a contradiction that I could express such high esteem and praise for
the poet and her work, while writing that I think her later work is "campy"
or even "bad." In my mind, one does not necessarily preclude the other.
Today I feel at peace with this dichotomy, but that has not always been the
case. Over the years I have struggled with the seeming incongruence be-
tween early Sexton and late Sexton, between brilliant and bad Anne.

Sexton's later work reveals an artist who is, at turns, vulnerable and confi-
dent (perhaps overly so); sloppy and exact; frantic and sedate; original and
redundant; genius and fool. These dichotomies should not be equated with
overall failure; we have the privilege of experiencing the warm, completely
gutsy life of a poet willing to bare all right there on the page. After winning
the Pulitzer Prize for *Live or Die* in 1967, after publishing the intense *Love
Poems* (1969) and the inventive *Transformations* (1971), Sexton spent the
next three years traveling around the country giving emotionally charged
readings, raising two daughters, divorcing husband Kayo, coping with the
mixed blessings of fame, struggling with depression and addiction. These
challenges impacted her writing and her own editorial eye: her work be-
came less critically successful, but the process as a whole provides a picture
of what it meant, for Sexton, to be a famous poet, what it meant for her to
lead a complicated life while staking out a place in the poetry business.

There are three major concerns I grapple with when reading late Sexton.
The first is her overreliance on a handful of tropes, which, after a while, turn

into what could be deemed annoying props—techniques that collapse under the weight of raw genius and the exposed nerve endings of depression, addiction, and emotional binging. The first trope that blips on the radar is the use of parallelism, repetition, and refrains. Structures, certain constructions, individual words, phrases—all are echoed and cloned, again and again, at a frightening pace from *The Book of Folly* onward. Another trope is the use of the demonstratives *that* and *those* to introduce noun phrases. Also, while trudging through Sexton's last few books, beware of epithets! They come left and right and below the belt. Then there's the plethora of honorifics. And finally, the Nazi references and images—vaguely offensive, overblown, and gratuitous.

The sheer number of undeniably bad lines and images, as well as the use of some bizarre figurative language, is the second major concern. Again, the word "campy" comes to mind. Sexton's associations and metaphors spill forth like drunken ramblings, oftentimes to riotous effect. At certain moments, I pause and whisper to myself: *Where was Max?* What is even more disturbing than the loss of Sexton's own critical eye (dimmed by alcohol, prescription drugs, emotional problems, and the high of fame/overconfidence) is the fact that Maxine Kumin (who intimately workshopped Sexton's poems) allowed or even encouraged Sexton to believe in the value of so many bad lines and poems.

The third and last major concern is the issue of Sexton's public persona and the performative aspect of her readings. Middlebrook provides many details, anecdotes, and stories about Sexton's "live to the hilt" ethos—information, I'm convinced, that creates a certain impression of the poet, imparts a glamorous, almost movie-starrish mystique to her life and work. She was a beautiful, sexy woman who possessed a fiery style, as well as fragility; she was a poetic Cinderella, bursting onto the national poetry scene having begun only a few years earlier, teaching herself how to write a sonnet after watching a PBS show on TV between house chores. There is no doubt that many Sexton fans, especially those who came to her work after her death in 1974, experience the poet not only on the page but also vis-à-vis the recordings of Sexton—recordings which became popular twenty years after her death (the first audiobook, titled *Anne Sexton Reads*, was released in 1993; the second, *The Voice of the Poet: Anne Sexton*, in 2000). Her voice on these recordings reveals a multifaceted personality; made at various points in her life, they provide auditory glimpses of a young woman, an older woman, a drunken/stoned woman, a lighthearted woman, a depressed woman. These recordings—especially those from the latter part of her life—shape who Anne Sexton is for listeners and greatly impact their experience of her work.

## Tropes Gone Wild

Parallelism, Repetition, and Refrains (Oh My!)

In "The Ambition Bird," the first poem in *The Book of Folly*, Sexton begins eight consecutive stanzas with "He wants," and uses a parallel structure to list all of the various acts said bird wishes to do. This is a strong poem; the repetition and parallelism on display can hardly be viewed as failures. Other techniques employed in the poem work well. The speaker's voice is confident, the figurative language fresh, and the serious and resolute tone speaks to the subject matter: mortality and "the business of words." The first line, "So it has come to this," an allusion to *Hamlet*, commands attention (*CP* 299). Yet, by the third poem of this same collection, "Oh," the repetition technique already calls too much attention to itself: "See the mark, the pock, the pock!" (303). In the next poem, "Sweeney," repeated words multiply like tribbles: "Lord. Lord"; "Fan, fan"; "Yes. Yes" (304–5). The repetition of words within lines is something that Sexton was fond of from the beginning of her career; she used the technique sparingly and to great effect. But here she is becoming overly enamored of this convention.

At the same time, Sexton begins to rely quite heavily on refrains. This technique made many of her early poems memorable, poems like "Music Swims Back to Me," "Her Kind," and "Little Girl, My String Bean, My Lovely Woman." In "Mother and Daughter," though, repetition runs amok as whole lines repeat in a heavy-handed effort to create a mood-inspiring refrain: "Question you about this" (305). This phrase is repeated in five more lines of the poem. "The Firebombers" struts a parallel structure: "We are America. / We are the coffin fillers. / We are the grocers of death" (308). An easy trick to start a poem with. "Anna Who Was Mad" unearths a treasure trove of laughable dwindling repetitions: "Forgive. Forgive. / Say not I did. / Say not. / Say" (312). Followed in the next stanza by these lines: "Eat me. Eat me up like cream pudding. / Take me in. / Take me. / Take." It does not help that she ends the poem with the same facile tactic: "Write me. / Write" (313).

The first poem in "The Jesus Papers" section, "Jesus Suckles," utilizes a "No" refrain/repetition, a shortcut that betrays the poet's laxness, which will appear in various poems throughout all of Sexton's last collections (337–38). She opens *The Death Notebooks* with "Gods," a poem about her search for a religious connection, and makes a refrain out of her futile search results: "No one" (349). In *The Awful Rowing Toward God*, Sexton uses this trope as a poem title: "Not So. Not So." It reverberates three times in the poem (472–73). In the title poem of *45 Mercy Street*, the "No" refrain appears again (with a twist—as the less emphatic "Not there") in six separate lines (481–83). Wait, this routine is not dead yet—the sixth line of "Bayonet": "No. No" (515). And it is still kicking in two separate lines of "'Daddy' Warbucks": "No. No" and "No. No" (544). At last, in "Demon," Sexton bleeds this "No" trope dry in two separate, consecutive lines: "No. / No" (550).

If repeating words twice within one or two lines doesn't tip off a drowsy reader, not to worry—Sexton begins to repeat words three, even four times, which gives the impression of a stuck record. Consider these "greatest hits" from various poems in *The Death Notebooks*:

never, never
forever, forever
Beware. Beware.
moving deep into (repeated twice in two lines)
I know that much (repeated in three separate lines)
blooming, blooming, blooming (a triple Lutz!)
The sun as red as (repeated three times in three consecutive lines)
touch them (repeated at the end of four lines)
Bury them (repeated in five separate lines)
la de dah (repeated seven times in "Hurry Up Please It's Time")

*The Awful Rowing Toward God* and *45 Mercy Street* are rife with similar examples. Here are the crème de la crème: "And others, others, others"; "Never. Never. Never. Never. Never" (Yes, *five*!); (the return of) "Beware. Beware"; "Many boos. Many boos" (you said it, Anne); "Is it true?" (this serves as the poem's title and appears thirteen times in the poem); "*Baa. Baa. Baa*" (Sexton's talking to sheep here); "and danced and danced and danced" (envision frenetic lamé-clad disco dancers in the catastrophic film *Can't Stop the Music*); and a personal favorite: "was, was, was, was." After chronicling this trope to the bitter end, I have to pose the question: what *was, was, was, was* Anne thinking?

For many years, I assumed that she must have been unaware of the habitual devices in these later poems, that she lost the ability to judge her own work, that she wrote too many books too quickly. But in a 1973 letter to artist friend Barbara Swan, Sexton responds to comments about *The Death Notebooks*: "I am interested in what you said about the nine psalms at the end. I worry about them. I'm afraid they are excessive or maybe just plain bad writing" (Swan 85). This proves that Sexton did question the quality of her writing. She was not blind to the possibility of badness.

## That (Demonstrative) Girl

Another device Sexton grows increasingly fond of is the use of noun phrases introduced by the demonstrative adjectives *that* or *those*. She had flirted with this technique in both *Live or Die* and *Love Poems*, an extension of her usually effective creation of metaphors. But her love affair with the trope really takes off in *The Book of Folly*—"I am drinking cocoa, / that warm brown mama"—as a way of stepping or speeding up her metaphor-making (*CP* 299). So much so, you cannot help but notice how smitten she is with this formula throughout the poems in *The Book of Folly*, *The Death Notebooks*, and *45 Mercy Street*. Eerily (you can almost hear the theme music from the movie *Jaws*), the device is notably absent from *all* poems included in *The Awful Rowing Toward God*—her use of it falls silent before resurfacing in the *45 Mercy Street* collection.

In *The Book of Folly*, Sexton's reliance on her new lover is hard to miss. "Going Gone": "the lips, / those two small bundles" (311). "Dreaming the Breasts": "my milk home, / that delicate asylum" (314); and "your great bells, / those dear white ponies" (315). "The Red Shoes": "their feet, those two beetles" (316). There is a veritable demonstrative body parts fest in "Killing the Spring": "My eyes, those two blue gods"; "My eyes, those sluts, those whores"; "My hands, those touchers, those bears"; "my ears, / those two cold moons" (321, 322). The trope takes a "smelly" turn in "Angels of the Love Affair": "Angel of fire and genitals, do you know slime, / that green mama who first forced me to sing, / who put me first in the latrine, that pantomime / of brown where I was a beggar and she was king?" (332). "Jesus

Raises Up the Harlot" supplies the following (poorly written) unpleasant-ness: "He lanced her twice on each breast, / pushing His thumbs in until the milk ran out, / those two boils of whoredom" (340).

An examination of *The Death Notebooks* and *45 Mercy Street* yields an endless crop of these noun phrases introduced by a demonstrative adjec-tive: [time] "that Nazi Mama"; [death] "that final rocking"; [sand] "that soft smother"; [a father's eyes] "those gun shots, those mean muds"; [a po-tato] "that charm, / that young prince"; [a penis during intercourse] "That theater"; [God] "that washerwoman"; [an abyss of fear] "that God spot"; [a heart] "that witness"; [rose petals] "those mouths of honey"; [mother's milk] "that good sour soup"; [windows] "those sky pieces" (to be fair, that's pretty good); [a brain tumor] "that apple gone sick" (*not* good); [soil] "that great brown flour"; and, the end of the road, [isolation] "that metal house."

## She of the Overused Epithet

Another trope Sexton wears out is her use of epithets. They make their first appearance in the second poem of *The Book of Folly*, "The Doctor of the Heart," where they are used to convey an accusatory tone: "You with the goo on the suction cup. / You with your wires and electrodes"; "You with your zigzag machine" (301). A few poems later, in "Mother and Daughter," we get, "you with your big clock going" (306). In the "Angels of the Love Affair" series, however, this construction morphs into an "epithetal free-for-all," which is then employed in poem after poem in this and in subsequent collections. The device announces itself with great fanfare in "Angel of Fire and Genitals": "Fire woman, you of the ancient flame, you / of the Bunsen burner, you of the candle / you of the blast furnace, you of the barbecue / you of the fierce solar energy" (333).

In "Angel of Blizzards and Blackouts": "You of the snow tires, you of the sugary wings"; and (pronoun shift) "She of the rolls that floated in the air, she of the inlaid / woodwork all greasy with lemon, she of the feather and dust" (335). An inundation, to say the least, of superfluous details. Later, "The Furies" gives us these self-referential lines: "me of the death rattle, me of the magnolias, / me of the sawdust tavern at the city's edge" (364). It is as if Sexton is *avoiding* writing by relying on this meager shorthand. From "Praying on a 707": "You of the bla-bla set" (378). Bla-bla, indeed. In a letter, Sexton said she "always thought the poem stunk" (*SPL* 410). Why, then, did she publish it? From "Hurry Up Please It's Time": "You of the songs, / you of the classroom, / you of the pocketa-pocketa, / you hungry mother, / you spleen baby!" (*CP* 389). The poet simply cannot help herself.

Honorifics "R" Us

*The Book of Folly* ushers in another trope of note: Sexton's use of the honorifics "Mr.," "Mrs.," and "Ms." "Oh" greets us thusly: "Hello? Mrs. Death is here!" (303). In "The Other" we meet "Mr. Doppelgänger" (317). The poet goes name-crazy as she cranks out poems and collections, almost always in a mocking or self-mocking manner, as in "Mrs. Sexton went out looking for the gods" (349). She introduces us to "Mr. Death" in "For Mr. Death Who Stands with His Door Open" (351–52). In one single poem, Sexton's grandfather is referred to as "Mr. Funnyman," "Mr. Nativeman," "Mr. Lectureman," "Mr. Editor," and (this one is good if you are a doctor about to clean an area before surgery) "Mr. Iodineman" (361). "The Furies" gets all Halloween-esque with "Mr. Bone man" and "Mr. Skeleton" (364). "Mrs. Sarcasm" prays on a 707 (379). "Hurry Up Please It's Time" treats us to ten instances of "Ms. Dog"—Sexton's alter ego, God spelled backwards (386–87).

Ms. Dog reappears in *The Awful Rowing Toward God*. Sexton gets her colloquial on—to wit, these lines from "Is It True?": "Ms. Dog, / why is you evil?" (448). The creation of "Ms. Dog" and the dialectical "why is you evil?" could be a tip of the hat to John Berryman's *Dream Songs* (1964), in which he employs the imaginary characters Henry and Mr. Bones as speakers. It is presumed that both are aspects of Berryman himself; if Mr. Bones is not, then perhaps—some critics say, taking their cue from "bones"—he is Death who stalks the poet. Similarly, Sexton's "Ms. Dog" functions as an alter-ego, an abject woman in search of spiritual salvation. The poet exhausts the trope in *45 Mercy Street*. "Mr. God" fails to save her in "Praying to Big Jack" (492). In "Sheep," she addresses "Mr. Ba-Ba," and mixes honorifics with epithets: "you yellow man, / you grease ball of thistles, / you yes sir, yes sir three bags full" (503). Sexton continues to mix tropes in "The Wedlock," and goes out with a bang: "Mr. Firecracker, / Mr. Panzer-man. [appropriated from Sylvia Plath's "Daddy"] / You with your pogo stick, / you with your bag full of jokes" (510).

*Frau* Poet!

The most problematic "trope gone wild" in Sexton's later work is her determination to employ distasteful Nazi imagery and references. As David Trinidad has pointed out, it is almost as if Sexton was trying to "out-Plath" Sylvia Plath, who had introduced Nazi imagery (judiciously) in her *Ariel* poems (29). Although Sexton used a couple of Nazi images in *Love Poems*— "Oh my Nazi, / with your S.S. sky-blue eye" (*CP* 187) and "you dragged me off by your Nazi hook" (207)—by the time she wrote the poems in *45 Mercy Street* she was living in her own private Holocaust.

The trope rears its ugly head in *The Book of Folly*'s "The Doctor of the Heart." Sexton refers to said doctor as "Doktor" in the first line, and later in the poem she injects an emphatic "Herr Doktor!" (301, 302). In "The Hex," she presents a frighteningly odd image of the speaker encountering a "Hitler-mouth psychiatrist climbing / past . . . [her] like an undertaker" on the stairs (313–14). The first Nazi image in *The Death Notebooks* appears in "For Mr. Death Who Stands with His Door Open": "that Nazi Mama with her beer and sauerkraut" (351). Sexton then goes beyond the Valley of the Dolls with a pair of rhyming lines: "I went out popping pills and crying adieu / in my own death camp with my own little Jew" (352). "Hurry Up Please It's Time" provides this gratuitous little jingle: "When mother left the room / and left me in the big black / and sent away my kitty / to be fried in the camps" (390).

Clearly on a Nazi roll, Sexton lets loose. "After Auschwitz": "each Nazi / took, at 8:00 A.M., a baby / and sautéed him for breakfast / in his frying pan" (432). "Praying to Big Jack": "you of the camps, sacking the rejoice out of Germany" (492). "Walking Alone": "and your chin, ever Nazi, ever stubborn" (514). In "The Break Away," Sexton imagines "a gas chamber for the infectious Jew in me" (518). Things turn psychedelic in "The Stand-Ins" ("the swastika is neon") and overheat ("he turns on an oven, / an oven, an oven, an oven") (526). Sexton's speaker in "Killing the Love" commits a Nazi-like crime: "The Camp we directed? / I have gassed the campers" (529). The despondent speaker of "The Lost Lie" "roam[s] a dead house, / a frozen kitchen," and "a bedroom / like a gas chamber" (533). Finally (and thankfully), the speaker of "'Daddy' Warbucks" suffers a metaphorical death after "swallowing the Nazi-Jap-animal" (544). Perhaps a fitting end for this particularly troublesome trope.

## The Fright Wig

The second major concern in late Sexton hinges, oddly enough, on a wig. If a reader can't see the *awfulness* in these lines of "The Lost Lie" in *45 Mercy Street*, "Oh love, / the terror, / the fright wig, / that your dear curly head / was, was, was, was" (533), then any conversation about the *undeniably bad lines and images, as well as the use of some bizarre (sometimes comical) figurative language* is moot. There is something spooky about this "fright wig," so Warhol peering out from beneath his spiky rug. There is something shocking and wonderfully bad about the image (and let's not even revisit the quadruple "was")—it makes me laugh every time I read it. Perhaps my own sensibility damns me; my reaction to this image (and others like it) is predictable, given my penchant for the absurd, the bad, the campy. I know I'm not alone. I have a few friends who, over the years, have pointed to their own findings, offering up gems like these two lines in "Mary's Song": "I will give suck to all / but they will go hungry" (382).

There is a particularly graphic image in *The Book of Folly* that always makes me think of poor little Regan in *The Exorcist*, projectile vomiting that green goo at handsome Father Dyer: "When truth comes spilling out like peas / it hangs up the phone" (317). The personification of truth hanging up a phone makes it even weirder, cartoonish. And seriously, if you read "The One Legged Man" just as it is written, even *without* a camp sensibility, you are still left with a pretty hilarious scenario: a man loses his artificial leg, and he writes it letters, feeds it supper, strokes it like a woman. Picture it. Take it in. Let's move on.

*The Death Notebooks* is teeming with similar bad lines and images. In "Baby Picture": "I crouch there, sitting dumbly / pushing enemas out like ice cream" (363). Yuk. In "The Fury of Sunsets": "why am I here? / why do I live in this house? / who's responsible? / eh?" (376). A bewildered, moonshined Granny (from *The Beverly Hillbillies*) comes to mind. In "Hurry Up Please It's Time": "I am cramming in the sugar" (386); "I am God, la de dah" (386); and (the pièce de résistance) "To make a bowel movement is also desirable, / La de dah, / it's all routine" (392). No comment.

"Cold wigs blew on the trees outside" (390) is an ominous Bad Anne line, toward the end of *The Death Notebooks*. These dangling wigs mark the path as we journey further, into the morass. Sexton produces a most bizarre, unforgettable bad simile in "Rowing," the first poem in *The Awful*

*Rowing Toward God* (which, incidentally, David Trinidad once dubbed *The Awful Writing* About *God*): "but I grew / like a pig in a trenchcoat I grew" (417). There was a time when I was so amused by this image of a trenchcoat-wearing pig (as it is slightly reminiscent of the dressed-up pigs that Joan Crawford procured for daughter Christina's childhood birthday parties), that poet Lynn Crosbie made a bracelet for me—a brightly colored pink and green number—with tiny plastic lettered beads spelling out "PIG IN A TRENCHCOAT"; it is my first (and only) piece of "Bad Anne Jewelry."

As if Sexton needed to top her trenchcoat-wearing pig, she launches *45 Mercy Street* with "The Falling Dolls." Need I say more? A deluge of dolls raining down from the sky? Pure *bad* genius. I cannot help but think of Jacqueline Susann's three "dolls" (Anne Welles, Neely O'Hara, and Jennifer North); in *my* mind the three women are scurrying down a Manhattan street, shielding their enormous falls from dolls—pills!—that pelt them like bullets. Granted, this is my own imagination talking. I cannot help it! This is one of the joys of reading late Sexton: the zaniness of the images and scenarios wear you down after a bit, like a strong martini, and you start to *feel* it. The world becomes a surreal kaleidoscope of bizarre associations, juxtapositions—a Sexton-induced effect—a new reality in which reader slowly turns into receptor of *Bad Anne-isms*. Out on the farm, or at the county fair, you no longer see just a trenchcoated pig, but rather you see (like the one described in "Hog") a "brown bacon machine," a purely Sexton creation (CP 498).

Once, during a Provincetown summer, friend and fellow Sexton fan David Trinidad came to visit me. We spent a morning holed-up in his rented apartment watching *The Story of Esther Costello*, a later Joan Crawford film. It is a real hoot, as Joan essentially plays Anne Bancroft's role in *The Miracle Worker* (Joan as humanitarian, educator, and martyr—you dig?), and she seriously overacts, frantically spelling words (in some unidentified and heretofore undiscovered method of sign language) into the palm of an adopted deaf mute daughter's hand. (I know, it's a lot to take in.) Later that same day, David and I read out loud to each other the entirety of "The Break Away." I think I can speak for the both of us: we highly recommend this to all aficionados of Bad Anne. (It occurs to me now that perhaps the warm-up activity for such a recitation should be a viewing of *Esther Costello*.)

Just take a peek, sometime when you are feeling a little down, at "The Break Away" (CP 518–26). There are these little blue and green chefs (on

Anne's kitchen wallpaper) who come to life and call out, "*pies, cookies, yummy*" (520). (There are several photographs of these chefs in *Anne Sexton: The Last Summer.*) Some daises arrive ("like round yellow fish") at the speaker's house the day of her divorce; they wait "like little utero half-borns" and "stand for a love / undergoing open heart surgery / that might take / if one prayed tough enough" (519, 520). Just a second: I thought the daises were like fish, no, like utero half-borns? OK, so they stand for love? That might take? If one does *what*? Spoiler alert: a couple of stanzas later, those daises will fade and dry up, become flour, "snowing" themselves onto the table, snowing lightly, "a tremor sinking from the ceiling," just as "twenty-five years [of marriage] split from . . . [the speaker's] side / like a growth that . . . [she] sliced off like a melanoma" (521–22). Whew! The poem reads like one of those scripts written as late Joan Crawford vehicle: *Sure, it's plausible* (says the writer pitching script), *Joan's character will teach the girl to communicate, like this, "Clap clap, Esther, clap clap," invent a new sign language system, create a worldwide charitable foundation, marry a playboy, fight off his advances toward an ever-changing-for-the-gorgeous Esther, and sacrifice her own life so that other deaf mutes like her adopted Esther (rounded up in the green hills of Ireland) can lead better lives too.* I digress. Again, I blame (credit?) Bad Anne; sometimes it *is* more fun to just let yourself go off on a tangent and roll with it.

Within the first eight months of 1970, Sexton had written seventeen long poems comprising *Transformations* and, within the last four months of the year, made headway with two other volumes of poetry, *The Book of Folly* and *The Death Notebooks*. Middlebrook says that *The Book of Folly* appealed to readers who had grasped the associational method Sexton employed in some of the poems in *Live or Die*. *The Death Notebooks* was intended for posthumous publication (though it ended up going to press in Sexton's lifetime). Sexton wanted to write "surreal, unconscious poems" for *The Book of Folly*. "At the same time . . . [she started] *The Death Notebooks*, where the poems will be very Sexton . . . intense, personal, perhaps religious in places" (qtd. in *AS* 338). So at the very least, the tangential aspect of these later poems was intentional. While she was writing poems for these two collections, she was teaching a poetry seminar at Boston University, she was on the road several times with her new musical group Her Kind, and she was on a daily dose of Thorazine. Additionally, a factor to consider when evaluating the poems in *The Awful Rowing Toward God*, Sexton wrote *all* thirty-nine poems in just twenty days. Linda Gray Sexton commented on the furious pace of her mother's composition: "often she wrote two or three poems in a few hours. . . . The days of spending months over a single stanza were gone" (*SPL* 390, 391).

So who's responsible, eh? Does Sexton deserve all the blame? To this day, if I share a new poem with a friend, I'll make him swear beforehand that he won't "Max out" on me. Meaning, where in hell was Maxine Kumin during these last few years of Sexton's poetic production? Sexton and her lifelong poet friend had their own poetry hotline (a private phone line in their studies) in order to critique each other's work in progress. It is documented that Kumin indulged or even encouraged Sexton's weaknesses. Other poet friends and editors gave Sexton honest and, I dare say, accurate criticism of her later poems (much of which Sexton ignored).

Jon Stallworthy, Sexton's editor at Oxford University Press, reluctantly chose to publish *Love Poems* in England after its publication in the United States. He had serious reservations about the manuscript. Middlebrook quotes Stallworthy as saying that he remembered the manuscript as a definitive turn for the worse in Sexton's art: "I liked the poems less and less and less; they weren't as carefully worked as before. She had learned to write, with Robert Lowell, with such fluency in a compact metrical structure; now the poetry began to get looser and more inflammatory, and I found it harder and harder to hear any sort of musical structure" (*AS* 301). I have never considered the poems in *Love Poems* sloppy or exaggerated in the way Stallworthy means. True, the poems in *Live or Die* are different from earlier collections; they are "looser," more confessional. It is true, too, that there are roots in *Live or Die* and also in *Love Poems* of some of the tropes that are the cornerstones of Bad Anne (Nazi imagery, repetition and refrains, demonstratives and honorifics, and some questionable figurative language). Overall, though, the two collections are successful. *Transformations*, which followed *Love Poems*, is an inventive collection of fantastical (as well as veiledly confessional) adaptations of Grimm's fairy tales.

For devotees of Bad Anne, however, the train starts to leave the station with *The Book of Folly*, picks up speed with *The Death Notebooks*, hits full steam ahead with *The Awful Rowing Toward God*, and suffers a total smashup with *45 Mercy Street*. But there in the wreckage, if you look closely, are, as previously mentioned, those lucky charms to be found. I am thinking of "The Furies" poems in *The Death Notebooks*. "The Fury of Sunrises" is a beautiful poem. The refrain "lighter, lighter" works (especially when heard in the recording of Sexton reading it [more on this performative aspect a little later]) extremely well; she evokes the kind of drowsiness that accompanies rising in the early morning (CP 377–78). The imagery and figurative language in the poem is fresh, exact: "Darkness / as black as your eyelid" (CP 377). In the middle of "The Hex," these two lines gleam like diamonds: "Thirteen for your whole life, / just the masks keep changing" (314). Even at the very end of her life, Sexton still had similar flashes of genius in what I think of as unsuccessful poems. For instance, in "Admonitions to a Special Person," these wonderful lines (which for a long time adorned my refrigerator door) jump out in quiet perfection: "To love another is something / like prayer and can't be planned, you just fall / into its arms because your belief undoes your disbelief" (608).

Middlebrook quotes James Wright's response to Sexton after he received an affectionate letter and the manuscript of The Awful Rowing Toward God. "I have no intention of excusing your bad verse and bad prose," he wrote. "There are some poems here that I think are fine. There are some that I think are junk" (AS 367). Wright also jotted a lot of marginalia on individual pages of the manuscript, scratching deep black X's through pages he disliked, and Sexton reacted with chagrin to his exhortations. Then she passed the manuscript onto Maxine Kumin, who defended much of what Wright attacked. "Maxing out" on her friend, Kumin wrote comments on manuscript pages to counter Wright's honest advice: "I like this poem—it isn't intended as a deep theological investigation but a way of hoarding up the good signs, or omens to keep going" (368). Middlebrook notes that Sexton's process of "image mongering" made reviewers of The Awful Rowing Toward God dubious about its finish. Middlebrook includes one critic's assessment that Sexton "continues to go over the top with words, letting them fill her pages like breeder piles. Having set up the situation in a poem, she lets the networks of associations do the rest" (388).

According to Middlebrook, Kumin "encouraged more than she disparaged" (368). Encouraged her to be bad? Maxine Kumin cannot be solely blamed for Sexton's creative negligence. In addition to her daily dose of Thorazine, Sexton was on a morning-noon-and-night, self-prescribed regimen of alcohol. Middlebrook, on the impact of alcohol on Sexton's work, writes:

Alcohol helped generate the curves of feeling on which her poetry lifted its wings, but it dropped her too, into depression, remorse, sleeplessness, paranoia—the normal host of furies that pursue alcoholics. More serious for her poetry, it deprived her of "the little critic" in her head that she had formerly summoned to the task of cut, cut, cut, expand, expand, expand, cut, cut, cut. She had the drunk's fluency but not the artist's cunning. (380)

She goes on to identify loneliness as the other "killer" of Sexton's art. Sexton's extreme neediness at this stage repelled many dear and longtime friends. Few of them enjoyed her company after she had been drinking: "alcohol made her imperious, paranoid, and sensitive to slights, given to quarreling and tantrums" (380). Her friends lost patience with her "midnight suicide threats" and her failure to perform simple chores, such as going to a store or mailing a letter (*SPL* 389).

The harder she tried to keep people close to her, the faster they pulled away. Sexton's poems of this period read like drunken late-night phone calls—"addressed to specific auditors, whose forbearance if not affection she could elicit by a pathetic appeal" (*AS* 380). She was met more often than not with indifference. This was Sexton's dance of death, as she herself acknowledged in "The Red Dance": "Words were turning into grease, / and she said, 'Why do you lie to me?'" (*CP* 531).

## Anne Sexton, Starring Anne Sexton

In 1952, Bette Davis starred as Margaret Elliot in *The Star*, just two years after her critically acclaimed portrayal of Broadway diva Margo Channing in *All About Eve*, a performance for which Davis was nominated for an Oscar. Much to her disappointment, she lost. Had she won, it would have been her third Academy Award for Best Actress. In *The Star*, Davis acts *super hard* (gunning, no doubt, for that elusive third Oscar) and turns out a campy depiction of a has-been Hollywood movie star aching for (guess what) another Oscar. In one hilarious scene, a drunken Bette, I mean Margaret, grabs her statuette and exclaims, "Come on Oscar, let's you and me get drunk!" She proceeds to take Oscar on a ride through her former Beverly Hills neighborhood, pointing out various stars' homes to him along the way as he teeters precariously on the dashboard, hostage to her spastic steering wheel maneuvers: "On your right, ladies and gentlemen, is the home of, of Mitzi Gaynor, rising young movie star. How young can ya be?" Bette's playing of Margaret Elliot mirrors Anne Sexton's playing of herself in the last years of her life. Whenever I view this scene in the movie (which is easily found on YouTube), I envision Anne piling into her old red Cougar, planting her Pulitzer certificate on the dashboard, and, with a bottle in one hand and a lit cigarette in the other, careening around the suburbs of Boston, past other PoBiz stars' homes, pointing out to her Pulitzer pal the family residence of Miss Sylvia Plath.

The publication of Middlebrook's biography of Sexton did much to create this *Anne as Bette as Margaret* movie star aura. One of the most memorable tidbits in the book, one that I read and reread many times when I first got my hands on it in 1991, is the story of Sexton's performance at the five-day Poetry International Festival in London in July 1967 (a trip she kicked off by setting up photographers to take "surprise" publicity photos of her departure from the gate at Boston's airport). Allegedly a bit tipsy, and perhaps on too many pills, Sexton went over her allotted time for the ten minute reading at the prestigious event, pissing off none other than W. H. Auden. When she finished reading, Jon Stallworthy recalls, "she laid down her book, threw wide her arms like a pop singer embracing her audience, and blew them a fat kiss. . . . two thousand people . . . looked at her in disbelief and horror. It was the most grotesquely ill-judged gesture I've ever seen at a poetry reading" (*AS* 278). Hopefully some of the members of that audience saw the appeal of Sexton's gesture, a kind of captivating Auntie Mame chutzpah.

Other details in the biography immediately mesmerized me. Sexton's friend Lois Ames, in an attempt to calm the poet's nerves before opening night of a stage production of *Transformations* in Minneapolis, offered her a tranquilizer, which, according to Ames, "cracked . . . [Sexton] up. She opened her big purse and showed me an enormous stock of pills—bottles and bottles of pills" (374). I found descriptions of Sexton's appearance equally enthralling. For that same *Transformations* event, "Sexton looked smashing in a floor-length dress printed with giant red hibiscuses" (374). For a reading arranged for her at Sanders Theatre by the Harvard Literary Club, Sexton looked "stunning in a black jersey top that wrapped her body and a long black-and-white skirt slit to the knee" (390). So glamorous. So Jackie O. What can I say? Starved.

Sexton had become very successful at securing high profile national readings. She packed houses wherever she went, and she enjoyed receiving top payment for such events. She perfected a flamboyant and captivating reading and performance style, despite tremendous stage fright. She dressed in beautiful clothes and traveled with an entourage most of the time. Her readings were carefully rehearsed, including introductory notes to poems and conversational banter with the audience. Sexton was well aware of the "show biz" aspect to her poetry world. In her aptly titled essay "The Freak Show," Sexton had this to say about/to poets giving featured readings: "You are the freak. You are the actor, the clown, the oddball. Some people come to see what you look like, what you have on, what your voice sounds like. . . . Some people hope you will do something audacious" (*NES* 33).

When Caedmon Audio released a cassette tape titled *Anne Sexton Reads* in 1993, I, like many others who had never had the good fortune to hear Sexton read her poetry live, was able to experience her bewitching voice and smoky incantations. These studio recordings were made in May 1974, five months before her death. Sexton's voice is mature, Salem cig deep, theatrical. When I first popped that tape into my Walkman so many years ago now, she had me at "Her Kind," the first poem on the recording. She *is* possessed; she sounds confident, self-assured, and completely at peace with her witchy-ness and demons. The poems that follow represent the best of Sexton's work from the beginning of her career. She reads "Music Swims Back to Me," "The Truth the Dead Know," "Letter Written on a Ferry While Crossing Long Island Sound," and "Self in 1958."

Toward the end of the tape, however, Sexton delves into her later work (which then would have been her more recent work); some of the "Jesus" poems from *The Book of Folly*; "Gods" as well as a couple of the "Furies" poems from *The Death Notebooks*; "Rowing" and "The Rowing Endeth" from *The Awful Rowing Towards God*; "Divorce, Thy Name Is Woman" from *45 Mercy Street*. These poems *sound* less credible; the dramatic, smoky voice that heightens the experience of hearing the earlier poems works against her here—it highlights the flaws of the writing. The force of her voice and tone, aimed at the dubious lines and images, causes these later poems to implode. For an example of this, have a listen to "The Play." Her embarrassing delivery of words like "soliloquies" and phrases like "many boos" is bound to make you squirm, or laugh uncomfortably.

Seven years after the release of *Anne Sexton Reads*, another cassette, titled

*The Voice of the Poet Presents Anne Sexton,* was released by Random House Audio. The collection includes "rare archival recordings" of Sexton reading a variety of her poems—poems from early and midcareer collections and a few from her late period. Unlike the cassette by Caedmon, which contains poems recorded during one studio session, *The Voice of the Poet Presents Anne Sexton* consists of poems recorded over the span of Sexton's adult life. You can hear a much younger, more strident sounding Sexton (I've always called this Sexton "telephone operator Anne" because of her clear, efficient tone and pronunciation), as well as Sexton later in life—her voice deeper, aged. The real difference between these two Sextons is that the latter was obviously bombed when she made the recordings. The audience and background noise make it clear that they are live readings. On the one hand, the listener has a visceral understanding of what one of Sexton's highly publicized readings was like; on the other hand, he is confronted with the fierce addiction with which Sexton struggled—she sounds drunken and overmedicated, slurring her words, at moments befuddled. Heartbreaking, yes; and yet, after a few listens, you can still hear Sexton the performer—a poet who is aware of the pageantry of a reading, aware of her audience and of her own central role as performer. You can hear Anne Sexton performing Anne Sexton. These recordings make up the last act in Sexton's greatest production: the creation of an intensely personal, confessional body of work that is irrevocably connected to the poet herself.

◆ ◆ ◆

A few years ago, a 1968 interview with Joan Crawford was uploaded to YouTube. In it, an older Joan (in thick pancake makeup and pink cowgirl outfit) is wheel chaired off a jet bridge at an American Airlines gate inside Los Angeles International Airport. She is helped into a battery-powered cart that has "AA" painted on the front (funny, given the fact that Crawford is so obviously shnockered). An interviewer hops into the forward seat, sits facing Joan. When the cart starts moving, he inquires about her broken ankle. She explains that she tripped on the lip of a staircase. "So it's broken, Miss Crawford?" he asks compassionately. "Shhhhattered!" she responds without irony. The rest of the interview is painful to watch (but of course I have, over and over). She is a movie star. And a train wreck.

As Crawford aged, she had a hard time evolving as an actress. She became a caricature of herself; the more refined qualities she exhibited in her early films lapse into histrionics, campiness. Sexton suffered a similar fate. The intensity with which she wrote her earlier confessional poems—her attention to precise figurative language and exact images, her ability to rework and edit poems—was sure and sound. In middle age, after the Pulitzer, after the wear and tear of addictions, her genius becomes unhinged. She forgets herself; her poems become formulaic due to their reliance upon a handful of tropes and persistent use of ludicrous images. There are whispers in her late poems of the singular brilliance on display in the early work. Sexton's not the first poet to fall apart. William Carlos Williams once wrote that Walt Whitman "was a magnificent failure. He himself in his later stages showed all the terrifying defects of his own method" (135).

Whitman's "badness," like Sexton's, lives on. How many poets enjoy this sort of dubious legacy? Maybe the bad is really the good? Nah. Sexton turned into a mess, but what an interesting mess! Over the years, I have struggled to reconcile early/good Anne with late/bad Anne. I have moments of compassion and admiration while reading the latter, mixed with moments of despair and exasperation. I also have moments of sheer pleasure, savoring the supersonic campiness to be found in places. Bad Anne represents the sum of a lifetime lived to the hilt—an incredible genius on overdrive, exploiting her own poetic persona. Such nakedness could only come from someone who "was born / doing reference work in sin, and born / confessing it" (*CP* 63). Bad Anne lived by my golden rule for poets: *never be boring.* If ultimately you have to be a failure, isn't it better to be a magnificent one? Like Frank O'Hara coaxing Lana Turner, I want to exclaim, "Oh Anne Sexton we love you get up!"

## Works Cited

Conway, Jeffery, Lynn Crosbie, and David Trinidad. "Chain Chain Chain." *Saints of Hysteria: A Half-Century of Collaborative American Poetry*. Ed. Denise Duhamel, Maureen Seaton, and David Trinidad. Brooklyn, NY: Soft Skull Press, 2007. Print.

———. *Phoebe 2002: An Essay in Verse*. New York: Turtle Point Press, 2003. Print.

Koch, Kenneth. "The Art of Poetry." *The Collected Poems of Kenneth Koch*. New York: Knopf, 2005. 254. Print.

Middlebrook, Diane Wood. *Anne Sexton: A Biography*. Boston: Houghton Mifflin, 1991. Print.

Sexton, Anne. *Anne Sexton: A Self-Portrait in Letters*. Ed. Linda Gray Sexton and Lois Ames. Boston: Houghton Mifflin, 1977. Print.

———. *The Complete Poems.* Boston: Houghton Mifflin, 1981. Print.

Swan, Barbara. "A Reminiscence." *Anne Sexton: The Artist and Her Critics.* Ed. J. D. Mc-Clatchy. Bloomington, IN: Indiana UP, 1978. 81–88. Print.

Trinidad, David. "Two Sweet Ladies: Sexton and Plath's Friendship and Mutual Influence." *The American Poetry Review* 35.6 (Nov./Dec. 2006): 21–29. Print.

Williams, William Carlos. *The Selected Letters of William Carlos Williams.* Ed. John C. Thirlwall. New York: New Directions Books, 1957. Print.

# $\cdots 9$

## "The Speaker in This Case"

Anne Sexton as Tale-Teller in *Transformations*

JEANNE MARIE BEAUMONT

I must begin this essay with a confession. My first readings of Anne Sexton's *Transformations* did not leave me charmed. I had the impression (false, as it turned out) that the poems stayed too close to the Brothers Grimm tales themselves, and I was somewhat deaf to their rhythms. In short, I was not initially convinced that the prose stories were sufficiently *transformed* into poetry. Then one evening about fifteen years ago I had the chance to hear "The Frog Prince" performed by an actor at a gathering at which theater company members practiced their craft by reading poems aloud, and poets presented their work to the actors.[1] The actor's delivery of Sexton's poem was so tonally perfect and effectively paced that the wit and magic of it, the appeal of it as a theatrical utterance, and thus the achievement of it as a work of Sexton's poetic art, converted me on the spot.

I was subsequently able to return to *Transformations* with a new appreciation of it as a collection of small comic masterpieces: grotesque, erotic, sly, and playful at their best. With each rereading, the deeper into the woods I am able to travel with them, not just as poems, but as markers for where Sexton was in her life and her craft as she wrote them, and as a particularly revealing document of mid-twentieth-century culture and its adult psyches, for they are nothing if not culturally and psychologically preoccupied. They are, as Sexton herself called them, "artifacts" (*SPL* 324).

To create a unified book of fairy tale retellings, Sexton had to recreate herself as a tale-teller; not just a poet (even one prone to exaggerating and twisting details for the poem's sake), but a crafty spinner in the folk tradition, that is, one who tells tales in the community, about the community, and on behalf of the community. One who *knows* things. She needed to create a voice of credibility and experience, one that carries authority. The tale-teller's voice is often that of a wise elder, a beldam, a crone. If not Mother Goose, well, Mother Somebody. Ideally a reteller of fairy tales should also offer fresh insights or updated details to vividly connect the source tales to the teller's era. The voice that Sexton invents for *Transformations* is part stand-up comic (think Phyllis Diller expelling a sarcastically wicked *Hah*!) and part attractively sultry actor such as Patricia Neal or Anne Bancroft, cigarettes near at hand or at least heard in the voice.

Sexton was forty-one years old in 1970 when she was writing this book, and although not "old" by contemporary standards (by which fifty is "the new thirty"), she was referring to herself and thinking of herself as middle-aged; she admitted to tinting her hair to cover the grey (314). Only four years from her death, she was thus actually *late* in her own life and appeared to intuit that. "I'm so God damned sure I'm going to die soon," she wrote to Stanley Kunitz in January 1971 (336). It could be argued that *Transformations* is the book that divides her middle work from her late work and that the poet herself underwent a transformation in the years that followed its publication—one that did not have a happy ending for her.

The voice in *Transformations* can be characterized as acutely death-aware, and indeed "death" gets the very last word in it; its tone is shaped by the gallows' shadow. This is evident to any reader who traces its patterns of metaphor. Before discussing those, however, I want to pursue further this issue of tale-teller; for if these poems are experienced as dramatic performances, poems that come most alive when heard out loud (as fairy tales were traditionally passed along), the first question is *Who is speaking?* Sexton addresses this directly in the opening lines of the book: "The speaker in this case / is a middle-aged witch, me—/ tangled on my two great arms, / my face in a book / and my mouth wide, / ready to tell you a story or two" (CP 223). Sexton recognizes the question of "Who is speaking?" (and note it is not "The writer in this case") as a critical one that she must answer at the start. The witch identity is one she had claimed since her first book, in perhaps her most famous poem, the poem she began her readings with and named her band for, "Her Kind": "I have gone out, a possessed witch, / haunting the black air, braver at night" (15). Sexton cultivated this spooky-strong tone of voice throughout her work, although she used it selectively. In 1968, she wrote to editor Paul Brooks, "I am a witch, an enchantress of sorts" (*SPL* 292). In this same letter she matches the witch identity to a common bane of middle age: "If and when I have a next book I may have to ask for larger print as this enchantress is getting older and finds it hard to read the print at these poetry readings. See, even witches, those of us who survive worship and hanging, get old" (292).

In taking on her witch-speaker to re-spin the Grimm tales, Sexton is not so much the ferocious and hauntingly voiced younger witch of "Her Kind," but this more mature, sarcastic, "wised up" witch, seasoned if not yet wizened, with reading glasses low on her nose. When she says she is "ready to tell . . . [us] a story or two" (*CP* 223), she promises a cackling good time and sounds a bit like a character you might hear at a local bar, if not a local cauldron, *Boy, have I got a story to tell you.* . . . We lean in to lend an ear, for who doesn't love a good tale?

Not to be overlooked in that first line of *Transformations* is the key word "case." A simple word although a loaded one for Sexton, who saw herself as a "case" among "cases" both as a psychiatric patient and former asylum inmate, it turns up throughout her poems: "But our case history / stays blank" ("Unknown Girl in the Maternity Ward" *CP* 24); "I checked out for the last time / on the first of May; / graduate of the mental cases, / with my analyst's okay" ("The Double Image" 39); "Years of hints / strung out—a serialized case history—/ thirty-three years of the same dull incest" ("Flee on Your Donkey" 100). One of the most notable contemporizing aspects of *Transformations* is how Sexton turns the tales into representative "case histories." In putting the Grimm characters on the psychoanalytic couch, she modernizes their conflicts and dilemmas and places them among mid-twentieth century neurotics and psychotics. This aspect is emphasized by the often long introductory sections to each of the retellings. Many of these, which are indicated by a one-em indentation from the left margin and which Sexton referred to as "prologues," can be read as poems by themselves; a few, arguably, are more compelling than the actual tale retellings they precede. The prologues range from six lines ("Godfather Death") to seventy-eight lines for "Red Riding Hood."

Sexton often appears more interested or more emotionally invested in describing the prologue cases than the narrative details of the actual fairy tales, especially when the poems relate closely to biographical episodes from her life. A prime example is "Rapunzel," which has a sixty-line prologue that begins and ends with "A woman / who loves a woman / is forever young" (244–46). This case involves an older aunt who takes a rather possessive, controlling interest in her young niece. Sexton's complex relationship with her great aunt "Nana" is certainly being evoked here.[2] Other cases that Sexton refers to in the prologues include split personalities, adulterers, deceivers, insomniacs, amnesiacs, the maimed and malformed, the suicidal, the narcoleptic, and even the cannibalistic parent. In one of the longest and most poignant of the prologues, for "Iron Hans," Sexton offers a catalogue of "lunatics" and seems to gather them all under her wings, or skirts. Mother Somebody indeed:

> I am mother of the insane.
> Let me give you my children:

> Take a girl sitting in a chair
> like a china doll.
> She doesn't say a word.
> She doesn't even twitch.
> She's as still as furniture. (250)

She goes on to describe a half dozen others, each with such vivid specificity of symptoms and behavior that they could only have been witnessed by Sexton on the mental wards. It is like touring the asylum with one of the saner inmates. In a Hitchcock-like cameo appearance, she places herself among them: "Take a woman talking, / purging herself with rhymes, / drumming words out like a typewriter, / planting words in you like grass seed" (250). Sexton, *the speaker in this case,* is the beldam from bedlam (and part way back); her convincing authority as tale-teller in *Transformations* derives primarily from her inmate experience and the empathy for pathology she acquired as a result.

This association was readily understood at the time. When *Transformations* was developed as a chamber opera in 1973, with music by composer Conrad Susa, the scenes were staged as though occurring in a mental hospital (Brunyate). Having "patients" act and sing as Grimm characters not only makes theatrical sense but also works in terms of the core appeal of the tales, as well as the appeal of the poet to her core audience. Fairy tales have endured because they serve as explorations of, and metaphors for, a range of human behaviors and emotional states. As for the poet, it has been said, "The memory of mental institutions never left her" (*SPL* 281). Sexton told her editor that she received "hundreds of letters" from fans who, like her, had been patients in mental hospitals; she tried to answer every one and even developed sustained correspondence with a few (318).

In 1968, close to the time of writing *Transformations,* Sexton taught a class at McLean Hospital, a private mental institution in Belmont, Massachusetts (to which she herself would later be admitted). This connection could be why she tends to be more gentle and sober in the prologues of *Transformations* and to save her more cynical, cartoonish, and even cruel, images and commentary for the fairy tale narratives themselves. Writing about the prologues to Stanley Kunitz, Sexton explained: "The poems seem to grow out of the prologue to, as it were, take root in them and come forth from them" (333). We can thus view the prologues as a sort of growth medium of psychological material, which enabled Sexton to *graft* (a word linked in *its* roots to Greek *grapheion:* to write) her poems onto that already well-developed and thriving "stock plant" of the Grimm stories.

Some wondrously odd new foliage springs up amid the old Grimm forest as a result; for the two strategic decisions that Sexton made for *Transformations,* to create a tale-teller voice that remains constant throughout and to write prologues to recontextualize each of the stories, set Sexton's fairy tale series apart from those of other poets who have used this source material. More typically, poets writing a group of fairy tale poems choose different slants and approaches from tale to tale. Sara Henderson Hay, for example, whose collection *Story Hour* was originally published in 1963, writes some poems in the voices of characters; some from a remote narrator's viewpoint; and others as epistles, "court" reports, and interviews. In Hay's collection, it is the sonnet form of the poems, rather than a single tone or point of view, that creates the unity.

In my reading of hundreds of fairy tale-based poems while editing *The Poets' Grimm: 20th Century Poems from Grimm Fairy Tales,* the dramatic monologue or "persona" poem, spoken in the voice of a Grimm character, emerged as the most prominent approach taken by poets. But Sexton does

not choose that for *Transformations;* she maintains her classic folktale deliv-
erer's stance, even incorporating traditional lingo. After the prologues, she
begins a dozen of her retellings with the most conventional words of all:
"Once ..." or "There once was ..." or similarly, "Long ago ..." and "In an old
time / there was ..." Coming in as they do after the often emotionally edgy,
discomforting prologues, these familiar tale-openers have a soothing effect;
they evoke the childhood experience that Sexton refers to in her first poem
("The Gold Key") with the lines "Do you remember when you / were read
to as a child?" (*CP* 223). They also provide a clear signal that the prologue
is over and the actual fairy tale is beginning. In a "preview" or warm-up of a
sort, Sexton had used this wording throughout a section of the last poem of
the book that preceded *Transformations.* In "Eighteen Days Without You,"
in *Love Poems* (1969), each of the three stanzas that constitute the *December
16th* section has "Once upon a time" as the first line (218). Evidently it was
an ingrained, evocative phrase for Sexton that connected her to her own
childhood and, in this poem, to the childhood of her lover.

Two other artistic choices that Sexton makes are worth acknowledging
before delving into the issue of metaphor. First is that she does not do any-
thing fancy with her poem titles; the most common title of the Grimm fairy
tale is adapted, without embellishment, as the title for the poem. Clearly,
Sexton wanted a close alignment with the beloved tales. A shrewd pro-
moter of her work, she must have realized this would give the poems im-
mediate recognition-appeal for editors and readers. Second, Sexton does
not use quotation marks around dialogue, which keeps the poems flow-
ing and uncluttered and helps convey a sense of oral rather than "literary"
transmission:

> Oh Grandmother, what big ears you have,
> ears, eyes, hands and then the teeth.
> The better to eat you with, my dear.
> So the wolf gobbled Red Riding Hood down
> like a gumdrop. Now he was fat.
>    ("Red Riding Hood" 271)

Notice, too, how the first three lines speed up a part of the tale that in the
actual Grimm version goes on for about eight lines of dialogue between
Wolf (disguised as Grandmother) and Red.

Throughout *Transformations,* Sexton acknowledges that she is recounting tales that most readers will know well if not "by heart," and she is not interested in boring us with parts we can fill in ourselves. Though fairy tale plots often have a series of three repetitions, Sexton finds ways of abbreviating events to avoid narrative tedium. She might humorously condense, or will say something like, "Next came the ball, as you all know" (256). In this five-line passage, what attracts us is likely "gobbled . . . down / like a gumdrop" (271). With that in mind, let us blaze a trail into the forest of metaphor and simile that is one of the prominent stylistic features of the speaker of *Transformations.*

> And as [the queen] was sewing and looking out the window, she pricked her finger with the needle, and three drops of blood fell on the snow. The red looked so beautiful on the white snow that she thought to herself, If only I had a child as white as snow, as red as blood, and as black as the wood of the window frame!
> Soon after she gave birth to a little daughter who was as white as snow, as red as blood, and her hair as black as ebony. (Grimm 196)

This well-known scene from "Snow White" by the Brothers Grimm contains three similes. One will need to search a while, however, to find a similar thicket of simile construction (here defined as a comparison made with "like" or "as") within the best-known Grimm tales. Perhaps that is because in fairy tales the transformation of image is more complete. It is not the case, for example, that the witch's cottage looks like gingerbread to the starving Hansel and Gretel, but that it *is* gingerbread.

Sexton, however, whether inspired by this opening for Snow White, or more likely following her own inclinations, uses a plethora of similes in *Transformations.* The absurdist as well as the more brutal possibilities of simile help to "set the table" of tone throughout the book. The play with simile enables her to contemporize the tales and also to "stretch" them in often comic, if not comic book-like, ways. While considering the simile as the most basic grammatical formulation of a metaphor, it is crucial to note that all metaphors can be thought of as "transformations," one thing turning into another; although particularly simile-rich, the poems in this collection are full of metaphoric transformations of all types. One representative passage that combines simile with more direct metaphor could be regarded as a rather grotesque witch's brew of sorts: "Frog has no nerves. / Frog is as old as a cockroach. / Frog is my father's genitals. / Frog is a malformed doorknob. / Frog is a soft bag of green" ("The Frog Prince" CP 282). This mix of figures, including the insect world, the male body, and a common household object, is typical of the grab bag that Sexton reaches into to enliven her fairy tale versions. Here the effect is very much like a rapidly shape-shifting cartoon, with images that shrink, protrude, stretch, and sag. In this way, Sexton's fairy tales are not so very far from the popular Disney renderings of the tales, for animation enables a visual playfulness and surreal mutability that live-action does not. But Sexton is definitely Disney for grown-ups.

*Pretty as a picture, ate like a pig, easy as pie, like a bat out of hell*—similes are a common characteristic of vernacular or folk speech. Their use contributes a casual, intimate, colorful, and down-to-earth (even earthy) quality to a speaker's tone. By my count, there are at least 235 similes in the seventeen poems of *Transformations*. Separating these into categories according to what a thing or person is compared *to*, the two categories of similes that predominate are food and animals, especially dogs. As befits the tales, several refer to gruesome things, while other frequently occurring categories include the anatomical and/or medical, pop culture, and less commonly, high culture. There are also enough images of clothing and common household objects, such as flat irons, hairpins, pots, and Venetian blinds, to remind us of the original title of the Grimm Brothers' 1812 book: *Children's and Household Tales (Kinder- und Hausmärchen)*.

Here is one particularly rich harvest of simile conjuring the witch's garden in "Rapunzel":

with carrots growing like little fish,
with many tomatoes rich as frogs,
onions as ingrown as hearts,
the squash singing like a dolphin
and one patch given over wholly to magic—
rampion, a kind of salad root,
a kind of harebell more potent than penicillin,
growing leaf by leaf, skin by skin,
as rapt and as fluid as Isadora Duncan. (CP 246)

We can sense the delight that Sexton takes in embroidering Grimm's more general description: "Now, in the back of their house the couple had a small window that overlooked a splendid garden filled with the most beautiful

flowers and herbs." Quickly, the focus zooms to the crucial greens: "she no-
ticed a bed of the finest rapunzel lettuce" (Grimm 47). As Sexton envisions
the garden, all of the plants seem enchanted, and again, animated. Readers
of Sylvia Plath might be reminded of lines from "Fever 103°": "Love, love,
the low smokes roll / From me like Isadora's scarves" (Plath 231). (Not the
only time a Plath echo can be heard in *Transformations*.) Although Sexton's
use of Duncan may at first seem less ominous, those salad leaves will lead to
all the woes of the tale. And as charming as that singing squash image is on
its own, it also prefigures a vital element of the story: it will be Rapunzel's
singing voice that attracts her suitor. There is often a subtle method to Sex-
ton's mania for simile.

Sexton as reader placed a high value on metaphor, writing, "Subject mat-
ter itself is not as important as the genius inherent in a great metaphor"
(*SPL* 297). The metaphors that writers invent reveal what is on their minds,
their preoccupations, obsessions, the drift or "bent" of their particular "ge-
nius." They are thought-markers. A pattern in metaphors, as evidenced over
a poet's body of work, becomes an aspect of what makes that work recogniz-
able and distinctive. I would like to propose that the reservoir of imagery
that each poet has to draw on, accumulated over a lifetime of experience, of
reading, and of associations, will be as individual as a fingerprint. Hence we
might say of a poem of Sexton's, recognized although encountered without
her name attached, that "her prints are all over it."

To thus engage in some "finger-printing," we can detect in Sexton's imag-
ery patterns evidence of her as one of the, if not the preeminent, "poet-pa-
tients" of the mid-twentieth century. Certainly, the Robert Lowell of "Wak-
ing in the Blue" and the Sylvia Plath of "Tulips" and "In Plaster" would be
among that number. Diane Middlebrook states that as early as 1956, Sexton
"took on the role of patient, which she did not abandon for the rest of her
life" (35). In her poems, Sexton frequently drew imagery from the medical
realm and employed its vocabulary of symptoms, diseases, and treatments.
In addition to "a harebell more potent than penicillin" above, the list of
medical similes from *Transformations* includes:

as tight as an Ace bandage (*CP* 227)
as intense as an epileptic aura—(229)
as ugly as a wart (234)
wine . . . as warm as a specimen (240)

his crotch turned blue as a blood blister (244)
It appeared as suddenly as a gallstone (252)
The tree treated them like poison ivy (262)
as sure-fire as castor oil (274)
like a tongue depressor held fast (276)
his eyes fiery / like blood in a wound (281)

Sexton's keen sense of impending death, mentioned earlier, also emerges in her similes. Dorothy Parker's "Résumé" might come to mind when reading these metaphors from Sexton, a particularly disturbing association in light of what end lay ahead for her:

Pride pumped in her like poison (*CP* 225)
each [snake] a noose for her sweet white neck (226)
a sword as sharp as a guillotine (253)
It burned in their brains like radium (263)
and at each window secrets came in / like gas (269)
He was as heavy as a cemetery (272)
He was as awful as an undertaker (285)
as if it were Socrates' hemlock (285)
circling the abyss like a shark (294)

All that is missing is the carbon monoxide. That would come later. In 1970, Sexton was having too much wicked fun riding the wave of writing the poems to take notice of the undertow. "It's something quite strange and different, and I'm having an awfully good time," she wrote to her editor in July (*SPL* 319).

Sexton might have felt the fairy tale poems were "quite strange and different," yet her ubiquitous use of simile was only an exaggeration and elaboration of her earlier style, not a departure. Middlebrook terms the poet's propensity for similes a "Sexton trademark" (293). Additionally, references to fairy tale imagery can be traced throughout Sexton's earlier work. In a poem from her first book, *To Bedlam and Part Way Back* (1960), published ten years before she wrote *Transformations*, Sexton depicts her writing instructor (Lowell) as a prince of a man turned into a frog by his mental illness. In a reversal of "The Frog Prince," he squats "like a hunk of some big frog," while the students try to "ignore your fat blind eyes / or the prince you ate yesterday / who was wise, wise, wise" (*CP* 32). In "The Abortion" from *All My*

*Pretty Ones* (1962), she writes, "up in Pennsylvania, I met a little man, / not Rumpelstiltskin, at all, at all . . . / he took the fullness that love began" (61). In "The House" from that same book, Sexton describes "The aunt, / older than all the crooked women / in *The Brothers Grimm,* / leans by a gooseneck lamp" (73). And in the poem that follows, "Water," she states, "Under us / twelve princesses dance all night, / exhausting their lovers, then giving them up" (75), alluding to "The Twelve Dancing Princesses." Although fairy tales had long been lurking in Sexton's ready cauldron of images, it would take the crisis of writer's block in 1969 to turn her energies completely to the tales and to transform her into the poet who would reinvent them for her twentieth century audience, which is to say, into "the speaker in this case."

◆   ◆   ◆

Throughout the year before Anne Sexton worked on *Transformations,* she was immersed in the writing and rehearsals of her play *Mercy Street,* which opened off-Broadway at the American Place Theatre in October 1969. It may have been this process, which included collaborating with actors, watching her lines being performed, and rewriting to suit the needs of the stage that contributed to the theatricality of the fairy tale poems she would write the next year. The voiced quality that came across so clearly when I heard the actor presenting "The Frog Prince"—would it have been as sharp without this play production experience of its author? Yet, in the immediate aftermath of the play's New York run, Sexton complained about creative blockage. In a letter dated 26 December 1969, she lamented: "I'm blocked now. Nothing comes. A drought. No poems . . . none, nothing. I've written one poem since June and that one was so bad that I've lost it" (*SPL* 313).

Within about a month, however, she was sending two fairy tale poems to George Starbuck and begging for his feedback: "HELP. I am trying something different and would like to know if you think it works. I plan a whole series of poems, possibly a book if it comes to that, but I want to know if these two poems make any sense to you" (315). (See the timeline at the end of this essay for the progression of *Transformations* from writer's block to book.) As if by magic, the blockage had been removed; from a drought to a whole new book idea brewing—the "middle-aged witch" was stirring her potions once again and wondering if her spells would take effect. Did she still have it?

Sexton worked on the fairy tale poems throughout the spring and summer. She succeeded in placing some in mainstream publications, including *Playboy* and *Cosmopolitan*. But when in August 1970 she sent a sample of six poems to Houghton Mifflin, the enchantress failed to enchant. The publisher was not impressed, and the poet would need to do some arduous persuading before the book was accepted. Convinced of its importance, she wrote to her editor in its defense, "If I were to heed your warnings about *Transformations* and see my life work with that book omitted, I would be very sad. It would be a mistake." She even floated the idea of taking the collection to another press (326).

In a revealing passage from that same October letter, Sexton writes:

> I realize that the "Transformations" are a departure from my usual style. I would say that they lack the intensity and perhaps some of the confessional force of my previous work. I wrote them because I had to . . . because I wanted to . . . because it made me happy. I would want to publish them for the same reason. I would like my readers to see this side of me, and it is not in every case the lighter side. Some of the poems are grim. In fact I don't know how to typify them except to agree that I have made them very contemporary. It would further be a lie to say that they weren't about me, because they are just as much about me as my other poetry. (325)

By this point, Anne Sexton, "the Confessional Poet," was a recognizable brand. The publication of *Love Poems* in 1969 "was the first of her books produced in the atmosphere of celebrity" (*AS* 293), but it could be argued that the branding had occurred a bit earlier. Understandably her publisher was loath to mess with a successful formula. And though Sexton, too, knew her audience well, knew who wrote her fan letters and why, at this stage of her career, she was eager to branch out. She might also have intuited that her audience would get the message—that she was indeed the "mother of the insane" and that these were in effect her bedtime stories to her fans, to her legions of familiar cases.

Editor Paul Brooks had told her the new poems "lack the terrific force and directness of [her] . . . more serious poetry" (*AS* 338). (Perhaps he should have been sent an actor to perform them?) Brooks may have underestimated the passionate connection certain readers have to fairy tales and to Sexton. It seems clear, now that the poet's work and life are in fuller view, that the poems were indeed "just as much about" Sexton as her other work. Only Sexton could have transformed these particular tales in these particular ways. The poems have a *terrific*-ness all their own, and in them the *force* of the poet's imagination finds a canny new outlet. That *Transformations* went on to become one of her best-selling books, and remains in print today, is proof that Sexton was correct to deem it an essential part of her body of work.

Among the six poems Sexton sent in her August sample to her editor was "The White Snake." It is one of the shorter poems in the collection, and Sexton did not seem to regard it as one of the stronger pieces, but she must have had some confidence in it to include it. Nor is it based on one of the better-known Grimm tales, but that makes it an interesting poem to consider more closely. Why did Sexton want to retell this tale? What was her attachment to the material? How was it "about" her? Although many of her selections seem inevitable, including the popular tales of family dysfunction such as "Snow White and the Seven Dwarfs" and "Hansel and Gretel"; and some we might recognize as biographically relevant such as "The Little Peasant" with its plot of infidelity, or "One-Eye, Two-Eyes, Three-Eyes," about three sisters (Anne being one of three daughters), "The White Snake" would not leap out as an obvious choice. Yet it is rather prominently positioned as the third poem in the book.

The prologue of "The White Snake" is a lyrical and brief one—just eighteen lines—and it does employ the confessional first person. Notably, Sexton "names" herself twice as though, this early in *Transformations,* she is still concerned with identifying the speaker of the poems: "There was a day / when all the animals talked to me. / Ten birds at my window saying, / Throw us some seeds, / Dame Sexton, / or we will shrink" (*CP* 229). This beguiling fantasy might be less benignly viewed as a case of psychosis—*oh, she's hearing voices again.* It also depicts a return to a prelapsarian state (Eden allusion will return in the poem), a vision of a true enchantment, and a Dame Sexton who may be related to Dr. Doolittle.[3] Sexton in fact did hear voices—human voices—as a symptom of her mental illness. Middlebrook calls these Sexton's "acoustical ghosts" (327). So the detail of hearing voices may have been one of the attractants of this tale for her.

The birds heard at the window in the prologue come from Grimm, as does the next image, though less directly: "The worms in my son's fishing pail / said, It is chilly! / It is chilly on our way to the hook!" (*CP* 229). While in Grimm, it is the fish that play a key role, it is the worms that Dame Sexton hears, worms already feeling the chill of certain doom. With *It is chilly*, a grave tone is set straightaway, so much for the "lighter side." The worm also prefigures the snake. And is that "hook" another Plath echo? In any case it looms large and lethal as we suddenly find ourselves looking up at it.

True to the pattern of threes that dominates fairy tale plots, including this one, a third animal speaks in this prologue, not one from the fairy tale but rather one from the poet's own household: the Sextons had dogs, Dalmatians specifically. As might be expected, the dog addresses her more intimately: "Maybe you're wrong, good Mother, / maybe they're not *real* wars" (229). So far in this pastoral auditory fantasia, starvation, death, and wars have been conjured. The animals are stark realists, although the innocent dog is willing to entertain doubt (*Maybe . . . maybe*). The Vietnam War was ongoing while Sexton wrote; it is in the background like the hum of a TV. As did many writers (and many "good mothers" as well), Sexton had taken part in antiwar readings and protest activities starting about 1966 (*AS* 295). Grim news for real. The sobering prologue ends with its own epiphany of sorts: "And then I knew that the voice / of the spirits had been let in—/ as intense as an epileptic aura—/ and that no longer would I sing / alone" (*CP* 229).

The imagination of this prologue is appealing, with enough gravitas to keep adult minds alert despite the conceit of talking animals. Who are these spirits? They beg, complain, and try to console. One of the medical similes quoted earlier, that *epileptic aura*, seems a warning. The dangling "alone" of the last line feels as much a broken promise or a veiled threat as a comfort. (One wonders if Stephen Sondheim read this book before composing *Into the Woods*, with its haunting refrain, "No one is alone" [Sondheim 128].) A kind of Pandora's Box in reverse is suggested by the influx of spirits, or perhaps a private Pentecost, untangling the tongues of animal speech. Sexton's intoning is almost like a spirit-medium's in a trance state (with a Yeatsian aura) in these lines. Throughout this prologue, the speaker in this case, "Dame Sexton" and "good Mother," has subtly claimed her territory: she has a gift, for she can understand the talk of animals, she is possessed (*a possessed witch?*) with the voice of the spirits, and some new knowledge has come upon her. Perhaps this means she must speak on behalf of others, or rather, sing. *And then I knew . . .* her state has changed. And perhaps her stage as well. Could this be an indicator of how Sexton viewed her responsibility as a poet once she had heard the voices, the bells, and the distressed spirits of bedlam?

In an interview, Sexton spoke of having had two "these are my people" moments in her life. Middlebrook proposes a third: "Just as Sexton had felt the releasing recognition 'These are my people!' when she entered the mental hospital those many years ago, and again when she began her first poetry workshop, she now felt liberated and stimulated by the world of the theater" (*AS* 323). The thrill and the satisfaction that Sexton experienced writing *Transformations* may have arisen from the fact that she had found a way to encompass all three of these key realms of her experience. Her recognition of that as a rare and happy confluence may also have been why she fought for the book's publication so insistently.

While the source material of the Grimm stories provided a release from the myopia of the intense biographical material she had been mining for her play *Mercy Street* the previous year, it still offered a metaphorical world of family and social trauma she recognized. Its charm, however, resided in the fact that she could dramatize it and comment on it from a more amused, sardonic, and satiric distance. She would ever be the "mother of the insane," but she was also the crafty poet who knew how to spin a good story or two.

Another aspect of "The White Snake" that undoubtedly attracted Sexton was its focus on the act of eating as a plot-starter. In pointing out that one "major source of symbolism in *Transformations* was eating," Middlebrook links this motif to the ongoing trauma in the Sexton household around the poet's problems with food shopping and mealtimes (333). And, as Sexton launches into the actual tale telling, we encounter food linked to speech, a theme that the prologue already introduced: "In an old time / there was a king as wise as a dictionary. / Each night at supper / a secret dish was brought to him, / a secret dish that kept him wise" (*CP* 230).

Moving from talking animals to the simile "wise as a dictionary," the idea of language emerges as central to the story. And the idea of eating something "secret" to gain wisdom takes us back to Eden and the temptation of Adam and Eve. In this case, however, it is the serpent itself that is the forbidden fruit. For when the servant bearing the dish dares to "take a forbidden look" at the king's secret food, he finds the white snake. He yields to temptation and eats it. What happens next directly echoes the prologue:

> he heard the animals
> in all their voices speak.
> Thus the aura came over him.
> . . . . . . . . . . . . . . .
> A cold sweat broke out on his upper lip
> for now he was wise. (230)

That Sexton embellishment of the *cold sweat,* a clinical symptom that anyone who has had an anxiety attack will recognize, is tellingly on his lip, the organ of speech. This is wisdom of a particular kind, and though it may turn out one can hear too much, it initially brings some good fortune.

Sexton in compression mode turns about thirty lines of the Grimm story into five to speed through the next episode by which the servant finds a queen's lost ring and is rewarded with a horse and travel money. Then she moves quickly through the three encounters that the servant has with talking animals as he travels: he saves fish that are caught in weeds, he avoids trampling on a colony of pleading ants, and most disturbing of all, he kills his horse to feed some begging ravens, "gallow birds" as Sexton calls them.[4] All the animals he has helped have "covered him with promises" and placed themselves in his debt; the payoff will come in the next town, where a princess is holding a contest. A spoiled, sadistic young thing, she gets her kicks by giving suitors impossible tasks then having them killed off when they fail. Our hero, however—thanks to help from the fish, ants, and gallow birds—succeeds. When she drops her ring into the sea, the fish bring it up; when she scatters bags of grain in the yard, the ants carry "them in like mailmen" (231).

Sexton returns to the Garden of Eden connection she made earlier in the poem for the princess as her last test sends the suitor "out to find the apple of life" (232). In the Grimm tale, the princess, who scorns this particular suitor as below her in station, states that "he shall not become my husband until he has brought me an apple from the Tree of Life" (Grimm 70). The young man sets off on a second journey through three kingdoms, and just as he is about to fall asleep in a forest, a golden apple falls into his hands. Grimm has the ravens speak elegantly: "When we grew up, we heard you

234 · Jeanne Marie Beaumont

were looking for the golden apple. So we flew across the sea to the end of the world, where the Tree of Life is standing, and we've fetched the apple" (70).

Sexton plays fast and loose with the details here. Her re-visioning of this journey is much more cartoonish. She adds a trio of other animals—monkeys, pheasants, and turtles—none of which are helpful (and each of which might be read as satiric comment on certain social types), and Grimm's Germanic forest and kingdom landscape seems oddly melded with that of Disney's *The Jungle Book* (released in 1967). The rescue is somewhat anticlimactic: "He was prepared for death / when the gallow birds remembered / and dropped that apple on his head" (CP 232). One can almost hear the "bonk" of that apple. (Elsewhere Sexton includes such comic book words as "Kaboom," and "Poof!" but here she lets the reader supply the sound effect.) However it falls, with the apple now in the hero's possession "happily ever after" would seem sure to follow.

In the Grimm version, young man and princess divide the apple of life, she falls in love, and the tale closes: "In time they reached a ripe old age in peace and happiness" (Grimm 70). Paradise restored. But Dame Sexton does not often go along with Grimm's happy endings. It is the one part of the tales that she drastically revises, adding a contemporary edge, a cynical jab, or a few lines of mocking commentary. In bringing this tale toward its close, she adds an element of sexuality, as well as sarcasm:

> He returned to the princess
> saying, I am but a traveling man
> but here is what you hunger for.
> . . . . . . . . . . . . . .
> Their bodies met over such a dish.
> His tongue lay in her mouth
> as delicately as the white snake. (CP 232)

The words of the young man sound like those from a country song. (Did he acquire a guitar on his journey?) The proffered apple does work its love magic. And in her tongue-snake simile, Sexton neatly conjures back the titular white snake who gets forgotten in the Grimm tale. This not only brings the tale full circle symbolically, like a coiled snake itself, but also narratively as the work of the white snake in the plot has now been fulfilled. Perhaps our young hero will soon himself be a wise king who must have a "secret dish" of his power food delivered each night?

But wait, Sexton is not yet finished with her version. She has a bleaker picture to paint, a bluer and more bitter one:

> they were placed in a box
> and painted identically blue
> and thus passed their days
> living happily ever after—
> a kind of coffin,
> a kind of blue funk.
> Is it not? (232)

She entraps the couple in an odd monochrome malaise where they spend their days in a death-in-life state. The two are like cartoon characters who get depicted in off colors. Or might she have been recalling an often-reproduced nineteenth century painting by Henry Meynell Rheam from 1899, *Sleeping Beauty*? It depicts Beauty looking somewhat comatose in a pale blue nightgown wrapped in a darker blue blanket; hovering behind is her rescuer prince, dressed in a deeper royal blue. All a blue funk indeed, alleviated only by the pink briar roses pushing through a window. Or perhaps floating around in Sexton's pop-cultural brain zone was the melancholy Billboard hit from Europe that got frequent airplay in the late 1960s: "L'amour est bleu" (Love is blue) . . . *Blue, blue, my world is blue.* . . . [5] Whatever its source, the painted blue image is disturbing and hardly turns the pair into bluebirds of happiness despite that "living happily ever after," which she quickly undercuts with the last three lines of the poem.

This final image of domestic non-bliss is similar to the ending that Sexton provides for her royal couple in the poem "Cinderella":

> Cinderella and the prince
> lived, they say, happily ever after,
> like two dolls in a museum case
>
> . . . . . . . . . . . . . .
> their darling smiles pasted on for eternity.
> Regular Bobbsey Twins.
> That story. (*CP* 258)

The couple is again confined, in a museum case instead of a box or coffin, and the tone of sarcasm is indicated by the skeptical "they say," "darling smiles pasted on[,]" and ending jab of "That story." There are at least a half dozen other doll images in *Transformations,* and in Sexton's hands dolls are seldom charming childhood objects but rather images of blankness, dumbness, and coldness, manipulating or manipulated.

In an interesting document reproduced in *Anne Sexton: The Last Summer,* Sexton, composing a sort of autobiography/résumé (date for this is listed as "1965?") moves from the solace of fairy tales to her disdain for dolls in just a few sentences. Recalling her early school years, she types:

> At home, or away from it, people seemed out of reach. Thus I hid in fairy tales and read them daily like a prayerbook. Any book was closer than a person. I did not even like my dolls for they resembled people. I stepped on their faces because the[y] resembled me. I think I would have prefered [*sic*] to exist only in a fairy tale where poeple [*sic*] could change reality the way an actor changes his constume [*sic*]. (Furst 2)

Note that she also links fairy tales to the theater here. (And one wonders if "any book" might have included a Bobbsey Twins adventure?) The dollish image of Bobbsey Twins in the "Cinderella" ending echoes the twinning of "identically blue" in "The White Snake"; both convey a sense of a couple that have become too much alike to be interesting to each other.[6] Sexton presents a tarnished view of lasting marital bliss, and it might be worth recalling here what she said about these poems being "just as much about me as my other poetry." In these dreary, sour endings, she may have been unleashing some of her own dissatisfactions and disillusionment with her marriage and suburban domestic milieu. Within two years of the publication of *Transformations,* Sexton would initiate a divorce from her husband of twenty-four years.

In "The White Snake," Sexton defines herself as a speaker, indulges her flair for language and image, and plays the source tale like an accordion, radically compressing some parts while amusingly embellishing others. The tale's motifs of hearing voices and acquiring wisdom (language) via an act of eating, along with the Adam and Eve echoes, likely provided points of attachment and thus inspiration for her. Updating while deflating the ending gave Sexton an opportunity to vent some of her discontent with the idea of a happy-ever-after marriage. (*That* fairy tale!) But in this poem, as in most others in *Transformations,* Sexton basically stays faithful to the source tale and keeps the *purely* personal content just offstage. The same cannot be said about the final poem in *Transformations,* "Briar Rose (Sleeping Beauty)"; this poem deviates from the Brothers Grimm in significant ways and crosses into a different realm of personal association for Sexton. Placed last in the book, it begins to break away from the world of Grimm and shift us back toward the world (and woes) of Sexton and the poems that would follow in her next and final books.

◆ ◆ ◆

In the collection of the Museum of Modern Art one can find a 1963 advertisement, elegantly designed by Rolf Harder, for the drug Noludar. Occupying the lower half of the vertical ad is the head of a woman sleeping on her side. (Was Harder inspired by Constantin Brancusi's "Sleeping Muse"?) A young brunette, a virtual "sleeping beauty," she might even be taken at first glance for a young Anne Sexton. Superimposed over the woman's head are two circles, one inside the other, creating a full blue moon within a white crescent effect. The ad is predominantly blue, yes, a sort of *blue funk.* The copy reads "Noludar 300 synonym for safe, restful sleep." The small type under Noludar, the brand name, gives its generic active ingredient: methyprylon. (The ad was designed before the regulations for drug ads required the generic be at least half the type size of the brand name.) Noludar was a sedative-hypnotic, related to barbiturates. If you had insomnia or anxiety in the year 1970, you may have received a prescription. You cannot get it today in the United States. It has been taken off the market.

During the summer of 1970, Sexton worked on revising and completing the poems for *Transformations.* Some took as long as two months. "Briar Rose (Sleeping Beauty)" was written over a six-week period from 5 July to 17 August. She wrote that it was "a difficult poem for me"—a rare instance of Sexton understatement (*SPL* 321). Why was it difficult? And did the work on the poem lead to the mysterious attack she experienced sometime before 12 August? Noludar played a central role in that episode, which Sexton recounted in a 19 August letter. She describes how it began as a "very strange" and somewhat trippy feeling, which then accelerated to a state of confusion and delusion. At one point she was convinced that Maxine Kumin was dead. Kumin, alarmed, called Sexton's doctor. Sexton goes on to report that her doctor "told me to take two thorazine which certainly wouldn't have done much, certainly didn't. Joan came in and I took two thorazine and two noludar. Kayo was home suddenly and he was going to drive Joan home. I told him I might take my pills and go to sleep. He left with Joan and I took 17 noludar" (322).

As a result, Sexton had to have her stomach pumped out and spent a few days recuperating in the hospital. After this overdose her doctor took firmer control of her medications: "Dr. Chase has taken all my pills away from me and put me on much higher doses of thorazine[.] . . . It took me a while to adjust, but I find I'm sleeping quite well" (322). She continued to work on the Sleeping Beauty poem. Presumably, no more Noludar. But Thorazine, trade name for chlorpromazine (note that Sexton does not capitalize drug trade names in her letters), stayed in the picture as it had been for quite some time. Unlike Noludar, Thorazine is an antipsychotic drug, and one that is still marketed; it is indicated for treatment of schizophrenia and other psychotic disorders, including mania. Sexton claimed in another letter that it was "the only thing" that calmed her down (299). Despite that, poet-patient Sexton couldn't help but be envious of "Iron Hans," the wild man who turns out to be a gentle king in the Grimm tale and the Sexton poem:

> Without Thorazine
> or benefit of psychotherapy
> Iron Hans was transformed.
> No need for Master Medical;
> no need for electroshock—
> merely bewitched all along. (CP 254–55)

The ending of "Iron Hans" is one of the most purely happy of all of Sexton's fairy tale poems. But there would be no such transformation, no lifting of the spell, for Sexton. She could not "change reality" like a costume as she had wished as a child. And apparently she could not function for long without Thorazine.

Sexton, alas, was not Iron Hans; she was Sleeping Beauty/Briar Rose. It had been so for years. She had been dependent on pills to fall asleep for most of her adult life, and the overdose of sleeping pills that occurred while she was working on the Sleeping Beauty poem was hardly the first such incident, nor the last. Middlebrook states that "Dying perfect was what Sexton did every night when she took her sleeping pills, making herself a Sleeping

Beauty" (216). This image also comes up in a description of an experience that D. M. Thomas had with Sexton when she visited England. Invited up to Sexton's room, the young writer is witness to her nightly ritual of counting and swallowing her pills. He recalls: "'She said, "Please stay, in thirty seconds I'll be asleep." And in thirty seconds she was asleep. What struck me,' . . . [Thomas] added, 'was the theatricality of that goodnight, a very subdued eroticism about it. She was going to be Sleeping Beauty'" (282).

Sexton's sleeping pill habit was something she wrote candidly about. Here is the opening and ending of her poem "The Addict" from *Live or Die*:

Sleepmonger,
deathmonger,
with capsules in my palms each night,
eight at a time from sweet pharmaceutical bottles
I make arrangements for a pint-sized journey,
. . . . . . . . . . . . . .
with two pink, two orange,
two green, two white goodnights.
Fee-fi-fo-fum—
Now I'm borrowed.
Now I'm numb. (CP 165, 166)

Here is yet another fairy tale allusion, though not to a Grimm story; the *Fee-fi-fo-fum* evokes the giant from the English tale *Jack and the Beanstalk*. Was Sexton climbing the beanstalk to dreamland each night with the help of her magic seeds, pink, orange, green, and white? Or was that ogre death stalking her? Sleep and death, death and sleep. In the fairy tale *Briar Rose*, as Grimm titles it, the infant princess is cursed by the uninvited, revengeful thirteenth fairy/wise woman: she will prick her finger with a spindle at age fifteen and die, but this spell is countered by another fairy, who modifies the death sentence to a one-hundred-year snooze.

Imagine if you can the opening of Sexton's "Briar Rose (Sleeping Beauty)" spoken by Rod Serling, the host of the classic TV show *The Twilight Zone*:

Consider
a girl who keeps slipping off,
arms limp as old carrots,
into the hypnotist's trance,

into a spirit world
speaking with the gift of tongues.
She is stuck in the time machine. (290)

The "case" described in this poem's prologue is a female patient being re-
gressed by hypnosis. Somewhat like the "pint-sized journey" in "The Ad-
dict," this girl is "on a voyage." Via the time machine she goes back to find
herself as a "Little doll child," sitting on her father's knee. Again the poet
uses a doll image unfavorably to indicate the passivity of the girl who is be-
ing manipulated by "Papa." Another of Sexton's food similes also crops up
in this opening—the carrots from "Rapunzel" that were "growing like little
fish" seem the worse for wear now that we have reached the last poem of
the book. And the "gift of tongues" brings back a theme from "The White
Snake." Everything that is brought back from previous poems in the col-
lection, however, has a more ominous edge here. But spookiest of all is the
character of the Papa/King. The prologue ends with his creepy invitation to
the child, "Come be my snooky / and I will give you a root" followed by Sex-
ton's bitter comment, "That kind of voyage, / rank as honeysuckle" (291).

Following this disturbing scene, Sexton begins her altered retelling of the
fairy tale. One key change she makes is to delete the queen/mother almost
entirely, placing more emphasis on the king. Wanting to protect his child,
the Grimm king issues an order that "all spindles in his kingdom were to
be burned" (Grimm 186). But in Sexton's hands, the protectiveness turns
creepy. Yes, the king banishes spinning wheels, but also each night he

bit the hem of her gown
to keep her safe.
. . . . . . . . . . . . . .
He forced every male in the court
to scour his tongue with Bab-o
lest they poison the air she dwelt in.
Thus she dwelt in his odor.
Rank as honeysuckle. (CP 292)

The hem biting is particularly odd and conjures up sex-play, or at least a
father who holds a nightgown in his teeth like an animal lest his daugh-
ter escape. And what but obsessive jealousy could lead to every male hav-
ing to bleach his tongue with cleanser? Odor of "Dad-o" wafts none too

sweet—that honeysuckle seems to grow ranker (and make a dirtier pun) each time it appears.

Despite the king's stringent efforts, however, the tale proceeds as it ever has, with the teen princess pricking her finger and the whole kingdom falling under a spell. This is the only time that Sexton mentions the queen, "king and queen went to sleep," which echoes Grimm precisely as do many of the poem's lines that describe the sleeping spell that overtakes the kingdom. Dame Sexton does spin them a bit with her own contemporary vocabulary, "each a catatonic / stuck in the time machine. / Even the frogs were zombies" while also radically condensing this part of the tale so that the hundred years quickly pass (292–93). Then a lucky prince gets through the briars and kisses the princess

and she woke up crying:
Daddy! Daddy!
Presto! She's out of prison!
She married the prince
and all went well
except for the fear—
the fear of sleep. (293)

The "Papa" from earlier in the poem has now become "Daddy" (another Plath echo?), but despite this momentary, and revealing, confusion of identity, Briar Rose does marry the prince.

From this point on, however, Sexton refashions the story through her imagination, incorporating her own experience. Just where the Grimm tale draws to a happy conclusion, "the speaker in this case" introduces a bad case of royal insomnia, the lingering symptom of the princess's travail and time travel. It makes perfect clinical sense. If you woke up from a sound sleep and found it was a century later (or if you woke and found something unwanted happening to you), you might be leery of falling asleep again too. Sexton, not wanting to put the poem, and perhaps even the entire book, "to bed," continues the story beyond the source tale's ending for more than sixty lines. Like the poet herself, Briar Rose cannot nap "without the court chemist / mixing her some knock-out drops" (293). She is afraid of dreaming, and of visions of a crone, who may represent not just the vengeful fairy who put the curse on her but the aged self she will eventually become, or in some way—since she is actually 115 years old!—already is:

> . . . a faltering crone at my place,
> her eyes burnt by cigarettes
> as she eats betrayal like a slice of meat.
>
> I must not sleep
> for while asleep I'm ninety
> and think I'm dying. (293)

In an early poem, "Old," Sexton had written, "In a dream you are never eighty," but an older wiser Sexton seems to know better (69). This girl who takes her knock-out drops, "This trance girl," is in a state close to death: "You could lay her in a grave, / an awful package, / and shovel dirt on her face" (294). In conjuring this comatose buried-alive state, Sexton appears to be evoking her own overdose episodes. Did she compose these lines after her stomach pumping and hospitalization of August 1970, or right before?

As the poem and the book reach the final stanza, it becomes less clear who is speaking. Briar Rose and Anne Sexton seem to have melded together, and the tone gets painfully personal as the theme of parental abuse, which Sexton had explored in her play *Mercy Street,* reemerges. The speaker of the last stanza describes being tortured in the time machine:

> I was forced backward.
> I was forced forward.
> I was passed hand to hand
> like a bowl of fruit. (294)

Perhaps the reliving of selves through the historic lens of these nineteenth century tales has made the poet feel she has been on a type of time machine voyage herself. In these last pages of the book, through the revisioning of Sleeping Beauty, Sexton is beginning to be drawn back toward the autobiographical material that she was known for, and from which *Transformations* provided a detour for a while, or as she put it to her editor, "a kind of dalliance on the way" (*SPL* 326). It is not hard to imagine those eight rainbow pills she described in "The Addict" as being nails in a coffin (or is it a cross?) for Briar Rose's sleep:

> Each night I am nailed into place
> and I forget who I am.
> Daddy?

That's another kind of prison.
It's not the prince at all,
but my father
drunkenly bent over my bed,
circling the abyss like a shark,
my father thick upon me
like some sleeping jellyfish. (*CP* 294)

In a reversal, the princess who mistook the rescuing prince for daddy upon waking from the spell now finds her father leaning over the bed and "not the prince at all." And father is no prince, that is clear. The similarity of sounds in *prison* and *prince* suggests how thin the line is between the two options. This imprisoning, claustrophobic scene takes place in an underwater dream state, a murky subconscious, where the sharks lurk (to bite a hem?) and jellyfish wait to sting. And of course there is a cruder definition for being *nailed* that swims around in this passage. Something is altogether fishy here indeed.

Although the theme of resuscitation, even resurrection, is part of the source tale, in Sexton's version the new life seems as full of terrors as the old. Or to put it another way, one cannot escape one's past, one is drowning in it. It comes with you in the time machine; it survives any magic spell. The poem, and thus the entire book, ends with a fragment of prayer and a question "God help—/ this life after death?" (295). Desperate, skeptical, dramatic to the last curtain, it is an ending that is pure Sexton. Cue the blackout. All the Grimm has been left behind. The fairy tale phase of Sexton's writing life is over; it would be life and death, as well as God, that would occupy her for the four years she had left.[7] Knowing or at least intuiting this might have made this poem particularly difficult for Sexton to finish or even precipitated her strange attack while she was working on it. If there was going to be a Grimm character that Sexton would be in danger of "over-identifying" with, Sleeping Beauty/Briar Rose was the one.

Whatever struggles she had completing the poem, she wrote to her agent that "'Rapunzel' and 'Sleeping Beauty' are two of my best" (*SPL* 324). In this same letter she states, "Come to think of it I'm not even sure these are poems. I think they are artifacts" (324). "Artifact" is defined by the *American Heritage Dictionary* as "an object produced or shaped by human craft, especially a tool, a weapon, or an ornament of archaeological or historical interest." Most would agree that all poems satisfy the first part of this definition, but it is interesting to contemplate how the poems may have been *tools* for Sexton to explore her own psychological trauma; *weapons* to wield against the familial/societal/cultural forces that she felt had shaped or misshaped her; and *ornaments*, qualified by their imagery (from brand names to show biz figures) and tone (casual, sardonic, suave, and psychoanalytical), to be markers of her particular historic moment.

Something else in *Transformations* marks its cultural moment, subtly yet unmistakably to anyone who was young in that period: Hermann Hesse. He appears in the dedication, "*To Linda, who reads Hesse and drinks clam chowder*," and this is echoed in the introductory poem: "It is not enough to read Hesse / and drink clam chowder / we must have the answers" (*CP* 221, 223). Approximately the age of Sexton's daughters, I feel fairly confident stating that this Hesse work would most likely have been *Siddhartha* (I still have my high school copy on the shelf), and if not, either *Steppenwolf* or *Demian*. What it was *not* likely to have been was Hesse's shorter fairy tales, yet how interesting that Hesse's spirit hovers over the opening of Sexton's book. For like Sexton, Hesse suffered from various mental problems including depression, despair, insomnia, and suicidal impulses, and he had several stays in mental institutions. As translator Jack Zipes records in his informative introduction to *The Fairy Tales of Hermann Hesse*, the period of the First World War was especially difficult: "In 1917 he suffered a nervous breakdown and went to Sonnmatt, a private sanatorium near Lucerne, where he underwent electroshock therapy and numerous analytic sessions with a Jungian psychologist" (xiv). Hesse's first collection of tales, *Märchen*, appeared in 1919.

Admittedly, Hesse's approach to the fairy tale involved a deeper and more experimental exploration of essential global fairy tale formulae than Sexton's, but like her, and many writers working in the fairy tale tradition, Hesse "used fairy-tale conventions to gain distance from his personal problems" (xxiii). And, as in several of Sexton's *Transformations*, the mother figure is prominent in many of Hesse's tales. Zipes points out how the protagonists of his tales often move toward a "mystical mother" (xxvi). The title character of "Augustus" hears his mother calling to him as he is dying, while the narrator of another story, "The Difficult Path," ends up "quivering through infinity to the mother's breast" (100, 203). Whether Sexton knew any of these facts about Hesse's life, or his fairy tales, there is an eerie confluence, a kinship, that perhaps she intuited. Middlebrook notes: "When Sexton imagined that end, however, it was not as a turning to God but as a return to the arms of what she called a 'consecrating mother'; in one of her last poems . . . she imagined death as a walk into the sea: 'I wish to enter her like a dream, [ . . . ] sink into the great mother arms / I never had'" (395; brackets in Middlebrook). That is a vision Hesse would have understood.

As it was, Anne Sexton—the teller of tales, the "mother of the insane," "the speaker in this case" on behalf of all the sad cases—in the end performed her final Sleeping Beauty act by walking into the garage, sinking under car fumes not sea foam, swaddled in her mother's old fur.

### *Transformations* Timeline

1969—*Mercy Street* production (summer rewriting; October–November run).[8]

December 1969—Sexton writes that she has been "blocked" creatively for six months.

January 1970—Sexton sends two of the *Transformations* poems to George Starbuck.

March 1970—Sexton resends the same two poems plus two more to Starbuck.

May 1970—Sexton has about half the poems, that is, eight or nine, finished (including "The Maiden Without Hands," "Hansel and Gretel," "The Little Peasant," "The Gold Key," and "The Twelve Dancing Princesses").

August 1970—Prior to 12 August, Sexton has an odd episode, overdoses, and is hospitalized.

25 August 1970—Six poems sent to Houghton Mifflin: "Iron Hans," "Rapunzel," "Godfather Death," "The White Snake," "The Little Peasant," and "Hansel and Gretel."

September 1970—Sexton sends four new poems to her agent, including two of "her best": "Briar Rose (Sleeping Beauty)" and "Rapunzel." ("The Little Peasant" has already been bought by *Playboy* and "Snow White and the Seven Dwarfs" and "Hansel and Gretel" by *Cosmopolitan*.)

October 1970—By mid-month, Sexton has completed all seventeen poems for *Transformations*. She writes a letter defending the book to her editor Paul Brooks.

November 1970—Sexton sends the completed MS to Houghton Mifflin. She also sends it to Kurt Vonnegut, asking if he would write a foreword, which he does.

December 1970—On 22 December, the book is accepted for publication.

1971—Throughout early part of year, Sexton works with Barbara Swan on the illustrations.

1971—*Transformations* is published. Launch party at Sardi's, New York, 27 September.

1972—In November, Sexton signs agreement with composer Conrad Susa for opera.

1973—Opera of *Transformations* opens. In early February, Sexton asks husband for divorce.

## Notes

1. This was Verse Circus hosted by Inverse Theater company in Manhattan.

2. Although beyond the purview of this essay, Sexton's intense relationship with her great aunt Anna Ladd Dingley, or Nana as she was called, which included a "daily cuddle" and had a lasting emotional effect on her, is detailed by Middlebrook (*AS* 14ff.).

3. The film *Doctor Doolittle,* with its Oscar-winning song "Talk to the Animals," had been released in 1967.

4. The contradiction inherent in this tale, that his aid of the birds results in the slaughter of his horse, is one that Sexton passes over without comment. Other poets however, have found this troubling; e.g., Martha Carlson-Bradley in her poem "The White Snake" ends with the paradox "the horse he slays / to feed the fledgling ravens / mute in its own defense" (Beaumont and Carlson 37).

5. The 1967 song was composed by André Popp and perhaps most familiar in the orchestrated version conducted by Paul Mauriat that was a number one hit in the United States in February and March of 1968. (Information at http://en.Wikipedia.org/wiki/L'amour_est_bleu.) Once you've heard it several times,

it haunts you forever, which is why it immediately came to my mind when I read these lines of Sexton's.

6. The Bobbsey Twins, a long-lived series of children's books (1904–79), told of the (mild) adventures of a family made up of two sets of brother-sister twins; Nan and Bert were the older twins, Flossie and Freddie the younger twins.

7. It is interesting to note that the very first lines of Sexton's next book, *The Book of Folly* (1972), pick up the insomnia strand once again: "So it has come to this—/ insomnia at 3:15 a.m" (*CP* 299).

8. Timeline information is culled from *AS* and *SPL*.

## Works Cited

Beaumont, Jeanne Marie, and Claudia Carlson. *The Poets' Grimm: 20th Century Poems from Grimm Fairy Tales*. Ashland, OR: Story Line, 2003. Print.

Brunyate, Roger. "A Feminist Far from Grimm: Anne Sexton and Her *Transformations*." *Opera at Peabody*. Web. 22 June 2011.

Furst, Arthur. *Anne Sexton: The Last Summer*. New York: St. Martin's, 2000. Print.

Grimm, Wilhelm, and Jacob Grimm. *The Complete Fairy Tales of the Brothers Grimm*. Trans. and ed. Jack Zipes. New York: Bantam, 1987. Print.

Harder, Rolf. Noludar 300 Advertisement. Museum of Modern Art: The Collection. Web. 7 June 2013.

Hay, Sara Henderson. *Story Hour*. New York: Doubleday, 1963. Print.

Hesse, Hermann. *The Fairy Tales of Hermann Hesse*. Trans. and ed. Jack Zipes. New York: Bantam, 1995. Print.

Lowell, Robert. *Life Studies* and *For the Union Dead*. New York: Farrar, Straus, and Giroux, 1964. Print.

Middlebrook, Diane Wood. *Anne Sexton: A Biography*. Boston: Houghton Mifflin, 1991. Print.

Parker, Dorothy. "Résumé." *The Norton Anthology of Poetry*. Shorter 4th ed. Ed. Margaret Ferguson, et al. New York: Norton, 1997. 799. Print.

Plath, Sylvia. *The Collected Poems*. Ed. Ted Hughes. New York: Harper and Row, 1981. Print

Sexton, Anne. *A Self-Portrait in Letters*. Ed. Linda Gray Sexton and Lois Ames. Boston: Houghton Mifflin, 1977. Print.

———. *The Complete Poems*. Boston: Houghton Mifflin, 1981. Print.

Sondheim, Stephen, and James Lapine. *Into the Woods*. New York: Theatre Communications Group, 1987. Print.

# $\cdots 10$

## Anne Sexton and the Wild Animal

### An Exploration of the Bestiary Poems

DOROTHEA LASKY

### A Memory and Mental Wildness

In considerations of her work, both formal and informal, much is made of Anne Sexton as the mad female, the suicide victim, and the mess. As a poet, I have always had a problem with this simplistic take on her, infused, of course, with its rampant misogyny. I have always thought of her poems' personae as undergoing a kind of immortal performance with each poem, nuanced by the actions of her life, but also never the work of a simple wild force. After all, when a poet writes a poem, there may be a wild wind blowing through her, but when she actually conveys the meaning of this wind through words, there is something non-wild about this translation. We can call it intelligence—to know what is the perfect construction of language to convey a feeling, or we could also call it a type of rationality. Whatever we call it, it is not something a wild animal can do, and it is not something just any human could do or does. And so, I think we need to revise the ways in which we think of the wild when we consider Anne Sexton.

When I think of Anne Sexton, I think of a controlled force. I think of her line breaks full of targeted venom, a simple palette of imagery and language. I think of a poet who calculatedly paved the way for countless American poets after her in a manner that was cool and calm—boundless, but not crazy at all. When I think of Sexton I do not think of the mad woman she may have been—a woman I never knew—I think of the purpose of her madness. Of what wildness and for what reason, what wilderness she created in her poems. Of what purpose her life did serve for the poets to come after her. I think of the immortal construction of a shapeshifter *I* she made for us to help us get through our lives and with what tenderness she did this.

I must confess I first fell in love with Sexton's work through my love of Sylvia Plath. In the early 2000s, as an MFA student at the University of Massachusetts-Amherst, I was an eager volunteer at the Sylvia Plath Day festival held in Northampton, Massachusetts (the town of Plath's alma mater, Smith College). I helped organize the readings and speakers, hung flyers all over the town, and was one of maybe ten people to attend every event that day.

One of the festival panels included Kathleen Spivack who had taken the famous Robert Lowell workshop at Boston University with Plath and Sexton in the late 1950s. I do not remember what details she recounted of the actual workshop, in terms of what poems they read or what suggestions Lowell gave them, but I do remember Spivack describing Sexton vividly. Spivack said that she could not see Sexton in the class from where she was sitting, but that she remembered the sound of her bangles clinging and clanging as she moved her hands to speak. She was enchanted by the lively sound of them in her memory, but with her retelling I became bewitched by the ghostly sound of them in my imagination. There is a wildness to the sound of bangles moving up and down an arm. And I must confess, too, that at that moment I vowed always to wear an armful of bangles to every poetry workshop I attended or taught and to every reading I might be lucky enough to give. I have kept my promise to the ghostly sound of Anne Sexton, and it is a ritual I practice to this day, as an adult, accumulating hundreds and hundreds of rainbow-colored bangles to adorn my arms. The sound of bangles is a wild animal. Every time I find the poem, I hear the call of this bangle animal, and I give a little nod to Sexton that she's in the room with me, too.

It has been said that when Sexton first started writing poems as an adult in her late twenties, it was under the guidance of her psychiatrist, Dr. Martin Orne (*AS* 65). She had written poems as a teenager, but not as a young adult. It was Dr. Orne who encouraged her to write again. And when Sexton became depressed and suicidal, feeling as if her life had no meaning, he told her that it did because she could use her poems as a way to help others. It was with this spirit that Sexton wrote her poems. Some may say that she had no choice but to unleash the darkness of her mental health as a person, living in the world. But as a poet, she chose to put darkness in her poems, so that others like her might not feel as alone.

I do not in any way mean to suggest that Sexton wrote poems therapeutically to perform some therapy for her readers (not that I think there is anything wrong with that, however) or that that is the point of her work at all. There is much trapped in such a kind of art-making and poetry based in its therapeutic value, that it need not be "good." I think Sexton wanted her poems to be "good" and that she cared rather desperately about craft. What I mean to really say is that Sexton contained a wild animal in her lyric to perform a sort of *catharsis* for everyone, to empower her readers, people like her. Sexton sought to seek the spirit in the wild, to bring to her poems, to make her readers feel less alone.

This essay is about a group of poems that seek out the spirit of the wild from Sexton's posthumously published *45 Mercy Street* (1976) called "Bestiary U.S.A." It also compares these poems to the work of other poets who investigate the animal, like Sylvia Plath and Galway Kinnell. Sexton's "Bestiary U.S.A." is a collection of eighteen poems, each focusing on an animal: a bat, a hog, a porcupine, a hornet, a star-nosed mole, a snail, a lobster, a snake, a moose, a sheep, a cockroach, a raccoon, a seal, an earthworm, a whale, a horse, a june bug, and a gull. And in it, Sexton studies and describes each to seek out the spirit of each animal, to uncover what makes it wild and human, in order to empower the reader to take on its strength—to ultimately use each as a cathartic symbol. In each poem, Sexton, as she is in all of her work, is willing to let her lyric go wild, for the sake of this catharsis and empowerment.

## To Make a Bestiary Is to Serve a Wild I

The first bestiary was the Physiologus, a Greek text from the second century that was popular in the Middle Ages and influenced the form until the present day. In a bestiary, there is traditionally writing about animals, mythological and real beasts, as well as other natural elements like rocks and plants, paired with drawings. A bestiary seeks to find the divine in all creatures. There is oftentimes a moralistic purpose to the writing, as the animal has some sort of knowledge to give the reader, to help his or her human plight, with its natural structure and intention.

Although Sexton's bestiary poems do not include illustrations, it does read in many ways like a classic bestiary. She starts the section of the book off explaining that the purpose of the poems was to "look at the strangeness in them and the naturalness they cannot help, in order to find some virtue in the beast in me" (CP 497). This prefaces the purpose of the section, to have awe for these natural creatures, to find the goodness of Sexton's own wildness. She sets up in her poems this transfer of wildness of object-creature to her I to her ultimate empowerment of her reader. In these poems, her I looks at the takes on what it could be and gets strength from the animal, putting on the mask of the creatures.

In the course of all of these bestiary poems, Sexton makes a wild lyric I. I define this I as one with no real center and one where the reader has no way to predict where it will go. An I in a poem that is a shapeshifter. A persona that uses unexpected language and imagery, that is inconsistent, frightening, funny, and beyond the idea of a singular self. That is so wild it may not be a self at all.

It can be a difficult task to try and find a purpose of creating any grouping of poems, but bestiaries with their long histories, provide somewhat of a purpose. Sexton's I often explained how animalistic, beast-like it felt, how out of control it was, as in "Cigarettes and Whiskey and Wild, Wild Women," a poem from the same collection as the bestiary group (CP 537–38). Taking its title from a bar song, this poem is a type of transformation of the lyric I into a beast. The I starts off ready to sublimate itself, as in the first line, it is "born kneeling" (537). It expects mercy at the end of its sublimation, but life and its details does not give it, so the I must "plant ... [its] fires underground" and feed its hunger for mercy with writing "many words," through sexuality as it "let out so many loves," and get lost in alcohol (537). The culmination of this is that when the I looks in the mirror it sees herself in a rat's eyes as she writes:

Do I not look in the mirror,
these days,
and see a drunken rat avert her eyes?
Do I not feel the hunger so acutely

that I would rather die than look
into its face?
I kneel once more,
in case mercy should come
in the nick of time. (*CP* 537–38)

Sexton chooses the image of a rat wisely, as what animal is more the shadow self of what it means to be beast-like as a human. Rats feed off of our food, live in our houses with us, yet they try to do so sneakily and quietly, a reminder of our beastly instincts that are ever present, but under the surface most of the time. Rats do not expect our mercy, like a stray dog or cat would, they know we won't have mercy for them and will be disgusted by their tails and habits. They simply live seemingly without the expectation, although in Sexton's poem, she supposes a rat like her might deep down expect it. In the poem, the *I* becomes the rat, the unnamed hunger, one with the beast, containing a kinship to the wild, drunk in order to try and temper this uncontrollable hunger. The rat and the *I* still hope for mercy at the end of the poem, despite having learned it does not come easy, or at all.

In the poem, the *I* feels its undeniable hunger, hoping that mercy or love might save it from its animal self. In this way, the *I*, feeling its animal "hunger acutely" states it would "rather die than look / into its face," yet it does look its hunger in the face within the poem, shredding its sense of containment, becoming a wild principle that faces the darkness and shapeshifts into a rat for the sake of explaining this hunger and finding kinship and mercy with its reader.

Whereas "Cigarettes and Whiskey and Wild, Wild Women" demonstrates the ability of the lyric *I* to become the beast, Sexton's bestiary section uses beast imagery as an overarching mask for the *I*'s wildness and a way to understand a voracious restlessness and hunger—the heart of what it means to be a poet. In this respect, the bestiary poems are different from the others in their collection (and maybe in most of her poems, or at least many) that they take on the mask overtly. But they share a lot with this poem, in that the animals in the section display their obvious wild and natural energy to give a hinge for the *I* to rest upon and are in lots of ways like the rat in "Cigarettes and Whiskey and Wild, Wild Women."

Among her library, Sexton owned *The Book of Beasts*, edited from a translation of a twelfth century Latin bestiary by T. H. White and published in

1960. The book, written in clear prose, is an engaging and strange reference book, a swift 270 pages, describing animals both real and imaginary. It is curious to note that Sexton did not annotate this book, unlike books in her library (Golden 68).[1] Perhaps by the time she read *The Book of Beasts*, she had become more confident in using texts as guide to help her write her poems wildly. The cover of the book is also worth taking note of when considering Sexton's wild *I* and her bestiary poems.[2]

The image is at once frightening, powerful, and strange in its visual reference points, at least in part because it is a completely made-up beast with qualities of mythical creatures who might be in a traditional bestiary. It is at its face a fuchsia-winged goat creature, with a snake-like dragon tail, seemingly on fire with red flames. The animal may loosely reference a chimera, although then it would have a lion's head and an actual snake for a tail. It is also standing straight up, as a human would do, and evokes a creature both man and beast. It is interesting to think about how Sexton might have interpreted this image as she was writing her own bestiary. The "Bestiary U.S.A." poems showcase real animals, who all seemingly have superpowers, as in "Horse, you flame thrower, / you shark-mouthed man" (*CP* 507), infusing their wildness onto her persona.

Comparing the poems in her bestiary and this book, we can find many similarities and many ways that Sexton used the basis of the animal descriptions to embellish her own characteristic, performative wild *I*. In addition, if we look closely at three of Sexton's bestiary poems, particularly the three that best illustrate the abject nature of being a beast and can be considered symbols of Satan, we can see how her lyric *I* goes wild as it interacts with the mask of the animal.

In "Bat," the introductory poem in the section, Sexton compares her *I* with a bat, ultimately putting its bat-mask upon it, starting the description of the animal with:

His awful skin
stretched out by some tradesman
is like my skin, here between my fingers,
a kind of webbing, a kind of frog. (497)

Looking at *The Book of Beasts*, we can see where Sexton got this idea, as she later also describes the bat as "only a veil of skin from my arms to my waist," and her bestiary book explains the bat "is supported by a membrane, poised on which just as if on a flight of feathers it moves and weaves about" (White 141). Thinking and describing the bat this way, as an animal completely composed of skin, adds to its wretchedness and strangeness and makes it even more uncanny.

Sexton chose the bat to begin her bestiary section, but it is not the first animal in *The Book of Beasts* (Leo the Lion takes this place) and instead assumes a middle placement. *The Book of Beasts*'s bat is named Vespertilio, of the evening light. Bats are creatures of the night, doing their work when others are sleeping, and Sexton's *I* captures this nocturnal existence, as she writes: "I flew at night, too. Not to be seen / for if I were I'd be taken down" (*CP* 497). Here is Sexton's *I*, the lyric *I* and the poet is a night being who, if it were seen in the light of day, would be destroyed out of fear, so it flies (it writes and sings) "in the thick dark" (497). The *I* is wild, a thing that shouldn't be moving, "a pink corpse with wings" (497). It is something not to let roam free, because of its wildness, but is "something to be caught," controlled, and perhaps killed (497). Still the *I*, by the end of the poem, with its mask of the bat persists, living as the *I* of the poem does with the eternally dead, ready to do its work when no one is looking, "something to be caught / somewhere in the cemetery hanging upside down / like a mis-shapen udder" (497).

Being of the night and a "paltry animal" (White 140) may be why Sexton chose to begin her bestiary and include the bat at all. Just like the rat, the bat is an undesirable animal. It is not the grand lion, king of the jungle; it is the occult nocturnal animal, just as Sexton may have saw herself as a poet. *The Book of the Beasts* also describes how bats hang in groups, literally hanging onto one another, and if the top one is moved, they all disperse, doing this "from a certain duty of affection, of a kind which is difficult to find in man" (141). One could only assume that Sexton delighted in this sort of cynicism of humanity, a group of animals without mercy for the troubled and weak, and assumed the role of the bat to gain her strength. As the section commences, Sexton's *I* invokes the bat and becomes it and accumulates the energy of all of the beasts in the poems who function similarly among the animal kingdom—in this way, she speaks as she always does in her bestiary poems a range of brutal and repulsive feelings as a type of selfless and self-imposed group catharsis.

In the second poem of the section, Sexton invokes the "Hog," a beast that we associate with dirt and gluttony, and yet one which we desire to eat vehemently in pounds of delicious morning bacon, as Sexton describes it as a "bacon machine" (*CP* 498). Unlike how in "Bat," Sexton's *I* completely puts on the mask of the beast, the *I* in this poem looks at the hog with some distance. She addresses it directly in the first stanza, comparing it to soft and gross things, telling it is "leaking out the ears," has "eyes as soft as eggs," is a "dog's nightmare," and yet is ultimately sweet, in pursuit of its own bodily pleasure (498). In the second stanza, the *I* thinks of a grouping of hogs, all neatly put up to move "on the shuttle toward death," while it masturbates ("just as my mind moves over / for its own little death") (498). The seemingly self-involved, and perhaps pointless, pursuit of pleasure of the *I*, uncontrollable once it is "in the closet of my mind," is like the hog, gluttonous and fat with its unrelenting hunger (498).

In her copy of *Book of the Beasts*, Sexton would have found no full entry for hog, as hog is mentioned in only two notes. The first states that hog "approach[es] the nearest" (White 70) to humans in that it, too, can survive and prosper in every climate on the earth. The second note is more relevant to the wild Sexton sought to convey in her beast poems, as it mentioned that hogs (called swine and then their ancient name of *Hybrides*) are the animal who is most wild (90). Certainly these references would have influenced her writing of "Hog," with its heavy emphasis on gluttony, both for food and sex. But the book's connection of the hog as being most like the human and the wildest of the animals, creates an important tension for Sexton to have considered as she meditated on the idea of the animal. Just as much Christian symbolism connects the hog with the devil or the evil sins of the body, Sexton, too, made the hog into the shadow drives of the human in her and then was able to infuse these drives into her shapeshifter *I*, one that learned and accepted the lessons of the wild animal kingdom.

In these two poems, "Bat" and "Hog," Sexton explores the wildness of two mammals and their beastly abjectness, their wildness. Her lyric *I* has more kinship with the bat and the hog, as it puts its mask on by the end of the poem, both working at night and ultimately living with the dead to do this work. In "Hornet," Sexton looks closely at an insect, finding a connection to an animal more distant to her seemingly mammalian lyric *I*. She writes:

A red-hot needle
hangs out of him, he steers by it

as if it were a rudder, he
would get in the house any way he could
and then he would bounce from window
to ceiling, buzzing and looking for you. (CP 499)

Here, Sexton turns the hornet into a kind of stalker—the bug is not the
random animal most of us consider it to be, going about its business and
sometimes running into a human it cannot help but sting out of fear or
some other more benign instinct. The poem turns even more frightening
as Sexton considers the hornet's merciless intent. She structures the rest
of the poem with six "Do not sleep" refrains, where the *I* of the poem begs
the reader not to rest, for the hornet is "under the shelf" and "wants to slide
under your / fingernail and push in a splinter" (499, 500). By the end of the
poem, Sexton's hornet "wants you to walk into him as into a dark fire" (500),
suggesting the ultimate kind of moral and self-sublimation.

In this terrifying poem, the lyric *I* is not overtly present at all, as it is in
pursuit of the *you* of the poem. It can be assumed that the mask of the hor-
net has completely consumed the *I,* and now it moves along systematically
and horrifically, hunting the reader in an attempt only to cause it pain—a
completely wild lyrical element. Of the three, this poem is the most spell-
like, with its "Do not sleep," to the *you* (the reader) as a horrible warning
that to let its guard down, to expect the mercy of slumber, will be the space
in which to open the door for the hornet to submerge itself and infect the
reader. Even though Sexton begs us to "not sleep," the poem reads like a lul-
laby that could put us to sleep, if it were not about our doom at the hands of
the hornet. In addition, she repeats the phrase "he wants" six times, demon-
strating the animalistic desire of the hornet, an *I* that moves only to fulfill its
sadistic desires.

There is no direct reference to a hornet, either in a full entry or a note,
in *The Book of Beasts,* but there is a whole section devoted to insects. Over
the course of several pages, the book outlines a spider, a millipede, and a
silkworm. Some of the descriptions of what we might think of the more
sadistic animals, like a scorpion, give them a surprising tender side, as the
book explains, "The oddest thing about a scorpion is that it will not bite
you in the palm of your hand" (White 192). However, other bugs are given
the demonic instincts of Sexton's hornet, like how the leech "lies in wait for

people who are taking a drink of water and, when it slips down their throats or manages to catch on anywhere, it sups their gore" (191–92). We can see even more direct inspiration for the "dark fire" of Sexton's hornet in White's description of a Usia or "pig worm," as when it bites you "The place where it has bitten gets so fiery that you make water on the spot, when it has bitten you" (194). Here, we can see where Sexton may have gotten the idea to connect the insect with the fire of its sting or bite, but also the idea that the body and the insect are interconnected, as Sexton's hornet "wants to sew up your skin" and "make a home in the embarrassed hair" (CP 499, 500).

Although Sexton uses real animals in her bestiary poems and not the mythological or imaginary beasts that historically some bestiaries have used, there is nothing particularly scientifically correct about her descriptions of the animals' motivations. Quite the contrary, there is something inhuman—perhaps demonic—about them, particularly the three I have discussed here. All three of these animals—a bat, a hog, and a hornet—are satanic symbols. They all three move in the night (the bat working and flying, eventually sleeping in a cemetery, the hog and the I conflating only in the pursuit of nightly pleasure, and the hornet ready to inflict pain in the nighttime). They give a power and wildness to the I of the poems, as they form a kind of catharsis for the reader who seeks to better understand Sexton's I through their animal masks and eventual sublimation. Ultimately, Sexton's close looking achieves a kind of catharsis that is the whole point. All three poems ask: What happens when we see the demonic in animals? Does it help us to understand the lack of mercy Sexton's I argues many times over that humans have? Facing these questions "into its face" (537) is aided by the wild lyric I and aids us in understanding what it means to be human—an understanding Sexton tirelessly investigated in her work.

## Other Uses of the Animal, but Not as Wild

Other poets writing in the twentieth century used animal imagery in their work, but there are few that utilize this imagery for the same cathartic purposes. Plath's sequence of bee poems contains some of the same struggles as Sexton's poems, as the bees, little animals, contain a wild principle that the I of the poem must contend with. In "The Arrival of the Bee Box" (1962), Plath describes her uneasy relationship to the wild small world of a beehive, where she becomes a godlike figure by giving the wild bees some potential for escape. She begins the poem by describing this locked world of mad things:

> The box is locked, it is dangerous.
> I have to live with it overnight
> And I can't keep away from it.
> There are no windows, so I can't see what is in there.
> There is only a little grid, no exit.
>     (*Collected Poems* 213)

Here, the "box" of bees has to be "locked," because it is "dangerous" or wild. But then Plath lets us know, by the end of the poem, that even though "They might ignore me immediately / In my moon suit and funeral veil. / I am no source of honey," that by "Tomorrow I will be sweet God, I will set them free. / The box is only temporary" (*Collected Poems* 213). Whereas in Sexton's "Hornet" (the closest poem in the section to the bee sequence because it is about a stinging insect), the *I* has become completely conflated with the hornet's sadistic actions, Plath's *I* is distant from the bees, who are wild in their multitude but not purely evil. Her *I* can only imagine itself in conversation with them, the angry "Roman mob" with their "furious Latin," a "box of maniacs" (*Collected Poems* 213). Plath explains that she need not contend with them; they are not the hornet of Sexton's poem which will haunt and hurt when one sleeps, but animals that the *I* cannot feed if it so chooses to. Plath's *I* does not have to interact with the wildness of the bees, if it doesn't want to. On the face of the *I*'s statements, it is safe to even set them free from their "temporary" box, as if let loose, they will not be interested in her, who is not a "source of honey."

Nevertheless, there is something haunting about this last line, "The box is only temporary" (213), as it is unclear if the *I* feels safe knowing that the box is ephemeral and she can be in control of the swarm of wild animals if they are let loose, or if there is fear that they could overtake her at any moment. It is this mix of fear and confidence that infuses in Plath's lyric *I* in this and other poems, an *I* that is ready to harness the wildness and strangeness of being human, to display it as a type of catharsis for her readers. But whereas Sexton is ready to conflate her *I* with the hornet and get completely lost in the animal's wildness, Plath always maintains some distance, controlling the bright light of the wild in the laser sharp focus of her *I*.

One poem by another poet, written many years after Sexton died, has always struck me as a quintessential struggle with one's poetic and beastly self (the beast self forever inside of every poet). "The Bear" by Galway Kinnell is a sort of ars poetica, as Kinnell's *I* contends with a bear, whose wild animal comes to represent poetry. In the poem's first section, he describes the poet as a hunter, always on the hunt for a wild animal to trap and conquer:

> In late winter
> I sometimes glimpse bits of steam
> coming up from
> some fault in the old snow
> and bend close and see it is lung-colored
> and put down my nose
> and know
> the chilly, enduring odor of bear. (67)

In the poem, Kinnell's *I* tracks and hunts the bear, seemingly for physical nourishment, eating bear excrement dipped in blood at moments of weak hunger, until it finds the carcass, which it climbs inside and dreams the hallucinatory dreams of bears. Eventually, as the *I* wears the dead bear suit, it becomes one with the bear and wanders the earth for the rest of its days, "wandering: wondering" (70), living on his own wildness. By the end of the poem, the wildness is all of poetry, "that rank flavor of blood, that poetry, by which I lived?" (70). Kinnell ends the poem with this question, as he wonders what was that "blood" or "poetry" that sustained him through his journey, and by finishing the poem with this question it becomes unanswerable. Blood, beastliness, poetry, and wildness are all equally ungraspable in the poem. Just as Sexton explores the strangeness and wildness of the animals in order to become one with them in her poems, Kinnell becomes one with his own animal, writing poems only after he has become consumed completely by the bear's form. But while in Sexton's poems the transfigurations and transformations have already happened, Kinnell narrates the act of becoming an animal, as a kind of explanation of his poetics. Still, in both, the wildness of the animal is used as a symbol for the wild lyric *I* that speaks from a beastly place.

As is often a theme in poetry, the work of the animals in these poems (and the work of the *Is*) is either nocturnal or otherworldly. Plath's bees seem magical, always awake and ready to leave the box, always hungry for honey and to be free. Kinnell's bear is dead by the time the *I* interacts with it. Sexton's bat is working in the night, then sleeping with the dead. Her hog lies around, governed by its gluttony, which Sexton's *I* blends with its nightly sexual desires. Her hornet is the most gloaming creature of all, ready and waiting to inflict pain when its prey is sleeping, completely at its lack of mercy. Perhaps it is the long held image of a poet, writing his or her poems as a seer to the spiritual world through the night that makes all of these animals take on their magical and nightly qualities. Or perhaps it is the idea of mercy, explored in Sexton's "Cigarettes, Whiskey, and Wild, Wild Women," that connects these animals to this liminal dimension. After all, we all are at the mercy of our environments and what they contain at a place of thresholds. Perhaps it is mercy after all that is at the heart of the wild lyric *I*.

## Conclusion

Sexton has taught me so much about how to be wild when writing my own poetry, to think of the poem not as a place to display what I know, but as a place to become something else entirely, to get to the dark vortex that surrounds us all. During the times when I have wondered if I should keep writing, it is Sexton's urgency that rises to the defense of the poem, telling me we poets do what we do to sum up the so many voices into voice, to bring voice to the weak, the forgotten and maligned, the lost animal in us all. And when I am teaching young poets, it is Sexton who is often the guide for them, not only because she shows that a poem can include not only the beauty of the world but also that the poem is the perfect place for their most ugly feelings.

This discussion has only begun to tackle the richness of Sexton's bestiary section. It is to be hoped that future discussions will consider more of the poems in the section, her other poems in the book that contains them, her other work, other poets' poems to compare them to, and theories of the connection between animal imagery and the development of a wild lyric *I*. I do hope that this initial discussion may have laid the foundation for some thinking about this body of work and its relationship to her writing poetry as a catharsis.

Certainly, I do think it has begun the discussion of how she took on animal imagery as masks to better infuse her lyrical *I* with wildness. As Sexton explained in the beginning of the bestiary section, she looked closely at these specific animals, in order to better understand her own wildness.

In doing so, through the act of taking on their masks, she uncovered what elements appealed to her that she could use for her lyric *I*. Maybe this is the reason anyone might make a bestiary, to make an *I* withstand the shred of a metaphysical nature, a principle who must go to earth and back and beyond, within every poem. An *I* which has, come to its physical self expecting mercy, and keeps looking for it, despite all of the earthly forces that beg it to stop looking. Maybe this is the gift Sexton keeps giving her readers, her kindred, through the wide expanse of time.

## Notes

1. Richard Oram, email to Amanda Golden, 30 July 2015.
2. See the cover of the 1960 paperback edition at Amazon.com, web. 30 July 2015, <http://www.amazon.com/The-Bestiary-Book-Beasts-Illustrated/dp/Boo 1113G4O>.

## Works Cited

Golden, Amanda. "Anne Sexton's Modern Library." *Collecting, Curating, and Researching Writers' Libraries: A Handbook.* Ed. Richard W. Oram and Joseph Nicholson. Lanham, MD: Rowman and Littlefield, 2014. 65–76. Print.
Kinnell, Galway. *Three Books.* Boston: Houghton Mifflin, 2002. Print.
Plath, Sylvia. *The Collected Poems.* New York: Harper Perennial Modern Classics, 2008. Print.
Sexton, Anne. *The Complete Poems.* Boston: Houghton Mifflin, 1981. Print.
White, T. H., ed. and trans. *The Book of Beasts.* New York: Dover Publications, Inc., 1984. Print.

# Contributors

Jeanne Marie Beaumont is the author of *Letters from Limbo, Burning of the Three Fires, Curious Conduct,* and *Placebo Effects,* a winner in the National Poetry Series. She coedited, with Claudia Carlson, the anthology *The Poets' Grimm: 20th Century Poems from Grimm Fairy Tales.* Her poems have been published in numerous anthologies and magazines, including *Court Green, Good Poems for Hard Times, Manhattan Review, Ploughshares, The Year's Best Fantasy and Horror 2007,* and *World Literature Today.* She currently teaches at the Unterberg Poetry Center of the 92nd Street Y and in the Stonecoast low-residency MFA program in Maine.

Jeffery Conway's latest book is *Descent of the Dolls: Part I,* a collaboration with Gillian McCain and David Trinidad. His other books include *Showgirls: The Movie in Sestinas, The Album That Changed My Life,* and with Lynn Crosbie and David Trinidad, *Phoebe 2002: An Essay in Verse,* and *Chain Chain Chain.* His current work can be found in *Columbia Poetry Review,* as well as in the anthologies *The Incredible Sestina Anthology; Dream Closet: Meditations on Childhood Spaces;* and *Rabbit Ears: TV Poems.*

Jo Gill is professor of twentieth-century literature at the University of Exeter, UK. She is the author of *The Poetics of the American Suburbs, Anne Sexton's Confessional Poetics, Women's Poetry,* and *The Cambridge Introduction to Sylvia Plath* and the editor of *The Cambridge Companion to Sylvia Plath, Modern Confessional Writing: New Critical Essays* and, with Simon Barker,

*Literature as History: Essays in Honour of Peter Widdowson*. She is currently working on a new book on *Modern American Poetry and the Architectural Imagination*.

Amanda Golden is assistant professor of English at the New York Institute of Technology. She previously held the postdoctoral fellowship in poetics at Emory University's Fox Center for Humanistic Inquiry and a Marion L. Brittain postdoctoral fellowship at the Georgia Institute of Technology. She is the author of *Annotating Modernism: Marginalia and Pedagogy from Virginia Woolf to the Confessional Poets* (forthcoming), book review editor of *Woolf Studies Annual*, and has published in *Modernism/modernity*, *The Ted Hughes Society Journal*, and *Woolf Studies Annual*.

Christopher Grobe is associate professor of English at Amherst College. Broadly speaking, his research concerns the fluid and reciprocal influence of America's literary, performance, and media cultures. His book, *The Art of Confession*, was published in 2017, and his reviews and essays can be found in *PMLA*, *Theater*, *Modern Drama*, and *Public Books*.

Anita Helle is professor of English at Oregon State University, where she currently serves as director of the School of Writing, Literature, and Film. Her scholarship focuses on twentieth- and twenty-first-century American poetry, visual culture, theories of the archive, and narrative medicine. She is editor of *The Unraveling Archive: Essays on Sylvia Plath*, and her essays on material modernism have appeared in *American Literary Scholarship*, *American Literature*, and *Literature and Medicine*. She is currently working on *Photo-Signatures*, a book about poetry and photography after 1945.

Kamran Javadizadeh is assistant professor of English at Villanova University, where his teaching and research focus on twentieth-century American poetry. His work has appeared in *Modernism/modernity*, *Arizona Quarterly*, and *Yale Review*. His essay in this collection is drawn from his current book manuscript, *Institutionalized Lyric: American Poetry at Midcentury*.

Dorothea Lasky is the author of five books of poetry, most recently *MILK*, as well as *ROME*, *Thunderbird*, *Black Life*, and *AWE*. She is coeditor of *Open the Door: How to Excite Young People about Poetry* and several chapbooks, including *Poetry Is Not a Project*. Currently, she is an assistant professor of poetry at Columbia University's School of the Arts and lives in New York City.

Kathleen Ossip is the author of *The Do-Over,* a *New York Times* Editors' Choice book; *The Cold War,* which was one of *Publishers Weekly's* best books of 2011; *The Search Engine,* which was selected by Derek Walcott for the American Poetry Review/Honickman First Book Prize; and *Cinephrastics,* a chapbook of movie poems. She teaches at the New School in New York, and she is the coeditor of the poetry review website *SCOUT* (scout-poetry.com). She was a 2016–2017 Radcliffe Fellow.

David Trinidad's books include *Dear Prudence: New and Selected Poems* and *Peyton Place: A Haiku Soap Opera. Notes on a Past Life* is forthcoming. He is also the editor of *A Fast Life: The Collected Poems of Tim Dlugos.* Trinidad lives in Chicago, where he is a professor of creative writing and poetry at Columbia College.

Victoria Van Hyning is a British Academy Postdoctoral Fellow at the University of Oxford (2015–2018), and the Humanities PI of Zooniverse.org (Oxford), the academic crowdsourcing research group. Her book project is titled "Court to Convent: Early Modern English Catholic Women's Autobiography." She encountered the poetry of Anne Sexton for the first time as an undergraduate at Goucher College (Baltimore) where she studied English literature and creative writing (2002–2006).

# Index

CPSIA information can be obtained
at www.ICGtesting.com
Printed in the USA
FFHW022327051118
49301815-53526FF